Gail Resnik

AND

Scott Trost

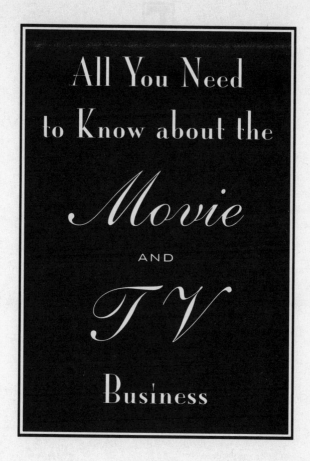

All You Need to Know about the *Movie* AND *TV* Business

A Fireside Book

PUBLISHED BY SIMON & SCHUSTER

New York London Toronto Sydney Tokyo Singapore

FIRESIDE
Rockefeller Center
1230 Avenue of the Americas
New York, NY 10020

FIRESIDE and colophon are registered trademarks of
Simon & Schuster Inc.

Designed by Jennifer Ann Daddio

Manufactured in the United States of America

5   7   9   10   8   6   4

Library of Congress Cataloging-in-Publication Data
Resnik, Gail.
All you need to know about the movie and T.V. business / Gail
Resnik and Scott Trost.
p.   cm.
"A Fireside book."
Includes bibliographical references.
1. Motion picture industry—Vocational guidance—United States.
2. Television—Vocational guidance—United States.   I. Trost,
Scott.
PN1995.9.P75R47   1996
791.43′02′9373—dc20   95-39804 CIP

ISBN 0-684-80064-0

Proceed with Caution

We give numerous opinions, suggestions, and advice in this book about navigating the sometimes treacherous waters of Hollywood. Please remember our key message, which is that you have to find appropriate professionals and representatives to support you in your particular situation. The business is constantly changing, requiring new responses to new circumstances. Accordingly, neither we nor our publisher are responsible for actions taken by readers as a result of the contents of this book.

Gail dedicates this book to her husband Don Goldberg for his unfailing love and support; to her mother Bertha Resnik, whose love of Hollywood lit the pathway to this book; and to her daughter, Maya, for bringing Gail so much joy.

Scott dedicates this book to his brother Lou for being a best friend; his father Lou, Sr., for the years of gentle patience; his mother Ann for her unique spirit; and his grandfather Claude Tillma for taking the time to help Scott write his first report.

ACKNOWLEDGMENTS

We both have Jeff Herman, our agent, to thank for taking us on as clients and building a bridge to our publisher. We also thank David Dunton, our former editor at Simon & Schuster, for taking a chance on us as a writing team; and Cindy Gitter, the editor who cheerfully inherited us, for her exhaustive editorial assistance.

In addition, we need to thank Gail's people: Alan Heppel, Steve Kotlowitz, Dirk Van de Bunt, and Harold Brook for their assistance in getting the business points right. Gail's dad, Arnold Resnik, for providing the foundation; Roberta Simon, Gail's sister and cheerleader; and her brother, Marshall Resnik, who taught her defense. Ted and Ruth Falcon, for support in life and work. LIL for years of dinners spent laughing about Hollywood. Trainers, coaches, mentors, and tormentors at Paramount: Bob Cohen, Richard Fowkes, Greg Gelfan, Ralph Kamon, Edith Tolkin, Kate Boyle Whitfield, and Vance Van Petten. Personal team: Ann Bartnett, Leigh Brecheen, Shelley Levinson and Bob Schumacher, Rachel Koretsky, Hugh McCallum, Debbie Pearl, Linda Reid, Stephanie Reynolds, Susan Ross, Luke Sader, Kathy Tol-

lefson, Clara Ukai, Susan Van de Bunt, and Linda Wohl. And Rosalind Russell, the first career woman in Gail's life.

And Scott's people: Al Fama, Robin Poole, Carmine Palazzo, Roy Gardner, Maryann Grasso, Dennis Grief, Dan Foliert, Steve Pizzello, Chet Migden, Dennis Hoey, Tony Snegoff, Stiefel & Company, Ed Dessisso, Duane Poole, Cheryl Mann, Richard Arlook, Stephen Galloway, Jay Shanker, Jim Jimirro, and Jane Tucker for their generous time and help. Tony Ferrar for being one of the best commercial agents in town and Junie Lowry for my first job. Friends and mentors: Rodney and Joan Vaccaro, Michael Capellupo, Leah Pinsent, Eric Edwards, Elkanah Burns, Lezlie Deane, Anna Densley, Holly Gagnier, Sam Whipple, Jeff Goldblum, Brett Harman, Pamela Dillman, Brennan Howard, Moon Hi Hanson, Mari Hulick, John Short, Lisa Kaminir, Eric Kohner, Hunt Lowry, Trudie Kessler, John Bridges, Massimo Mazzucco, Mark Pelligrino, Tony Savant, Fred Selbulske, David Nicolette, Barry Castro, Stephen Rowe, Karl Klare, Robert Merrick, Hoot Gibson, Al Jacobs, Rob and Maren, Elaine, Alexandra, Gregory, Charlotte, Ted, Cody and Mary, Gill, Tim, Hank, Sally and the girls, Blair, Marybeth, Michael and Paulette, Diane, the Corff's, Joe and Ellen, Helen, Jeff and Patty, Heather, Mal, Debra, Stephanie and Fred, Jane and Michael, Camille, Gaye and Margo, Donna, T.J., Mark, Kate, Mrs. Nelson, and my soulmate, Blake Arnold.

A special acknowledgment to Robert Carnegie, artistic director of Playhouse West School and Repertory Theater in North Hollywood, for freely sharing the fruits of his wisdom and experience. Without him this book would not have been possible.

CONTENTS

Contents

Contents

Contents

Contents

Contents

Contents

Contents

Contents

Contents

What It Takes to Work in the Movie and TV Business

What does it take to work in the movie and TV business? It takes a lot of qualities, such as desire, talent, business sense, dedication, street smarts, and a lot of heart. Those are only some of the basic minimum qualifications you need to fashion a career in what is referred to simply as "The Industry."

We've found that most books about Hollywood don't tell you much about how the business actually works, so we have tried to include the information that we wished someone had told us the first few years we were in town. There's a lot of ground to cover, from getting started to surviving failure and making the most of your successes. We describe the kind of character you will need to succeed in this business. We give an overview of the job opportunities and the industry. We offer our take on the politics of Hollywood and how to play the game. We even describe, in English (more or less), the legal ins and outs of the business.

SURVIVING THE DREAM FACTORY

The dream of a career in film and television lures thousands of young and not-so-young people to Los Angeles each year in a quest for fame and riches. Most probably come to pursue the ultimate and most elusive dream, that of acting in film and television. Many others come instead to direct, produce, write, or even to pursue less glamorous dreams as makeup artists, stunt men, camera operators, and grips. All these people set out, full of hopes, down the proverbial yellow brick road in search of the Emerald City we call Hollywood.

Unfortunately, like Dorothy in *The Wizard of Oz*, many of these young people lose their way and find only a barren land inhabited by a never-ending supply of wicked witches and nasty little flying monkeys, all the creatures who prey on the naïve and feed off their dreams, robbing them of their dignity, their money, and sometimes even their souls. Drama aside, many just never find anyone to give them a chance and drift away from the business. A few hardy individuals survive these hardships and get their first break, only to find that each new success brings more complex and difficult challenges.

A very select few break into the business and string together enough jobs to consider themselves a "working" actor, director, writer, producer, studio executive, agent, or cinematographer, although this status may only last a few years. The nomadic existence of the business may begin to take a toll, or the basic craziness that evolves out of the marriage of art and big money becomes overwhelming. A person may find himself back at square one—having depleted savings and emotional reserves—not to mention a few years older and therefore less experienced for many other careers.

Yet somehow, in the midst of a million tough-luck stories, a handful of people will achieve stunning financial and creative success over a lifetime. They will find joy and rewards every step of the way. Some of them will even become or create worldwide icons and stories that will live forever.

This book is for all these budding actors, directors, agents, studio executives, wardrobe people, best boys, and others who are considering a career in Hollywood. It is also for those who have already arrived and are still in need of guidance in a land where each new opportunity presents a myriad of new and greater dangers, together with exciting possibilities. It is even for those who have been around awhile, maybe even on a fast track, but are too embarrassed to admit they still have gaps in their knowledge of the business. If you have been doing business for years and still don't understand how profit participations work, you can sneak into a back room and read this book before closing your next deal.

Our purpose is to give you a realistic assessment of what awaits you in Hollywood, wherever you are on your career path. It is a guide to dealing successfully with lawyers, agents, unions, and the other business components of the entertainment industry. Our goal is to increase your chance of creative, financial, and spiritual survival in the money- and power-driven entertainment business.

With all due respect to the other centers of the entertainment industry, such as New York City, Chicago, Toronto, and Florida, we have focused this book on careers in Los Angeles. Much of the information we offer is applicable to those other areas, but some is not, due to local customs and conditions. If you plan to work in one of these other locales, be sure also to check local reference books.

We cover a tremendous amount of ground here, and frankly we don't expect you are interested in covering all of it with us. We've tried to set the book up so you can jump in and out, depending on where you are in your career. You can let yourself imagine you're in the game and look at what people concern themselves with from various places on the board.

If you are just starting out, then check out the introductory material in the beginning sections of this book. We discuss the

Introduction

many pathways to breaking into the business (there is more than one yellow brick road in Hollywood). The heavy-duty business material in the sections entitled "When You've Become a Working Professional" and "The Rules of the Game" is probably much too detailed for this stage of your career. Conversely, if you've been around for awhile, you might want to skip the suggestions on how to break into the business and head right for the dealmaking and business structure sections. Use the index for specifics, such as net profits or completion bonds.

Finally, let's be real. You probably cannot know all there is to know about the movie and television business. We certainly don't. However, you can learn who does what and how the game is played, whether it's for your information or your survival.

SECTION ONE

What You'll Need Before You Start

CHAPTER ONE

Be Prepared

You might be tempted to skip over this chapter. Much of what we say here is self-evident and simple. However, we are willing to lay odds that most success stories in this business involve heeding the simple truths we describe below. It may sound lofty, but this section is about character—the personal traits that you bring to the table. Looks, personality, or family connections may get you a job, but only character can build a career. All the sophisticated advice and technical information we give you in the later sections will be wasted if you don't have what it takes to take advantage of it.

Read this section carefully. Maybe even reread it if you find yourself at sea in your career. The solution to your problems is likely to be found at the source, which, of course, is yourself.

TRAINING AND EXPERIENCE

There is a reason why Hollywood has developed into the film and television capital of the world. The town has attracted, for several generations, the most qualified professionals in every branch of the industry. If you intend to compete with these people for the few jobs that are available, you stand a much better chance if you have learned your craft before you arrive.

Despite the hype, most creative talent must be skilled craftspeople to sustain a career in the business. Even if you are great in front of the mirror or at handling the family video camera, you need to be ready if you get a chance to show your stuff. Some people get noticed just about as soon as they hit town, and if they're not ready, they may find in retrospect that they've blown their one shot. Before you relocate, you should take every opportunity to gain the skills and experience you will need.

Yes, you can find training and gain experience once you have arrived, but as we explain below, Los Angeles can be an expensive city, both financially and emotionally. Better to take advantage of training opportunities in your less competitive and less expensive local community before setting out for Hollywood.

TALENT

The entertainment industry is a high-octane blend of the creative and the practical. Thousands and even millions of dollars ride on the ability of an actor to work himself up, in a moment's notice, to the appropriate emotional state for each *take*, each shot in a day's schedule. Even the lowly production assistant must be able to respond to a thousand competing demands each day on the set, demands that would set the busiest air-traffic controller spinning in a tizzy.

Beyond the skill that is necessary for these jobs, a certain inborn talent is required. Do you have that talent? Unfortunately, you cannot answer that question until you try the job. Imagination will not do it. If you take our advice and get training and experience before you come to Hollywood, you will have some indication of whether you have the talent and temperament for the career you are pursuing. If you build sets for your local community theater, you will discover whether you have a feel for building materials and tools. If you act in community theater productions, the roles you play and the response you receive will tell you whether others recognize the immense acting talent you are so sure you possess. These experiences can give you a clue to whether you have what it takes to succeed in the entertainment business.

One cautionary note for actors. We will give you our strong opinions about the state of acting and actor training in chapter 5, "First Steps." For now, let us say that actors especially should take anyone's opinion of their talent with a grain of salt. Most individuals in creative-talent occupations don't get tested before they hit L.A., but actors often start at home. Just because the local community theater director or even the teacher at your prestigious acting conservatory fails to see and reward your talent doesn't mean you don't have any. A few of these people have a good eye for recognizing talent, but most do not. Of course, the reverse is also true. Even if you've received nothing but praise and encouragement from local "authorities," you may very well get shot down in Hollywood.

COURAGE

This is no profession for the faint of heart. Rejection will be your frequent companion. Poverty may become a familiar condition. More than once your friends and family and even you will question your career. Every successful person in Hollywood possesses the courage to struggle with the demons of doubt, disappointment, anxiety, and low self-esteem each night, then each new day begin again.

PATIENCE

For every overnight success in Hollywood, there are a million people who must build their careers a pebble a day. Most so-called overnight sensations enjoy only a year or two of heady acclaim before they find themselves back at square one, no richer for the experience. When you see the names appear in that long list of credits at the end of a picture just remember that those people spent years toiling away at their craft in obscurity to earn that millisecond of screen time. The people who are likely to be successful in this industry will view their careers from the perspective of five, ten, even twenty years.

COMMON SENSE

While often work in entertainment demands that you exhibit the vulnerability, naïveté, and imagination of a child, the business of making a career for yourself requires the opposite. Many talented people will never be "discovered" because they lack business sense. You must have the maturity and smarts to navigate through the maze of agents, managers, casting directors, directors, producers, and others who stand between you and each job, or at least the common sense to choose your supporting team wisely.

A GOOD WORK ETHIC

Woe to the person who lounges in bed each day waiting for the job to come to them. This is a career path that demands constant salesmanship on your part, that demands you constantly train and hone your craft. The twelve labors of Hercules pale in comparison with what will be required of you to make a successful career in Hollywood.

A LITTLE HELP FROM YOUR FRIENDS

This may not be an absolute prerequisite for a career in Hollywood, but it sure helps. There are so many downs and so few ups in this business that a warm and loving network of family and friends can often make the difference in your emotional and financial well-being. If you can count on someone to come through in a crisis (and there will be many), you'll have that extra cushion that makes the difference between throwing in the towel and hanging in there one more day.

If you have all of the traits listed above, begin your journey today. You have a wonderful gift to share with the world. If you lack one or more of these qualities, do not count on some wizard to endow you with them when you arrive in Hollywood. Instead, stay home. Get a good education. Find a loving partner and raise healthy, happy children. Make a contribution to your community. Let that dream of fame and fortune remain just that—a dream. That's where it belongs. After all, even Dorothy knew there is no place like home.

Required Reading before You Come to Town

We've included a list of books in the appendix that you should read as you begin your career. These books will give you additional tips about the various crafts in the entertainment business and some perspective about life and the kind of character you will need to succeed. You don't have to read all of them before you come to Hollywood, but the more information you have, the better.

The Players

What are the careers Hollywood has to offer? Who does what, and to whom? What kind of life can I expect if I pursue one of them? Just what is a "best boy"? There are hundreds of jobs in Hollywood. This section will discuss a variety of the ways people work in Hollywood, from the players to the worker bees.

What's a "player" in Hollywood? Well, you've probably noticed that we've entitled this entire section "The Players," and we've described a wide variety of jobs available in the entertainment field. In the broadest sense, every person who participates in the game is a player. Even the pawn is a player in the game of chess, though a pawn certainly can't move like a king.

You've probably also heard the word player used to describe a person who has the power to make the rules, as in "He [or she] is a real player." Director Robert Altman's movie The Player was about a studio executive who had the power to decide which scripts were bought, and ultimately what movies were made. A true player in Hollywood is a person who controls the purse strings and creative decision making. A player could be the studio executive high enough on the power ladder to say yes or no. Executives aren't the only players in town. *A movie star who has the power to approve or reject other cast members can be described as a player. A producer who can pull together the financing for a picture or a director with final-cut clout (which we'll describe later in the book) is a player.*

As you can imagine, there are a number of ways to classify the work people do in Hollywood. In the first category are the people who work on the productions "above the line" or "below the line," terms we define in chapter 2. In the second category are the people who handle the business deals, addressed in chapter 4. Finally, in chapter 6, we discuss the people who train and prepare people so they can get into the game.

CHAPTER TWO

The People Above the Line

Every chicken coop has its pecking order, and Hollywood is no exception. One way of distinguishing status in the entertainment business is by identifying people by where their job title fits into the budget for a project. The compensation for producers, directors, actors, and writers is always inserted *above the line* in a budget, with everybody and everything else *below the line*.

What line is that? When budgets are prepared, the very first items inserted on page one are the costs of the *literary material* (the script and any book, article, or movie upon which the script is based) and the key *creative talent* (the creative people as opposed to business people). Note that in some contexts, *talent* can be a somewhat impersonal term used to refer to actors, as in "We're ready for the shot, let's get the talent in here."

In any case, there is literally a line in every budget separating the literary material, producers, director, and lead actors from the rest of the costs budgeted for the project. Thus we have the terms above the line and below the line.

Above the Line vs. Below the Line

There is a logical explanation for this seemingly haphazard structure. Typically a studio will know what a project will generally cost below the line, because it's relatively easy to predict what a camera crew will cost for ten weeks. However, the above-the-line costs for actors, writers, or directors can vary wildly. Talking in very round numbers, a low-budget motion picture for a studio is something less than $15 million, a medium-budget film is in the neighborhood of $15 million up to $35 million, and a big-budget film is anything higher. (Compare these numbers with the numbers the unions use for purposes of determining scale in chapter 10.)

Let's walk through an example. Perhaps the current powers that be want to make a low-budget picture, say $12 million below the line. They know that if they want to keep it low budget, the above-the-line costs can't be much more than $3 million. If the book and screenplay cost $750,000, then the executives know the cost for everyone else above the line has to be in the $2.25 million range.

TV producers go through a similar exercise to figure out their expenses, except that television budgets are generally smaller. For example, in *episodic* TV, the *pilot* (the first episode, which introduces the characters) for a half-hour show currently runs about $1 million to $2 million. You can halve that figure for a regular episode in the series and double it for one-hour episodes.

Whether we're talking about features or TV, the creative talent is defined by where each individual fits relative to that line. There's also a kind of unspoken hierarchy inherent in the words above the line and below the line in Hollywood. Above the line connotes the creative talent and the money. Below the line connotes the technical and other less glamorous elements of a production. For you sports fans, the terms are analogous in many ways to the terms *backs* and *linemen* used in football. Everyone knows it's the linemen who do the grunt work and are responsible for allowing the backs to move the football up and down the field. But it's the more visible backs who receive all the adulation from the fans, plus the higher salaries. So it is in Hollywood, too.

As you've guessed by now, being above the line means being higher in the Hollywood hierarchy, where money and creative control, the two great driving forces of Hollywood, reside. In this chapter, we'll discuss those people whose roles are above the line.

PRODUCERS

Everyone in Hollywood who doesn't call himself a writer calls himself a producer, unless, of course, he calls himself a writer/ producer. Even your Aunt Minnie can get a free option on the screenplay written by her gardener and call herself a producer. Of course, very few people in town actually "produce" anything, partially because Hollywood is full of wanna-bes, but also because it can take a long time for a project to be completed. In a town of illusions, it's hard to tell who's got the right stuff. In the meantime, it's impressive party chat to say you're a producer.

Note that here and elsewhere in the book we refer to individuals who produce as producers while we refer to the company that hires the producers as the studio. Even if the company only consists of three film students with high hopes, we'll call them a studio here for the sake of clarity.

Figuring out what a producer does is one of the lingering puzzles in Hollywood. A producer can fulfill any number of job descriptions, from putting the whole project together to making sure the elephants arrive at the set on time. Because producers are basically supervisors at whatever level they produce, no union or guild effectively governs the field of producing as they do for writers, directors, and actors.

Generally, a producer is in charge of pulling the production together at some level, bringing the creative elements together, and handling the million and one problems inherent with film and television development and production. For those people who actively produce, this can mean any number of activities, such as hiring the writer to write the original screenplay, selling the script to the studio, courting and signing the major creative talent, doing the budget, making sure the sets get made on time, hiring the crew, even making sure the cast and crew make it over the border for a foreign shoot.

PRODUCERS' CREDITS

If you've read the credits to any movie or TV project lately, you'll notice lots of titles with "producer" or some variation of the word in it, e.g., executive producer, associate producer, or production executive. We talk about credits in chapter 17, but we mention them here to help sort out the different kinds of producers in Hollywood.

Producer generally refers to the person who got the studio to finance the project and who then oversees the broad strokes of the production, such as pulling together the script and the major creative talent.

An *executive producer* title is perhaps the least descriptive; you really can't know what that person did unless you were involved in the production. An executive producer title could describe the person who actually raised the money to get the project made, or it may refer to the person who made one phone call to an executive at the studio and had nothing further to do with it. It could be used by an actor who simply wants an additional vanity credit in the project, or it could denote the person who actually sweated over putting the budget together and stayed on the set making sure someone cleaned up after that elephant. In TV, the executive producer is often the top deal-maker. As we said, it's hard to know if you weren't there.

An *associate producer* can also be anything, but often means someone involved in physically producing the project, making sure everything happens on schedule, and handling all the production problems that arise after the money is in place.

The *executive in charge of production* is generally someone hired by the studio to oversee the day-to-day production of a program, usually a television show.

A *production manager* is generally the person who orders the trucks and hires the crew (and is generally not above the line).

Supervising producers usually work on TV shows, and there can be half a dozen of them. They may be writers with ongoing responsibility for the scripts, or one of a multitude of high-level producers connected with the program.

Probably the key distinction between producers is whether they are what we call dealmaking producers as opposed to line producers. The former are basically high-level salespeople while the latter are actually involved in the day-to-day operation of a production.

Dealmaking producers work on the larger dealmaking level and put together enough elements to bring the project to a studio. If they can get control of a script (or at least a book or article on which to base a script) and perhaps the commitment of a director and/or famous actor, they'll pitch the project to a studio executive (which we'll discuss in chapter 15). If the producer can interest the studio in buying the project outright or at least option the right to buy the project, the studio will do something called *putting the project into development.*

_____

Optioning a Screenplay

When a producer options *a screenplay or a script (the two words are interchangeable), it means he gets the writer to agree, usually for a small fee (or no fee), to let him have the exclusive right to produce it. Many producers get writers to give them a free option, so they control the work but don't have to pay anything until the studio comes up with some cash. Note the sample contract in chapter 15 illustrating the kind of language a producer might use to option a story.*

_____

Selling Projects to a Studio

The goal here is to get a project made (also known as getting the studio to greenlight *the production) without spending any of your own money. When the studio buys the project, it will usually insist the producers assign all of their rights in the screenplay. At this point, the producer might take the money and run (though almost always taking a credit in the final project). Alternatively, a producer may remain actively attached to the project and become involved in the day-to-day production matters. In chapter 21, we discuss the ways that projects get put together.*

_____

In movies, a first-time producer who will not be involved actively with the production will generally make a small fee ($10,000 to $25,000), sometimes called a *finder's fee,* and rarely receives any profit participation (which we'll discuss in chapter 17). A more experienced producer who remains involved usually gets *development* money (i.e., compensation for his input while the studio hires writers and figures out whether or not to greenlight the production) in the $15,000 to $50,000 range. If a project gets the greenlight, the producer will receive another $100,000 to $350,000 or more with a participation in profits. Very successful or high-profile movie producers will sometimes get production deals, which we discuss in chapter 5.

In TV, most producers who are dealmakers will have a deal that pays them a per-episode fee in the $25,000 to $75,000 range, but that doesn't include royalties and other participations. Really successful producers will get long-term deals, which we'll discuss in chapter 17.

The term *independent* refers to a producer who works outside of the studio system and obtains funding from private investors such as banks (although doctors and shopping mall owners have been known to be financiers in Hollywood). Sometimes being an independent means that while you get your financing from a studio or a network, you still retain creative control over the project until it's delivered.

Truly independent financing allows the producer to keep more control over the project and perhaps sell off the rights to the various territories and media separately. A producer who has retained rights can make separate deals for all of the distribution channels to which the project might get sold, such as selling HBO (Home Box Office) the cable rights or selling a distributor the rights to distribute the film to movie theaters in Argentina. When distribution rights are retained, the independent will keep more of the money that comes in. In chapter 10, we'll talk more about how deals are set up.

Independent producers who retain rights to their projects are money and power brokers, the driving forces behind many productions. You can find these producers at restaurants, meeting rooms, film festivals, and trade shows, always wheeling and dealing to raise enough money to get a film made.

For every one of these true entrepreneurs, however, there are a hundred fakers and also-rans who are more bluster than substance. These are the ones who are most likely to exploit young creative talent or, at best, do them a disservice by tying up their time and creative output waiting for that elusive shooting date to be announced.

Line producers do the hands-on producing on a project, sometimes referred to as *line producing.* These people are generally more interested in the day-to-day operations than in putting the projects together, and a good line producer works regularly on production after production. While they may get main title credit, they're usually not in the "glamour pool" in Hollywood because they are the working class among the elite in town. This is probably because they actually work.

Line producers are responsible for building the cities, counting the costumes, and making sure the train leaves the station on time. They are hired by studios and independent producers to run things, so that the project comes in on time and within budget. More often than not, line producers, who do the detail work, make it their entire careers or end up in supervising roles at the studio, overseeing a group of other line producers. This isn't necessarily a path to becoming a player, though line producers control huge pots of money and have enormous responsibility. Salaries range based on experience: In movies, good line producers make in the $150,000 to $350,000 range, depending on the budget and their reputation. They rarely command profit participation.

Production managers or *associate producers* most likely have line responsibility; i.e., the responsibility for the details of production. It's also interesting to note that though the word "produce" appears in their titles and they do a lot of hiring and supervision, production managers are in fact members of the Directors Guild. We'll talk about unions in chapter 9.

Script Breakdowns

One of the responsibilities that are most likely to be associated with a production manager is the script breakdown. Just about the first thing a production manager does is read the script and analyze each scene to figure out the order of shooting the production. The order of shooting scenes is usually not the order in which they appear in the script. While television shot before a live audience is shot in a linear fashion (i.e., scenes are shot in the same order as they appear in the script), most filmed television and motion picture work is not linear because it's inefficient.

The production will be planned so that all the scenes in one location are shot at the same time. That way the production doesn't have to waste time and money going back and forth to different locations. Sometimes an actor is only available for a short period of time, so all the scenes involving that actor will be shot at once. Other times a certain location may be available for only short periods of time.

Here's an example of how a script might be broken down: Let's say the production manager has negotiated a location in a remote area of a national park for one week. Even though the script may call for one scene in the beginning of the picture and one scene at the end in this particular location, the production manager will try to schedule both scenes to be shot consecutively so the production doesn't have to go to the same location twice.

Remember that when a movie company travels to a location, it usually means lots of people traveling, from the director and camera and lighting people to the actors and their nannies and physical trainers. Organizing all these individuals doesn't always work according to location availability; the schedules of the lead actors, availability of equipment and props, and other factors may determine how the scenes are put together in the production manager's board.

The production manager gathers all the information required to get the necessary elements in place (such as the location and the performers). The information is then put on little strips of cardboard that are inserted in a board in shooting order. Presumably, computers will take over this function in the years to come, but as you can imagine, it can be a tortuous process to plan those ten to fifteen weeks of production. A skillful production manager can make or break a production.

———

As we mentioned, production managers are responsible for getting the budget together (which can be a sixty-page single-spaced document) and making sure the production stays within budget. They often play a liaison role between the director and the studios, since it's the production manager's job to blow the whistle if it looks like the project might go over budget. As you can imagine, this responsibility can require tremendous political savvy. When you get people arguing about art and money, it can be ugly, and a good production manager will keep the waters smooth and the production in gear.

Producers are the original wheeler-dealers in Hollywood. If you want to get into the game and you have no particular skills (other than the gift of gab), tell people you're a producer. You can hang out for a while, talk the talk, and probably get away with it, at least for the first half-dozen parties or so.

On the other hand, when someone tells you he's a producer, you may want to ask some questions, especially if you are contemplating doing some business with this person. What other projects has he worked on? What did he specifically do on that project? What is he working on now? How far along is he (does he have the money)? If this information isn't forthcoming, beware.

DIRECTORS

Most of us have some notion of what a director is. The director is the one who gets to yell "action" to start a shot and "cut" to stop it. He or she is the one who literally directs the action of a film or TV show. In theory, if not in practice, every shot you see, every word you hear has been created under the guidance of the director. Everyone on the set is at the director's beck and call.

Because of the nature of what a director contributes to a production, directors have always been pivotal players in the production of any film or television project. This power has been strengthened over the years by the Directors Guild of America, Inc., a potent force in mainstream Hollywood. Every ship needs a captain, and the director is in charge, at least once the camera starts to roll.

On movie projects, the director is usually the most powerful person on the set. Though the studio usually has final say on issues such as the budget, film length, and casting, the director is often the final, or at least the most influential, arbiter in making most creative decisions. This includes the form of the final screenplay, casting decisions, the look of the sets and costumes, where the camera gets set up, and in general the look of the project. Of course, how much clout any director has depends on his reputation and track record, not to mention the force of his personality. The director has to contend with the interests and strength of the producers and studio executives attached to a project.

The director's ability to choose creative elements often depends upon the stage at which a director gets attached to a project. If a director gets called onto a project at the last minute, everything may already be in place, and the director has to deal with the elements someone else set up. For example, with some projects the lead actors are already attached, so whether or not the director thinks a particular actor is right for a role, the director must work with that actor. The director may also have to deal with all the producers and studio executives vying to get their boyfriends, girlfriends, cousins, and other loved ones a part in the film. We'll talk about some of the approval rights an established director can negotiate in chapter 17.

In television, the studio and network executives tend to have more power than the director, since directors are often changed from week to week with a different director for each episode. Time is precious, since so much money is at stake. The role of the director can be minimized in this process and made to appear like just another hired hand on the set. So the TV director often will exercise much less control over production elements. It's not unusual to see the director acting as a glorified traffic cop, simply deciding where the cameras and actors will stand and move during a shot.

TV series usually have a small herd of producers who work on the show the entire season and are therefore more likely to be involved in many of the decisions made on the set. Some executives love to use the casting process as a place to mark their territory, and as a result, the director may have less authority in casting. Of course, in many television shows, the chief creative force is the writer/producer who also directs many of the episodes and therefore has a chance to control the overall development of the show.

Often you'll see titles like first or second assistant director or second unit director in the credits. These people are generally considered below the line, but we'll describe what they do here, since they work in tandem with the director. The *first assistant director* is just what it sounds like, someone who assists the director, usually making sure that everyone and everything is in place so the cameras can start to roll. They yell things into megaphones, like "Quiet on the set!" He or she is usually assisted by a *second assistant director* who manages the incredible mass of paperwork that is generated by a film. Either the first or second assistant director is usually responsible for directing the extras in a scene. The *second unit director* is the person who takes a separate crew to shoot distant locations or action sequences.

Actors

Most people know what actors do. Actors are the ones we see acting on the big or little screen. They lead the glamorous lives we read about in the gossip magazines. What you may *not* know is that thousands of actors toil away in Hollywood in relative obscurity and even make a decent living at it. For example, you may not have heard of John Short, but he has a list of Broadway, film, TV, industrial, voice-over, print, and commercial credits longer than your arm. (John Short actually exists. In fact, he is a friend of ours. More on John later.)

For most of you who come to Hollywood to be actors, your career above the line will last as long as an eyeblink at best. (Extra work doesn't count because it is considered below the line, which should give you a good indication of the status of extras in Hollywood.) Many never get a single job or even an agent, although they may spend thousands of dollars and a lot of time looking for them. Another large group will find work in small independent films, student films, occasional guest spots or featured roles in film or television, or possibly make a living off commercials. After a handful of these jobs, many actors will get discouraged and go home, take up other pursuits, or diversify into other jobs in the entertainment industry.

We don't mean to suggest that such a short-lived acting career is an unworthy one. One line on a popular TV show may allow you to return home as a conquering hero. If the show goes into indefinite reruns, you may receive congratulatory phone calls from friends around the country for the rest of your life. You came, you saw, you conquered (a little overstatement never hurt anyone), and you even have the tape to prove it. While everyone else in your neighborhood sat around on their butts and talked about it, you actually did it.

Let's go through that list of John's we referred to and talk about the different kinds of film and television acting jobs that you will be competing for (and when we say competing, we mean it).

———

John's Acting Resume

Film

Apollo 13	*Supporting*
Diggstown	*Supporting*
Welcome Home, Roxy Carmichael	*Supporting*
Gross Anatomy	*Supporting*
Planes, Trains, & Automobiles	*Supporting*
A Fine Mess	*Supporting*
Maximum Overdrive	*Lead*
Brenda Starr	*Supporting*

Television

Coach	*Guest Star*
The Torkelsons	*Guest Star*
Simple Folk	*Guest Star*
Brooklyn Bridge	*Guest Star*
The Cavanaughs	*Series Regular*
21 Jump Street	*Guest Star*

St. Elsewhere	*Guest Star*
The Other Lover	*Guest Star*
Newhart	*Guest Star*

Broadway
Big River	*Lead (Drama Desk Nomination)*

Commercials
List made available upon request. (John wouldn't be able to list all these jobs on a single page, since they include over seventy TV commercials and over forty voice-over jobs.)

ACTING ROLES

Let's go over some acting terminology. You should note that since the listed terms of roles do not have exact boundaries, they have a tendency to blur together. One actor's guest-starring role is another actor's co-starring role.

A *featured role,* for example, is the role of the waitress who comes over to the table and asks, "May I take your order?" This term refers to a small speaking role. Sometimes actors cheat and list their non-speaking extra roles as featured roles—anything to build that resume.

A *guest-starring role* is usually applicable only in television. The term *guest star* means the actor has more than a couple of lines but only appears in one episode or a few episodes as the same recurring character. Good agents and managers will often negotiate to have that featured role be listed as a guest-starring role in the credits.

A *co-starring role* is something meatier than a guest-starring role, but not a starring role.

A *supporting role* is usually used for film roles that fall somewhat short of a starring role. It can range anywhere from one line to several lengthy scenes.

The *recurring role* applies to an actor who appears in more than one episode of a TV show as the same character but who isn't a regular. It can be used in conjunction with the term guest star.

A *regular role* is used in TV to designate the actor who is one of the main characters and appears in most, if not all, of the episodes.

The *starring role* refers to the main actor with the big credits, although superstars will often command credits even higher than this one (see chapter 17 for more on this distinction).

OTHER TYPES OF ACTING JOBS

Commercials feature thirty-second stars who get paid lots of money to sell beer, fast food, cereal, laundry detergent, and cars on TV.

Voice-overs use the recognizable voices that wax rhapsodic on the radio or TV, or they provide the crowd noise in a movie. Cartoon voices are also included under this category. Voice-overs provide such a large source of income that some agents specialize in this type of work.

Industrial films are familiar if you've ever worked at a company and had to watch some boring in-house film or video about customer relations or a similar subject. Actors can earn a pretty good income making these films and, since many industrials are produced locally, it's a good place to get some on-camera experience wherever you live.

Print ads are seen on billboards, in magazines, at bus stops and other places where pictures of people are used to sell products. Some actors in Hollywood will use this type of work to supplement their incomes.

CD-ROMs offer a new type of acting work that is growing so fast the unions have already negotiated a contract setting wages and other benefits for these jobs. For those who have not entered the computer age, CD-ROM refers to a powerful new technology that allows you to put images and information on a computer screen. Companies have begun developing programs that do things like reenact the Battle of Waterloo (1815), with real actors in the roles of Napoleon, Wellington, and their troops.

Karaoke videos are the videos that play on big screens in Karaoke bars, featuring actors in low-budget mini-dramas that bring songs to life. This is a new source of acting work that has developed in the last few years.

Extra roles, last and unfortunately least, are speechless— and usually thankless. Extras may act on a set or soundstage, but they're usually invisible in a sea of faces or bodies.

There are about forty thousand actors in Los Angeles who are members of the Screen Actors Guild at any one time, and only 15 percent of them find work in any given year. These figures don't even cover non-union actors or non-union work. Still, there are people like John Short who earn a decent living doing what they love, even if they don't end up on the cover of *People* for their work.

CHILD ACTORS

Much has been done to protect child actors from the abuses they suffered in the early years of Hollywood. Perhaps the most famous or infamous event in the history of child actors was the scandal that erupted around Jackie Coogan. Coogan (who later became well known for his role in television on the *Munsters*) had great success as a child actor, both starring with Charlie Chaplin and being the lead actor in many films. When it was discovered that Jackie Coogan's parents had spent his considerable fortune, leaving him with nothing for all those years of lucrative labor, an uproar ensued. Stories surfaced about the abuse of child actors, from outrageously long hours and lack of education to the administration of drugs to keep them in line. As a result, the State of California has passed laws, and the unions have negotiated a whole range of protections specifically for children. These regulations provide for educational instruction of the child during a production, maximum work hours, the presence of parents or qualified guardians on the set, protection against sexual exploitation, health and safety rules, and a myriad of other regulations. In addition, the child's earnings are put in a trust fund, ensuring that there's money left by the time the child reaches maturity.

Because a child, when he reaches majority age, can void a contract his parent entered into, studios regularly go to court to have all child actor contracts approved. This gives them some assurance that they will be able to use the result of that child's services when the product is complete.

Most producers take these regulations very seriously, and as a result, parents can generally allow their children to work in Hollywood without serious concern for the child's health and safety. Still, abuses occur. Despite these regulations, however, two children were killed on the set of the motion picture *Twilight Zone: The Movie* in 1983. In the early morning hours, a helicopter crashed during a shot and instantly killed the kids and the actor Vic Morrow. The situation can only be worse in non-union shoots, and parents would be wise to exercise much greater discretion over their children working in non-union productions. It is naïve to think that production people are as interested in your child's welfare as you are.

Perhaps the more important issue for parents is whether to allow their children to seek acting work in Hollywood in the first place. The whole family will be affected by this decision. As we have discussed above, there is little continuity in this business. The child actor and even the child's siblings and parents will not be able to lead a normal life, which will become fragmented by the various demands of the business on the family.

School days will be disrupted by auditions. Families may be forced to split up or uproot themselves to accommodate shooting schedules in distant locations.

The papers are full of stories of what happens to immature people with lots of cash and the attention of adoring hangers-on. Other childhood activities and even childhood friends will be sacrificed. Of course, plenty of vices await these impressionable youngsters in Hollywood. The death of young actor River Phoenix from a drug overdose was just the tip of the iceberg.

Every parent who is considering this lifestyle should take the time to read several biographies of people who grew up as childhood stars. They are the best testament to the price a family must pay for this decision. Finally, just because your kid was the big hit in the local production of *Annie* doesn't mean the kid will succeed in the big time. Hundreds of thousands of other kids from other towns with just as much charm, spunk, grace, beauty, and talent as your kid are already in Hollywood chasing after those starring roles.

WRITERS

In Hollywood everyone who isn't a producer is a writer. Just about anyone you meet in Los Angeles calls himself a writer. It's a running joke in town that every actor, lawyer, police officer, doctor, and waiter has written a screenplay. It seems that everyone believes they have some great story to tell, so they buy a computer and go to work. Of course, the person you meet on the bus who calls himself a writer may have nothing but a story idea, often no more unique than "boy meets girl, boy loses girl, boy gets girl back." The more serious writers in this group will have written one or more unproduced screenplays, which they usually will be glad to show you if you express even the mildest interest.

Studio executives in Los Angeles regularly get scripts in

the mail, dropped on their car seats, thrown over fences, and stuffed into their kid's backpacks at the day-care center. Hopefuls *pitch* (make an oral presentation in hopes of selling their stories) to anyone they think has a connection to the big game. Stories regularly get pitched in locker rooms, restaurant bathrooms, and at weddings and bar mitzvahs.

Every project, whether it's film, television, video, commercial, industrial, animated cartoon, or CD-ROM, has one or more writers. They create the story, the setting, and the lines that everyone else involved in the project will use and attempt to bring to life on the screen. This translates into thousands of writing jobs in Hollywood every year.

In film, the writer's major participation is in "pre-production," which means the early stages of the project. The writer may be employed to write a script based on his own or someone else's story idea or on some other literary material, such as a novel. If the writer already has a finished script, called a *spec script* (as in "speculative"), a producer or production company may option the rights to produce a film based on the script. (More on options in chapter 15.) The same, or another, writer will be employed to write a series of rewrites and *polishes*.

Once filming starts, the writer's involvement is minimal. Sometimes the producer may hire a writer (sometimes a writer who has had no previous involvement in the project) to be available in case problems arise and some rewriting is needed. During post-production when the film is edited, the writer is rarely around to give input, unless he also happens to be one of the producers or the director.

In a television series, the writer is usually hired as part of a team, or several teams, to develop and write each episode. For one thing, hiring teams provides for some consistency in series television. These writers are often also the producers of the show and so have a great deal of creative control over the series from initial concept to finished product. All scripts are *tabled*, i.e., literally brought to a big table with regular series writers and producers and eventually the actors. The script is read in this open forum and "improved" by the input of everyone at the table. The writers who find themselves in this unique bullpen have to be resilient, but TV money can be good, and the residuals, which we'll discuss later, can make for a very nice living. There is also a significant amount of work in television for writers who submit spec scripts to different shows. The general rule is that hopeful (meaning unemployed) writers will prepare a writing sample, usually based on an established show. This gives producers, agents, and studio executives a sample of work based on familiar material.

A film writer can earn a wide range of money, from union scale (see chapter 10) to $1 million a picture. Most get minimal profit participation, although writers are notorious for getting frozen out of the profits on the most successful projects. Most writers of feature films get in the $150,000 to $350,000 range if the picture is actually produced, less for non-union work.

TV writers get anywhere from scale to $25,000 or more per episode, sometimes up to $100,000 for a half-hour pilot. The largest sums are earned by the writers who are hired to write the *bible* for the year, meaning a general outline of where the series will go, what story lines will develop, and how the characters will change.

For writers at the top end of the business, the financial and creative rewards are great. However, except for a few select staff positions at the studios and larger production companies, the writer's employment, like most jobs in Hollywood, is piecemeal and sporadic. Most of the successful screenwriters and TV writers toil away for years in relative obscurity. This explains why writers have a love/hate relationship with the movie and TV business. Almost everyone understands that the basis of every production is a script, and without a good story the film or TV project will not shine. Unfortunately, writers are usually the low persons on the totem pole from a power perspective, whether or not they make the big bucks.

In Hollywood, unlike publishing or the theater, the word is not sacred, and there is a well-documented disregard for the sanctity of the writer's work. Directors and producers often view scripts as outlines or starting points at best, for what they will eventually put on the screen. Many projects will employ a score of writers to rework the script, and most of the writers will never receive credit for the finished product. Most scripts are rewritten until they are unrecognizable even to the original writer. This is why Hollywood has always been considered the ultimate sellout for so many writers—the money can be there, but the writer has no control over what happens to his work after it leaves the computer. For this reason, many writers become directors: It's the only hope any writer can have of shaping the final product.

CHAPTER THREE

The People Below the Line

As we indicated above in chapter 2, *below the line* refers to those people in the business who have the more technical jobs. These are the people who run the cameras, hang the lights, monitor the sound, set the props, build the sets, dress and make up the actors, transport the equipment, serve the meals, and perform a myriad of other behind-the-scenes tasks. Thousands upon thousands of these people are employed in the business, and many of them enjoy successful and fulfilling careers.

We describe below many different jobs, but some general comments can be made about all of them. First, someone who is willing to work hard and keep his or her nose clean has a very good opportunity to secure more or less steady employment in this part of the business. Second, the lifestyle can be a semi-nomadic one, particularly in the movie end of the business. A person must be able to move from project to project, from city to city, and know how to sustain themselves during the sometimes lengthy periods of unemployment. Third, these jobs are not for the faint of heart or the physically unfit. The hours on the set are long, and the demanding work requires that you keep yourself in top physical condition. Finally, for below-the-line people, the glamour of working in the entertainment industry is vicarious at best. These folks are the grunts. As reward for their work, their names roll on that long scroll at the end of a film, when the audience is already filing out of the theater.

What follows is a brief description of some of these jobs.

CASTING DIRECTORS

Technically speaking, casting directors are listed above the line. That is, they're listed in the above-the-line section of the budget with the writers, producers, director, and major actors. The reasons for this are, we can only assume, traditional. They may have something to do with the fact that casting directors work closely with directors as a team. But even though they appear above the line with regard to the budget, very few casting directors operate with anything like above-the-line status, nor do they earn anywhere near the money of most above-the-line players. Very few casting directors are considered players in Hollywood, though they can have enormous influence over the careers of less-established actors.

Casting directors are hired by production companies and studios to find and then screen actors for film or television projects. They may also participate in the contract negotiation once an actor has been hired. The casting director's creative input is in presenting the pool of actors selected to read for each role, although the director and producer usually make the final casting decisions.

The casting director's job is to make the difficult determination about whether a particular actor is appropriate for a given role. The decision of whom to call in for a given role is usually made based on minimal information: usually sex, looks, and personality.

The casting director may meet an actor at a *first reading*, where the actor is auditioning for a specific part. However, the first contact an actor has with a casting director is often at a general interview, during which the casting director just wants to meet the actor but isn't considering that actor for a specific part.

If the casting director likes the actor's looks and reading, the actor may be called back to audition again for the director and usually several others involved in the production. (In some cases, the casting director has the authority to cast certain parts without consultation.) Depending on the project, the actor may be called back to audition several more times as the group of persons on the other side of the evaluating table seems to grow exponentially.

We don't have a particularly high regard for methods many casting directors use to select actors. Typically, the actor comes to a bare office. He or she must read the lines as the casting director mumbles back the other character's response. It's not a great way of judging that actor's ability. Really good casting directors have a keen eye for talent and find ways to enliven the audition process to get more out of an actor.

Most casting directors get their start by working as an assistant for a casting director and, with a few exceptions, most casting offices are a two- or three-person operation. When a project is being cast, these folks work at a harried pace, breaking down the script to determine what roles must be cast, consulting with the director and producers, sending out a list of roles to be cast to the *Breakdown Services* (chapter 5), sorting through the hundreds and even thousands of submissions from agents and managers, setting up multiple auditions, conducting the auditions, and negotiating the contracts.

During their down time, casting directors fill their days and nights conducting general interviews with actors they haven't met before and attending films, plays, and showcases to seek out more talent. The way a casting director makes himself useful to a director is to have a large stable of actors they can suggest to the director during the casting process. So the best casting directors make sure they know who's available, and they generally have the names and faces of hundreds if not thousands of actors at their fingertips.

The casting director's survival depends on presenting the director with an assortment of creative, talented, and interesting actors, so they need actors as much as actors need them. Casting directors can also be quite loyal. Because they labor with such a lowly status in the industry, they sometimes have a natural sympathy for actors. Many actors' careers are made by one or more casting directors taking a personal interest in them and bringing the actor in to read for project after project.

Casting directors are usually hired on a freelance basis on movies. They are brought in, usually for about $25,000, to cast the featured actors. They bring recommendations to the director and producer, who in turn have the final say. The casting director obviously makes a large contribution to the picture and is often accorded *main title credits* (in the beginning of the film), as opposed to *end title credits*.

In TV, casting directors are usually not only involved in casting the series regulars but also enlisted throughout the life of the series to bring in actors for featured roles. Studios often employ their own casting people to oversee the freelance casting directors and to assist with casting decisions.

PRODUCTION ASSISTANT

Look for the people carrying the walkie-talkies around the set and you've found a *production assistant*. Production assistants (PAs) are the troops who work under the supervision of the production manager. They are the worry warts and the busy bees, making sure everyone is where they need to be, transporting actors and crew from parking lot to trailer to set, getting the reams of paperwork signed by the right people, making up and distributing the call sheet for the next day's shooting schedule, making the late-night telephone calls to announce costume fittings, changes, and on and on ad infinitum.

While some people make a good career out of working as a production assistant, this position is considered a perfect hands-on entry-level job for people who have ambition to move into the production end of the business. Scratch below the surface of any successful producer and you're sure to find one of his or her first jobs in the business was as a production assistant.

FIRST AND SECOND ASSISTANT DIRECTOR AND SECOND UNIT DIRECTOR

We mentioned these people when we talked about directors in the above-the-line section. The *first and second assistant directors (AD)* work as assistants, while the *second unit director* will take a film crew on location and actually direct the action while the director of the film is shooting the rest of the production.

DIRECTOR OF PHOTOGRAPHY

We all know who the director of photography is. The *DP*, or *cinematographer*, is the person behind the camera actually shooting the film, right? Well, not quite. The DP is the person responsible for translating the director's vision into a series of moving images. The DP coordinates all the elements of a scene that make up these images: the lighting, the set, the camera position and angle, and the movement of the actors. An incredible number of variables come into play in how a scene is shot, and it is the DP who must be on top of all of them. Even a small decision, such as what kind of film stock to use for a particular shot, can mean success or failure artistically and financially for the film.

The scope of this responsibility necessitates a close working relationship between DP, crew, especially the director, the *gaffer* (who's responsible for the lighting), the *production designer* (who designs the set), and the people immediately under the DP: the *camera operator* (who actually handles the camera), the *key grip* (who is responsible for moving the camera around), and the *first assistant camera operator* (who keeps the camera focused).

The path to becoming a director of photography is a very competitive one. People work for years advancing up the ranks, from assistant loader (who loads the film in the camera) to second assistant camera operator to first assistant camera operator to camera operator, then finally to DP. The rewards are commensurate with these efforts. A director of photography is one of the highest paid positions in the business. A top level photographer can make in the $200,000 range and up per picture. The work can be one of the most creatively satisfying ones. It can also be a path to becoming a director, which we will talk about later in chapter 5.

Camera Operator, First and Second Assistant Cameramen

These are the people who operate and care for the camera and film stocks. The *camera operator* is the person who sits behind the camera and moves it on its tripod to follow the action (along with the dolly grip, who moves the dolly to take the camera in whatever direction is required). The camera operator's eye is the one that sees what is being shot, which also gives him the authority to call for another take if something looks wrong on a shot. The *first assistant camera operator* supervises the camera crew and is also responsible for keeping the camera focused. The *second assistant camera operator*, or *loader*, takes care of the film stock and camera equipment, handles the paperwork, loads the camera, and sets up the slate at the beginning of each scene. Talk about teamwork. These people, along with the dolly grips and the boom operator, must be more coordinated and in sync than ballet dancers in the most intricately choreographed performance.

GAFFER AND BEST BOY

These have to be two of the more curious names in the business, but the actual work involved is integral to any production. A *gaffer*, sometimes called the *key electrician*, is the person who is responsible for the lighting. The gaffer takes direction from the director and the director of photography and supervises all aspects of the lighting operation, from getting all the right electrical equipment to the location and setting it up for each shot (called "pre-rigging") to operating the lights during the shot and breaking it all down. As far as we can tell, the name gaffer came from the term "gaffs," which refer to the beams above the stage where the production is being shot.

The *best boy* is the gaffer's right-hand person who handles everything, including lights, cables, cranes, generators, lighting filters, and crew. As with most of the below-the-line jobs, the gaffer and the best boy get their start and experience in the business by doing the grunt work of laying cables and operating lights.

KEY GRIP

The *key grip* is the third part of the camera triad, together with the director of photography and the gaffer. He and his crew are responsible for moving the camera before and during the shot. He also helps out the gaffer by setting up all the *diffusion* (the filters, scrims, and nets that go over and around the lights) and other lighting paraphernalia, such as reflectors.

Good grips are vital to a production because they are the Mr. (or Ms.) Fix-its. They can usually be identified on a set by the tool belts around their waists. If someone needs a piece of tape, a screwdriver, a piece of plywood, it is the grip who magically supplies it and, depending upon how strictly the union is supervising the production, often takes care of the problem.

The key grip has a team of grips at his disposal: his right-hand man, called the *best boy grip;* the *dolly grip,* who is responsible for the dollies and cranes that move a camera during a shot; a *rigging grip,* who sets up the rigging from which lights are hung, called "greens" or "beds"; and the *hammers,* the grunts with the tool belts.

Like the gaffers, the grips do much of the physical and sometimes dangerous work on a set. Someone who is contemplating a career as a grip better enjoy getting his hands dirty and better hope that his body can take the years of stress and strain that's involved.

PRODUCTION SOUND MIXER

Much of the art of a film, especially with the improved sound systems in most theaters, depends on those subtle and elusive waves that move through the air and titillate the inner organs of our ears, producing sound. It is the *production sound mixer* who must capture as many of these sound waves as he can on a set.

The production sound mixer is easy to identify. He or she is the one sitting behind an array of recording equipment with a pair of headphones on. On every take, after the command, "camera rolling," everyone waits for the simple cue, "speed," before the director can call "action" and start the scene. The production sound mixer is also the one who you will see pleading with everyone on the set to be quiet for a few seconds at the end of a shoot so he can get a clean recording of the background or ambient sound to use as filler between gaps in the dialogue.

The production sound mixer is usually assisted by the *boom operator*, the ever-present assistant who attempts to set the wide array of microphones that must be close enough to pick up the dialogue but far enough away not to be seen in the shot. Also present is the *cable person*, who does everything the boom operator can't get around to doing. These people must have strong arms and backs to hold those long poles with microphones suspended over the actors, called the *boom poles*. They must also know what everyone else is doing on the set, so they can stay out of the way but still get their job done.

Production Designer

The color, size, and shape of the set, locations, costumes, props, and everything else that's seen in a film is the responsibility of the production designer. This is the person who translates the words of the screenwriter and the mental images of the director into a visual reality. Much of the production designer's job involves coordinating and focusing the activities of the various people who are directly responsible for the various visual aspects of a film, from location scouts, set designers, and property masters to set decorators, costume designers, makeup artists, and hair stylists. The production designer's assistant is called the *art director*. Obviously, these folks can have a huge creative impact on the finished product.

Set Decorator and Property Master

The *set decorator* "dresses" the set with appropriate items, like the drapery in a bedroom. The *property master* is in charge of the objects on the set that the actors use (usually referred to as *props*), plus some of the smaller miscellaneous items. If weapons are used in a film, it's the property master who is responsible for their care and handling.

LEAD PERSON AND SWING GANG

The *lead person* supervises the buying/renting, care, placement, and transportation of the set dressing. The *swing gang* is his group of foot soldiers whose job is to get this work done.

MAKEUP ARTIST AND HAIR STYLIST

No mystery here about what these people do. The real question is how, at six o'clock in the morning, the makeup and hair people manage to successfully make up and style the six principals for the walkthrough of their scene, as well as the thirty-five extras who must be ready in fifteen minutes to practice their scene. Besides that, they must match the black eye on the lead actor if he had the fight in the last scene, even if that scene was filmed three weeks ago. Plus they're responsible for making up the swamp monster, which takes six hours of prep time. You get the picture. The good makeup artists and hair stylists earn every cent they make.

WARDROBE

The *costume designer,* in close consultation with the director, production designer, makeup artist, hair stylist, and director of photography, determines and designs the costumes and oversees construction and acquisition of the costumes. The *key costumer* assists the costume designer and is responsible for fitting the actors on the set. The *set costumer* hangs around the set to make sure the actors look good in their outfits, to find out what scenes are coming up so that the appropriate costumes can be ready, and to ensure "continuity," i.e., that everyone is wearing the same thing in this scene as they were wearing the day before when the same scene was being shot.

These people can be identified by the Polaroid cameras they always have on hand to snap shots of the actors in their costumes.

STUNT COORDINATOR

We're certain you have a pretty good idea what a stunt coordinator does. He or she plans the stunts and supervises the stunt men and women, who perform the physical actions too dangerous for the actors to perform. Stunt people often have specialties, from jumping off buildings to car racing. They also have a union that makes sure they are well paid and that the stunts are performed as safely as possible. Good stunt people combine meticulous planning with casual disregard for the inevitable bumps and bruises and occasional broken bones of the profession. Bad ones don't last long.

SCRIPT SUPERVISOR

Another critical person on the set is the *script supervisor,* whose job it is to make sure all the shots match by making meticulous notes about the scenes. For example, if an actor is smoking a cigarette in a scene, and the director chooses to shoot part of the scene from another angle, the script supervisor will note exactly how much of the cigarette had been smoked, so there's continuity between the two angles. The script supervisor ensures that the actors follow the script and will feed them their lines if necessary.

PRODUCTION ACCOUNTANT

Maybe not on the set, but certainly within range, is the *production accountant,* assigned by the studio to watch the daily progress of the shoot and keep accounts of all the cash flow. He travels to the distant locations and is generally there for the entire schedule of production.

STAND-INS AND EXTRAS

While the crew is setting up a shot, they need some people to sit or stand where the actors will be. This is what *stand-ins* do. These people are often selected for their physical resemblance to the actors, at least in terms of size and shape. It's a necessary but very unglamorous job. Stand-ins never actually appear in the film.

Extras are all the background people in a shot. The distinguishing line between extras and principal actors—a very strict one in union projects—is whether or not the person has a line of dialogue. As we mentioned, the fact that extras are considered below the line is indicative of their rather low status. Some inroads have been made with the inclusion of extras in the Screen Actors Guild, but the fact remains that most people in the industry view extras and principal actors as two separate classes. This fact is reflected in the rather disparate income each is entitled to in a job and the difficulty extras have in moving up the ladder into speaking roles. Agents and others are not impressed by a resume filled only with extra credits. On the other hand, if you want to see what it's like on a set, extra work will get you a front row seat—and it includes meals!

Other jobs on the set include *caterer, dialect coach, animal trainer, wrangler, transportation coordinator and captains, choreographer, unit publicist, still photographer,* and *studio teacher.*

Are you tired of reading about below-the-line jobs? We

hope not because now we'll describe some below-the-line people who work primarily off the set but whose work is critical to the success of every film and TV project.

MATTE PAINTER

Who is responsible for creating a background or landscape when it is too expensive to film a real one or the film uses unreal backgrounds, such as in science fiction films? Why, the *matte painter*, of course. In the old days the matte painter lived up to his name. He really did paint for a living. However, with the introduction of computer-generated images and backgrounds in film, the tools at a matte painter's disposal have expanded to the computer terminal.

PRODUCTION ILLUSTRATOR

Another visual artist who is employed in the entertainment business is the *production illustrator*. This person is busiest in the pre-production stages, primarily creating *storyboards*, drawings that show the sequence of shots in a scene. These storyboards can be used by producers to sell a film concept, by directors to see how their mental vision of a film looks in pictures, by directors of photography to plan the breakdown of the camera shots, by production designers to plan their sets and locations, by production managers to make up the schedule of shots, and by the visual effects folks to design their lifelike sequences.

VISUAL EFFECTS PEOPLE

We talked about one of these folks above, the matte painter. Others include the *visual effects producer*, the *visual effects director of photography*, the *pyrotechnic* people, and the *model* and *miniature builders*.

If you really want to sound knowledgeable, you'll know the difference between visual effects and special effects. *Special effects* are created on the set. The wind, lightning, and rain machines that are used to simulate a storm are tools of the special effects team. *Visual effects,* also called *special visual effects,* are created off the set and then incorporated into the film in post-production.

Visual effects people work in their own studio and spend a lot of time talking about blue screens. When the studio wants to show Superman flying, they'll hoist the actor in a harness in front of a screen that is literally blue, then superimpose what they shoot against another background. It's the technique used to create traveling matte photography, animation, computer-generated images, and front and rear projection. Weather reporters use it to show you the cloud patterns moving across the weather map. It's a technique that combines artistic sensibilities with great technical expertise and innovation.

A Note about Animation

Animation has experienced a boom in the industry in the last few years, thanks in large part to Disney's megahits Beauty and the Beast, Aladdin, The Lion King, *and* Pocahontas, *as well as the huge success of* The Simpsons *and* Beavis and Butthead *on television.*

These animated projects provide a great deal of work for writers, producers, and actors, not to mention animators. Animators display a wide variety of skills. Some draw the beginning and ending images for a scene (the key cells), some do the drawings in between the key cells (yes, they're called the in-betweeners), and others do the coloring. Nowadays, much of the drawing work is done overseas to take advantage of the much cheaper labor there.

FILM EDITORS

Almost everyone has a rough idea of what a *film editor* does. He or she is the one who takes all the different scenes that have been shot, then cuts and splices them back together to make the final film. Although it may sound simple, the actual process is incredibly complex—technically and creatively—involving many people and usually taking much longer to complete than it took to shoot the film.

The director calls "print it" when he's satisfied with a scene that has been shot. This is a critical call, because it determines which shots will be developed and possibly used in the final product and which shots will be discarded and never used at all. At the end of a day of shooting, the film is taken to a lab and developed. All those takes that were deemed worthy by the director are printed and delivered to the editor. These "dailies" (so called because this procedure is done every day) are viewed by the editor and often many others at the end of each day. The editor and others review dailies to determine what kinds of problems need to be fixed and to reassure themselves that everything is going according to plan. The editor is looking for all sorts of things—that the color matches from reel to reel and camera to camera, that the actors' movements and the objects on the set match previously shot scenes, that everything called for in a scene has been shot, and that the sound quality is consistent throughout. A good editor at this stage of the game can save a production thousands of dollars and ensure that a director's vision of his or her masterpiece is actually being realized.

As the production is moving along, the editor, in consultation with the director, begins cutting together a *work print* until they have a very rough finished product, called appropriately enough, the *rough cut*. All of the work is done on duplicate copies of the original film, which is too precious to work with since one mistake could ruin the original footage. The editor keeps working on this rough cut as special sound and optical effects are added, as scenes are reshot, and as the production company begins gearing up its publicity campaign with a *release date* that always seems too soon to get everything finished.

When everyone is finally satisfied, too worn out to care anymore, or out of time, the editor makes a list of all the cuts that must be made and turns this list over to a *negative cutter,* the person who will take the original negative and meticulously cut it into its final form (discussed below). From this, *answer prints* will be made that will be distributed to the movie houses to be viewed by (the studio hopes) millions of paying customers.

Because of the technical and creative expertise involved, the job of editor has evolved into a highly skilled and competitive position. People work for years as *film librarians, apprentice editors,* and *assistant editors* to learn the craft and advance up the ladder into the coveted position of editor. Because of the highly collaborative relationship with the director, many directors will use the same editor in film after film. An editor's lifestyle can be one of the most demanding in the business. As that release date looms closer and closer, editors will spend hours upon hours in the cutting room, often under enormous pressure and sometimes not sleeping for days, in order to get the film out on time.

With the rapid advance of video and digital technology, editors are increasingly using computers to do the work they used to do by hand. The days when editors handled actual film stock, cutting and splicing it, are fading fast. Anyone who is thinking about a career as an editor would be well advised to learn about these advances and make sure they are up to speed on the latest film editing advances in the computer field.

A few people should be mentioned at this juncture. We just talked about the negative cutter, the person who cuts the original negative of the film into its final form. He or she is assisted by a *breakdown operator,* who does much of the actual physical work of handling, caring for, and storing the film, as well as the careful paperwork that must be done to ensure that anyone can find a particular reel or scene when needed. These folks are usually supervised by a *foreman.* The handling of actual film is possibly one of the least creative aspects of the business but one of the most critical. If an original negative has been damaged, it can never be repaired completely. For a negative cutter, one fingerprint smudge on one frame of film is a major mistake. The negative cutter, along with the *librarian,* is also responsible for keeping track of where the film stock is. When thousands of feet of film for scores of movies a year are involved, this can be a daunting task.

The *color timer* and the *hazeltine operator* work together in much the same way as the editor and negative cutter to set the color balance, density, and contrast of a film. The color timer consults with the cinematographer, director, and producers to determine their preferences, then sets about making the necessary adjustments on a positive work print. When the color timer is satisfied the work is complete, the hazeltine operator makes the adjustments on the original negative. Much of the mood of a film is determined by the colors and the shades of light and dark, so a good color timer can make an important contribution to the success of the project.

POST-PRODUCTION SOUND

As we mentioned above, while the moving images in a film get most of our attention, the sounds that we hear in the theater can have a profound effect on our movie-going experience. We've talked about the folks who are responsible for capturing the sound during the actual filming—the production sound mixer, the boom operator, and the cable person. Now let's meet the people who work on the sound after the film is "in the can."

Supervising sound editor, as the name suggests, is the person who coordinates all the different sounds that are put on the final soundtrack, except for the music, which is handled by the *music editor.* In addition, there are *sound mixers,* who add all the soundtracks together in the final edit. As with visual effects, the sound editor must have many people helping him and a lot of technology at his or her disposal.

The *ADR editor* does the "looping," which is the recording of voices after filming. Also called *ADR,* additional dialogue replacement, this process is used if an actor's dialogue needs to be redone because of some technical problem on the set, such as a jet plane passing overhead during an intimate love scene; or some of the dialogue may have to be replaced to give an R-rated film a PG rating. Looping voices for crowd scenes is called *walla.* The name apparently derives from the idea that "walla" is the sound that a crowd makes when its members are all talking at the same time.

The *foley editor* is responsible for producing the right sound for different kinds of footsteps, as well as other sounds that are difficult to record on the set. You will see foley editors in special studios that have several kinds of surfaces, such as concrete, marble, and gravel. There's a screen overhead for the foley person to watch as they try to match their footsteps with those of the actor in the scene. In the days of Fred Astaire movies, there were specialists in *snaps and taps* who actually made the tapping and snapping sounds to match the movements of the dancers. The people who do foley are also responsible for creating a multitude of sound effects in their studio, such as wind, rain, and thunder.

A *rerecording mixer* mixes together all the different sounds that have been recorded to make the final soundtrack for a movie. Obviously, this person will work closely with the sound editor and the director to mix the sound to their specifications.

Sound editors and mixers, like film editors, work in a high-pressure environment in which time and money are at a minimum and many people are looking over their shoulders, second guessing their work. This job demands a strong but very flexible ego and the ability to put in long hours. The competition for good sound jobs is fierce, so make sure you're ready for a long-term commitment and plenty of hard work.

COMPOSERS, ORCHESTRATORS, AND MUSICIANS

These are the people who write the music, determine which instrument plays what, and then sit down and actually play it. We all know how important music is to a film. Who is not inspired by John Williams' music in the *Star Wars* trilogy or terrified by his music in *Jaws?* What you may not know is that Hollywood attracts some world-class musicians and composers to work in film and television. Since the music is added near the end of post-production and time is at a premium, musicians are expected to walk into a recording studio, tune up their instrument, get several pages of original music they've never seen before, and then play it flawlessly the first time. The musician who needs some work on his or her sight-reading need not apply.

There are also many people who work full time at the studios in music departments, obtaining the rights to music to use in television and movie productions. We'll talk about some of them in the section called "Studio Employees" below.

TECHNICAL ADVISERS AND RESEARCHERS

Because each movie and TV show has to create a realistic world, producers have always brought in people to supply the accurate details. Technical advisers are people with expertise who are hired, usually on a freelance basis, to advise the creators on how to make the production more accurate. For example, we know a psychic who was hired to advise the producers of a movie on ESP. He gave them information on the phenomenon and gave the writers and actors ideas about how to portray psychics. Retired military people have often found work as technical advisers, and of course more than one doctor has gotten some work showing movie and TV people how to make their hospital dramas look like the real thing.

Somewhat related are jobs as *researchers*. Researchers might be librarians or graduate students or *Jeopardy!* types who wander into Hollywood and get hooked up with some production because of their skills. Some people do it on a freelance basis, but many of the *reality shows* (discussed below) keep skilled researchers on staff. *Clearance businesses* keep people in more or less permanent jobs reviewing scripts for accuracy and making sure that the scripts don't inadvertently defame people. For example, if the script is a murder mystery and the murderer is a doctor from Albuquerque named Louis Prout, the researcher will check the Albuquerque phone book to find out if there's such a doctor with that name. The studio lawyers and producers will make the final decision about whether to change the script or the name, but meanwhile almost every script for major movie and television productions is checked, which keeps some researchers consistently employed.

STUDIO EMPLOYEES

There are thousands of people who work in the studios in more or less stable positions. They don't get credit on screen, but they have health insurance, vacation days, and generally decent salaries, and they often retire with pensions and health intact. They even get to see a movie or television star once in a while.

Studio employees are generally grouped into the category of *overhead*, because they're not budgeted separately on a production. Instead, the studio will charge a flat fee for providing the use of all of its employees and charge an overhead fee (usually 15 percent) to each production.

We talk about some of these people in chapter 4, when we discuss the studio executives, production executives, and lawyers, but there are plenty of other jobs to be had at the studios. We'll mention just a few here.

There are entire departments with specialties such as *marketing*. The marketing department prepares all the advertising campaigns for the movie and television productions. You see their work in the billboards, posters, and other promotional materials. If you understand that a studio will spend in the ballpark of $10 to $15 million to promote each film, you can imagine the resources and the clout available to the people who do this work. Naturally, the huge amount of money flowing through these departments makes everyone nervous, so higher-level jobs tend to be somewhat unstable. We discuss the marketing activities in more depth in chapter 20.

Beyond marketing, there are also departments that oversee the film and television distribution, making sure the prints and videos get there on time. There are people who work on the *trailers*, which promote movies, and the *promos*, which promote television shows. There are *anti-piracy* experts who try to make sure no one but the studio makes money from its properties.

Other staff people who work at the studios include *credit administrators*, *casting administrators*, *contract administrators*, *music people*, *construction crews*, *projection people*, *file people*, *mail people*, *messengers*, *food service people*, *telephone operators*, and *security guards*.

At any one time, there will be two thousand or more permanent employees of a major studio and a smaller but still significant number at the lesser production companies. There are many more categories of jobs, and as we've said, lots of people spend their whole working lives at a studio. They might not really have much to do with actual production, but they like the environment of a studio lot.

————

A Few Words about Reality Shows

We've directed most of our discussion to jobs people find in traditional narrative motion pictures and television: that is, productions that tell a story. This book wouldn't be complete without a mention of the work people find on shows that are based on reality, as opposed to fiction.

Of course, television news and documentaries, which have had a long history in television, are the granddaddies of this category of production. The children of this tradition are Hard Copy, 20/20, Rescue 911, *and* Stories of the Highway Patrol. *Sometimes talk shows such as* Geraldo, Oprah, *and* Ricki Lake *are also included, but they've become so pervasive they enjoy their own status as a type of production.*

Reality shows are enjoying a huge popularity now, and therefore they provide a great career path for some. All of these shows use directors, writers, producers, on-camera talent, researchers, clearance people *(people who get permission to use footage or photos in the stories), and technical people behind the camera. Many of the people who work on these productions have a background in journalism. The pace can be hectic, but the work can be steady. People tend to get work on a yearly, half-yearly, or quarterly basis on these shows, depending on the stability of the show and the creative talent's contractual clout.*

————

CHAPTER FOUR

The People Who Do Business

AGENTS

There are agents and there are agents, and you can't lump together high-powered agents at Creative Artists Agency with your struggling, one-person creative-talent agency in Encino, California. If you are one of the chosen few with a hot agent, you can sit back and wait for your next script to arrive via personal messenger. (Of course, the script might be for a sequel to *Bimbo from Mars*.) In contrast, even though most agents don't play at the heady levels of the top people, they're still crucial in Hollywood, because most deals at the higher levels are negotiated by agents. Some agents help their clients find work. In the case of actors, we'll discuss below how most acting jobs are actually funneled through the agencies.

Agents vs. Managers

One key difference between agents and almost all other players in Hollywood, except for lawyers, is that they are regulated by state law. In the state of California, the Talent Agencies Act in the Labor Code requires individuals who procure employment for artists in entertainment fields (except those that procure only recording contracts) to be licensed as talent agents by the labor commissioner. In addition, an agent must be franchised by the unions to represent union members. Agents procure work as opposed to managers (who are not subject to licensing and whom we'll discuss below), who are supposed to counsel and direct the careers of the creative talent.

BIG AGENCIES VS. SMALL AGENCIES

There are three agencies that are currently considered the dominant forces in Hollywood: Creative Artists Agency (CAA), International Creative Management (ICM), and the William Morris Agency. All three have at least fifty agents. These three and the few respected mid-level agencies (mostly made up of big-agency veterans) are focal points for the power brokering in Hollywood. It's a widely held cliché that one of the classic ways to start your Hollywood career on the dealmaking side is to begin in the mailroom of one of these agencies. The idea is to become someone's assistant, then maybe a junior agent, and finally an agent with a client roster at the top. This happens to be one cliché that's true. Most agents do start in the mailroom, where they can be watched and sorted and selected for the rarefied atmosphere of high-powered agenting.

Most agents work within agencies as opposed to going solo. The smaller agencies generally specialize in one type of client (e.g., writers), and are thought to provide more personal service, though they may not have the clout of the big three. Big agents will represent their clients in all aspects of movies and TV, including commercials. Fees are generally 10 percent of each deal, and packaging fees are 5 to 10 percent of the budget of the project. Some people are more comfortable with a smaller agency, feeling they get more attention, whereas others prefer the implied power and clout of the big agencies. Some successful agents are so big (or ornery) that they work alone. We discuss the process of choosing between kinds of agents in chapter 7.

What do agents do? The top agents at the top agencies in town are some of the major players in the business. Their calls get answered, their demands get met, and they are just as important to the process as any person in Hollywood. Their power is based on the desirability of their clients, the collective clout of their agency, and the force of the individual personalities of the agents. Their power allows them to make deals for creative talent according to their rules. Their wisdom allows them to guide their clients' careers.

In addition to doing deals on an individual basis, agents *package* their clients so that a studio is forced to take a number of their clients for an individual project. For example, if the studio wants a particular actor for a TV series, they have to take a producer and team of writers represented by the same agent. This earns the agency license fees (in television, 6 percent of the license fee plus a percentage of the profits is typical).

A powerful agent sets the pace for dealmaking in town. The big agents not only complete huge deals for the individuals they represent, but they also broker the buying and selling of entire companies worldwide. Why are agents such an important part of the game in Hollywood? Perhaps the fundamental reason is that most creative talent aren't necessarily businesspeople. The studio is much more comfortable doing business with an agent, because they want deals done efficiently and with as little ego damage as possible done to the creative talent. No studio executive wants to tell an actor that she's only worth X dollars and there's no way she can get main title billing, so the task falls to the capable agent. A good agent knows what the traffic will bear and can generally get his client most of what the studio will give.

A bad agent can weaken or destroy his client's career by sheer incompetence.

We'll talk about the deal points agents negotiate in chapter 13. Do agents get their clients work? Not as much as you might think. It seems that only the most powerful agents are in a position to make suggestions to the studios that their client's work get read or seen. A good agent submits clients for the appropriate jobs, has the connections and clout to get them a meeting or an audition, takes the time and trouble to do the necessary follow-up to secure the job, and usually negotiates the contract once the creative talent is hired. Most agents do whatever they can to power-lunch and network their clients into jobs, but it's clear that most people get their own work, especially at the beginning of their careers.

AGENTS AND ACTORS

Actors have a special relationship to agents because most acting jobs are actually funneled through agents. These jobs are listed by the casting directors in the daily Breakdowns, a list to which only the agents and managers have access. (We'll discuss the Breakdowns in chapter 5.) Do most agents have the training to recognize real creative talent? Do they have the necessary intelligence to understand the finer points of entertainment contracts? Do they have the will and imagination needed to propel creative talent to the top? Well, no. Their training, if any, is haphazard. Almost all represent scores of clients they've never seen act or direct and have a hard time keeping track of. They'd just as soon drop all their less than successful clients for the few who've grasped the golden ring.

Almost everyone needs an agent to play the game because the studios don't like dealing with creative talent directly, and doing your own deal is like sending the lamb in with the lion. Agents are regulated by state law, so there is some protection against incompetent or unethical behavior, but anyone who wants to make it in Hollywood has to learn to choose an agent. Getting them to effectively represent you is a fine art that must be learned.

MANAGERS

Just what do managers do? We're talking here about managers who manage overall careers of creative talent as opposed to business managers, whom we'll discuss below. No one seems to have a good answer to this question except to say that managers take a 10- to 20-percent bite out of all your paychecks before taxes, whether or not they do anything to help you get a job, or they take a hefty producer's fee in place of a commission. Managers attach themselves primarily to actors in Hollywood, with the intention of providing career guidance of some sort. Another place you see managers is, of course, in professional sports such as boxing and wrestling. By law, managers are prohibited from submitting an actor for roles or negotiating contracts; this is supposed to be exclusively the domain of agents. However, this law is broken with great regularity.

A good manager, who usually represents only a handful of clients, does what good agents used to do. They gain the actor access to auditions. They pressure the right people to get them cast. They negotiate the best contracts. They give sage advice to help the inexperienced and inept fashion ideal careers. They have the ability to see strengths and match creative talent with the right projects.

If it sounds too good to be true, it's not. A good manager is worth his or her weight in gold and is just as rare. The mediocre ones are hardly worth the money. The bad ones can be really bad. Many actors in particular experience their first taste of the rampant sexual and financial exploitation that exists in Hollywood at the hands of someone calling him- or herself a manager. Unlike agents and lawyers, people can call themselves managers without having any license; managers are completely unregulated and are not subject to any form of professional scrutiny. If an agent or a lawyer rips you off in some way, you may be able to get his or her license revoked. A bad manager can pave the way to a short trip to palookaville. The point is you have to educate yourself in Hollywood and vigorously pursue those people who can help your career. Both good agents and good managers are well worth the cut they take out of the pie and are usually indispensable to a successful career.

BUSINESS MANAGERS

Business managers, as opposed to simply managers, are enlisted by creative talent who have established careers and who need help managing their often complicated financial affairs. The business manager keeps track of the flow of money, pays the bills, makes investments, prepares tax forms, and helps set up the legal mechanisms, such as incorporating the creative talent, to ease tax burdens. For this they usually take a percentage. Just be aware that unless they're CPAs or regulated by some other professional standards you'll have no recourse when your money suddenly disappears.

While the idea of one person supervising your financial affairs, freeing you to concentrate on your career, may appear to be the most cost-effective and sensible approach, this advantage can be outweighed by the risks of putting all your precious financial eggs into one basket. For every business manager who's provided his client with financial security, there's another who has literally ruined his client. Unless your business manager is exceptionally well trained and completely insured, you run the risk of a single act of negligence, incompetence, or thievery destroying your financial security. Don't believe it could happen to you? There are dozens of stories of creative talent at all levels who have naïvely believed the same thing and are now paying the price.

We recommend following the lead of the studio executives we know, who use an accountant to keep track of their money and prepare their taxes, a stockbroker to manage their investments, a tax attorney to structure their financial affairs, a secretary to pay their bills, and a certified financial planner to help them invest. These people are well trained to perform their jobs, can be supervised more easily, and usually work for organizations that have deep pockets should disaster strike.

LAWYERS

Your lawyer, if good, is often the difference between cashing in on your rightful share of the goodies or watching the fruits of your labors devoured by others. The top lawyers can be major brokers in town, setting up the deals as well as negotiating. It's not unusual for high-level creative talent to rely on their lawyers to make their deals.

There are lawyers negotiating the deals on both sides of the table. For almost every deal made in Hollywood there's at least one lawyer on the studio side and one lawyer working in tandem with the agent representing the creative talent. The role of the lawyer for creative talent is most often nailing down the finer points of a contract once the major points, such as compensation, have been negotiated.

However, in today's Hollywood many lawyers have become superstars in their own right, pulling together deals and setting the pace for the industry. Lawyers are definitely players in the good old boys and girls network of the entertainment business, which has created potentially huge conflicts of interest when they represent clients on both sides of the table.

We'll discuss what studio lawyers do under the section

below on studio executives. As for lawyers who represent creative talent, entertainment law is a specialty practiced full time by no more than a few dozen people, certainly less than one hundred. There are a few law schools in Los Angeles, San Francisco, and New York that prepare lawyers for this kind of work, which is a combination of contract and *intellectual property law* (mostly copyright and trademark law, with some antitrust and international law issues thrown in).

It's not so much what they learn in school that makes an entertainment lawyer especially capable. It's experience in the detail of the sometimes Byzantine structure of typical deals, from profit participation to credit. We'll talk more in chapters 13 and 17 about the kinds of deal points lawyers negotiate. Of course, the more people on your team, the more people take a bite out of your earnings. Most lawyers still operate on an hourly basis (and fees range from $100 to $600 an hour), but some take a percentage of your compensation (5 to 10 percent) instead. While most working actors use an agent, a manager, and an attorney to promote and protect their career, a small percentage of well-established actors will jettison their agents and managers and rely exclusively on their attorney to act in all three capacities.

While an attorney might not be helpful at the start of a career, even if you can afford to hire one, many new creative talent fail to add a lawyer to the team early enough. When you land that first lead in a pilot or sell your first script, you'll be so grateful you'll sign for a box of Cracker Jacks. Bringing in an attorney to help negotiate the deal can be the furthest thought from your euphoric mind. Three years later, however, as your show wins its second Emmy and your face is being used to sell T-shirts and coffee mugs, or they've made a best-selling doll based on a character you created, you're still living on a diet of peanuts and caramel popcorn, looking for the prize in the box but not sharing in the profits that should have been yours.

Fortunately, lawyers are so much a part of the scene in Hollywood that the studio will be reluctant to do business with you if you don't have decent representation. This attitude reflects not so much generosity as a practical understanding that creative talent without lawyers generally end up unhappy creative talent, and unhappy creative talent is not good for business in the long run. We'll talk about finding and using an attorney in chapter 7.

STUDIO EXECUTIVES

Studios and independent production companies employ hundreds of people in various capacities to attract creative talent, bring material into the studio, make deals at all levels, oversee production, and generally guard the company's assets. As you make the rounds, you're most likely to hear the following terms.

CREATIVE EXECUTIVES

Any title in Hollywood that contains the word "creative" would have to be a misnomer. The studio refers to their cadre of mostly young, highly polished, and usually deeply ambitious soldiers as *creative executives*. They put deals together, develop projects, and deal with creative talent in contrast to the people who handle the nuts and bolts of production *(production executives)*.

Creative executives work day and night swimming in the waters of the dealmakers and creative talent, trying to make their own careers by coming up with the next big hit. They have lunches with agents and creative talent and listen to pitches from writers or producers trying to sell scripts. They read scripts themselves or, if they're high enough on the totem pole to have them, they get their assistants to write brief summaries of scripts called *coverage*. If they get something going or work for someone who does, they'll spend their time worrying over the budget and smooth-talking the creative talent into fulfilling the studio's wishes. A large portion of this job is what is referred to as *spin*. Sometimes it seems spinning at high speeds is about the only ability most creative executives have. Mostly the phrase has to do with the ability to control creative chaos through hype and manipulation. In a world of illusion, the greatest illusionists are sometimes the creative executives.

It's a heady world. These people, rarely beyond their mid-thirties, spend every waking hour doing deals and schmoozing in an attempt to get a project produced. If only because of their age, these are people who have little experience in anything, let alone film production. Yet these are the people who ultimately rise to positions of power in the industry through force of personality or blood relations, if not creative vision. If they are effective, creative executives have the ear of the powerbrokers and thus can have the first and sometimes the last word on who gets hired or fired on a project or whether a project gets made at all. Their role is to seek out good properties and good people and seduce them into attaching themselves to the studio. Once a project is set up, they become the liaison between the production and the studio. They are often assigned to the set to keep everyone happy, to convince reluctant actors to drop their pants on-screen or jump off a bridge for some artistic purpose higher than their petty concerns for modesty or safety.

The bad news about creative executives is that many of them seem to get caught up in their own hype and end up behaving badly. Anyone who's seen Robert Altman's film *The Player* has a sense of the moral values of some of this breed. If anything, that film was a mild and loving reflection of what can be some pretty ugly behavior. We don't think many creative executives kill people who annoy them, as did the main character in that picture—at least not literally—but we've seen some fairly predatory behavior. Although not unique to creative exec-utives, some people with this job description seem to practice a particularly virulent form of sexual harassment, otherwise known as employing the casting couch. We'll talk more about some of the hazards of playing the studio game in chapter 14.

The good news about creative executives is that many of them have a good eye for material and creative talent and the chutzpah, or nerve, to put it all together in projects. The im-portant thing to know is that creative executives at studios are definitely players, and even the lowliest of them has a shot at moving a project or a creative talent forward if they're good enough.

BUSINESS AFFAIRS PEOPLE

These people are mostly lawyers who have managed to escape drafting contracts and taking care of the boring minutiae of a production. Instead, these driving people spend most of their time on the phone with agents and lawyers tying together the guts of each deal for all the actors, writers, and directors hired to work on a project. *Business affairs people* answer to chief executives and do the bidding of the creative executive on a production. Their job is to have an awareness of the fiscal con-fines of the project and to hold the line on each deal so the studio doesn't give out too much money, power, or credit to any individual.

If the talent representatives are doing their jobs, there is almost no contact between business affairs and creative talent. It's considered a breach of etiquette for a business affairs person to talk to the creative talent directly during the dealmaking process. Of course, it's inevitable that some business affairs peo-ple and creative talent cross the line in order to close a deal.

Here are a few things to remember about business affairs people:

- First, their sole responsibility is to pay the creative talent as little as possible and to give the studio maximum freedom to develop, produce, and advertise the project. In a real sense, the business affairs people set up the structure of each project. If they give someone too much money or creative control, others will get less.

- Second, once the studio executive, casting director, director, writer, and/or producer decide they want to hire someone for a position, the business affairs person is under tremendous pressure to close the deal quickly. They will have to have some very strong reasons to justify to all those people why someone is too expensive or troublesome to sign.

- Third, all business affairs people talk to each other and tell each other what the other studios are paying for a particular creative talent. This may not sound like appropriate behavior, but it's a widespread practice. The savvy creative talent representatives know that the studio can check out their claims of past salaries.

In the rollercoaster world of Hollywood dealmaking, negotiating with studio business affairs is the real test of your representatives.

PRODUCTION EXECUTIVES

All studios have their own in-house producers, whose job it is to watch the purse strings. These people can visit sets or be permanently assigned to a production, particularly in television. Most often, these people are not decision makers with power to control above-the-line creative talent, but they can have enormous influence on which below-the-line creative talent is used. Usually, the studio production executive will have the relationships with the local unions representing the crew and teamsters, even the catering business.

The *production executive*'s job is to watch the dollars being spent and blow the whistle if costs are getting out of hand or if the production team is doing something that is likely to get the studio into trouble, such as working kids too many overtime hours or bribing the wrong city officials. A good production executive has been a production manager or some other type of producer and knows how much it should cost to rent that crane or how many days a wardrobe person is needed.

THE MOST IMPORTANT PERSON IN HOLLYWOOD

The most important person in Hollywood is somebody's assistant or secretary. We're not kidding.

By now, you may have gathered that the secretaries and assistants of today are likely to be the casting directors, studio executives, and agents of tomorrow. More often than not, people in entry-level jobs in the industry are simply on the first rung of a long career ladder. Whether or not they're on their way to somewhere else, they are the gatekeepers to the offices where the action happens. Any creative talent who does not take the time to develop relationships with them is at best missing out on a golden opportunity and at worst making a dangerous future enemy.

Secretaries and assistants are the people who do all the busy work. They answer and screen calls, open and read the mail, file all the paperwork, and control the schedules of their bosses. Those with higher abilities, luck, connections, and/or ambitions may read scripts and/or spend all their free time schmoozing and making contacts. They are often included in the important decision making that goes on.

The key here is to know that it's not necessarily so important where you start as where you end up, and in Hollywood the important thing is to know who the players are and what current rules are in place. Most often the best place to learn this is working for the players. Most secretaries and assistants read the trade papers and follow the game. Starting at the bottom may have gone out of style as the first rung in the ladder of career success, but it's still a part of the Hollywood program. There's no shame in starting as someone's assistant. You can't play the game until you know the ropes, and anyone with any experience in Hollywood knows that today's assistant is tomorrow's vice president of production.

SECTION THREE

Getting Started

The first steps you take when you arrive in Hollywood can affect your entire career. If you haven't built a stable foundation, you'll have a very tough time when the going gets rough as it inevitably will. In particular, because film and television is such a collaborative art form, your success in obtaining work in Hollywood will be in direct proportion to the strength of your relationships with the people who hire you, your peers, and the others with whom you work.

CHAPTER FIVE

First Steps

GETTING SETTLED

You need a home and a car in L.A. Finding a home in town should not be too difficult. Nine million people live in Los Angeles County, and within a couple of days, you should be able to find a place to live too. There are scores of publications that advertise house and apartment vacancies, including the local newspapers.

A good way to start is to pick up your handy *Thomas Guide*, a detailed, multi-page map of the Los Angeles area. You'll need it. L.A. is vast. Does it matter where you live? Not really. The "L.A. area" is really a collection of areas, basically separated by the Santa Monica Mountains. Hollywood, Beverly Hills, Santa Monica, and the west side are all "the City," while Burbank, Studio City, and surrounding areas in the San Fernando Valley are called simply "the Valley." There are studios spread all over the area, from Santa Monica and Hollywood to Burbank and other points in the Valley. You could work anywhere. And no one is going to care much about your address until you hit the player ranks.

One of the best sources of information about cheap places to live is a publication called *The Recycler*. You can pick one up at most any convenience store or newsstand. Buy one of the San Fernando Valley edition *Recycler*s for cheaper places "just over the hill." Some places are naturally safer than others, so do some homework and keep your eyes open.

What about transportation? Remember those nine million people in Los Angeles County? Just about every one of them has a car, and you'll need one too, especially to survive in the business you are entering, in which each new day can mean miles of travel around the city. To put it mildly, the public transportation system leaves a lot to be desired and isn't a viable alternative if you expect to make it to meetings on time. You would be well advised to arrive with a car or have the cash to purchase one as soon as you get there.

FINANCIAL CONSIDERATIONS

Life is not cheap in Los Angeles. Even if you are sharing an apartment, you will be spending $350 a month, probably more, on accommodations. The insurance rates on that very necessary automobile are sky high in L.A. Food in grocery stores is not extraordinarily expensive, but L.A. is a place where people congregate more in restaurants and coffeehouses than at home, and the price of your daily double cappuccino can add up. And don't forget your cable TV and the price of all those movies you will be seeing. You're in the business now, and you'll want to keep up with all the new shows and films.

The most important financial factor to consider is the irregularity of work in the business, especially for people just breaking in. Almost everyone we know has underestimated the time it will take to earn a living solely from jobs in the industry. In fact, it is safe to say that the majority of people, especially actors, will *never* earn a living in the business. Even for those who do, it will take many more years than they anticipated, and they will likely hit several dry spells along the way.

This means it would greatly behoove you to have some cash reserves when you arrive. Supportive family members who will loan you a little money during the tough months and years will also help.

A day job (i.e., a job you take while waiting for your break) is pretty much a necessity for most people. If you have other job skills, so much the better. There are many entry-level jobs in the industry, although not necessarily in the area you want to pursue. An actor who works as a receptionist at a film lab may make a few contacts and learn about a certain part of the business but simultaneously despair about not getting the opportunity to pursue his acting career. Many people start their climb as someone's assistant or a production gofer. However, there are many stories of folks who came to Hollywood with one ambition, only to find themselves through happenstance pursuing entirely different but equally satisfying careers in the business.

The catch-22 of any day job is the need to make ends meet conflicting with the flexibility needed to pursue your desired career. How can you be available for auditions or pickup assistant work if you are stuck behind a desk all day? Who will hold a job for you when you leave for six weeks to work on a film shoot? The most flexible day jobs we know of are flight attendants, temporary secretaries, and, of course, that old standby, waiters and waitresses. The point is, find yourself some solid means of support, so you don't starve to death or get forced into some compromising positions before you become an overnight sensation.

Read the Trades

There are several trade papers in L.A., and many can be picked up at your local convenience store or newsstand. These publications are helpful not only to get a feel for the business and to learn the names of the players, but also to get leads on work opportunities. Many below-the-line folks and even some above-the-line people obtain work by contacting production companies about upcoming projects they read about in the trades.

Daily Variety *and the* Hollywood Reporter *both give daily coverage of the entertainment industry and offer listings of shows and films in production.* Dramalogue *and a relatively new periodical,* Backstage West, *review theater, film, and TV shows and list casting calls for most theater productions, some film and television, commercials, and student films. They are an excellent source for finding entry-level work, although much of the time for little or no pay. The* CD Directory *by Breakdown Services lists casting directors in town. The* Hollywood Creative Directory *includes agents and managers, feature writers, directors, and guides to TV movies and miniseries.* Film & Video Production *is a monthly periodical that covers film, TV, music video, and commercial productions. The* LA411, *also known as* The Blue Book, *lists all sorts of businesses serving the entertainment industry, like rental houses, and laboratories. Production people in the commercial field keep track of developments in* Shoot Magazine *and* Advertising Weekly. *Composers and arrangers read* Score Magazine. *Even popular publications like* Buzz *and* Premiere *are helpful.*

To get a complete feel for what resource materials are available, visit one of the Samuel French bookstores in Hollywood or in Studio City. If you are an actor, make sure you pick up *The Working Actor's Guide,* a yearly publication that is chock-full of information. If you're a lawyer, check out the *Entertainment Law Reporter.* Everyone has a specialty, and there's plenty of information on every area of the entertainment business. Take the time to educate yourself.

LETTING THEM KNOW YOU'RE IN TOWN

How do you get noticed once you've arrived? Here are a few methods: telephone calls, letters, headshots and resumes, personal appearances, postcards, anything respectable and not too silly to get their attention. Don't forget classes, seminars, and parties. All of these techniques are likely to yield a low percentage response, but remember that salespeople consider a 1 percent response rate a success for a mass mailing. You should operate with the same expectation—one response out of a hundred inquiries is a success.

One of the best ways to let people know you are in town is to immediately get involved in some project in almost any capacity. Low-budget productions are always looking for help, especially if you are willing to work for free or next to nothing. Not only will you show people what a hard and trustworthy worker you are, but you will also begin to get a feel for working in the business and for whether or not you have the temperament for it.

DO I HAVE TAPE OR FILM OF MY WORK?

One tool agents, managers, casting directors, and others use to evaluate your abilities is a videotape of work you've already done. Every office has a videotape player; and directors, producers, and even technical people are expected to have some samples of their work to show. The working actor who is still having to hustle to get work usually has assembled, at great expense, a tape containing short clips of his or her roles in film and television.

Now, you may be thinking, "All I have is a videotape of my work as Tony in *West Side Story* at the Davenport Community Theater. Can I use that?" No, not unless you want to get laughed out of town. Nor do we advise you to spend the money and time taping that scene you do so well in class. Nor is there much sense in producing a 15-second tape containing your extra work on *Divorce Court*, or the fabulous footage you shot at the family picnic last year. Until you have produced at least one piece of professional work that shows how you look on camera and gives some indication of your acting ability, it doesn't make sense to spend hundreds of dollars making a tape. *Professional* refers to work in film or television or extremely well-produced student and independent films. Anything less than that in terms of quality, and the tape will only undermine your chances of getting a role or securing representation. When asked if you have any tape of yourself, just politely say no. Don't be embarrassed about being a beginner in Hollywood.

One other point. When you do get film and TV work, make sure you get a tape recording of high quality. Similarly, if you work on a low-budget or student film, ask to get a tape of the film. For television work, many videotape duplication studios in town provide *air checks*, in which for a reasonable fee, they will record the TV program on which you appear and provide you with a copy. These studios are also the place you want to go when putting your tape together. The technician you use can make all the difference between a mediocre tape that does nothing for your career and an outstanding tape that gets you jobs.

WHAT ABOUT STUDENT FILMS?

Hundreds of talented people are flocking to the film schools in Los Angeles to get their start in the business. Some of these schools include the American Film Institute (AFI) and programs at the University of Southern California (USC) and the University of California of Los Angeles (UCLA). Part of the training is learning to shoot low-budget short films and videos, scores of which are being shot every day in Los Angeles. We talk more about the individual schools in chapter 6.

Some of these projects are first class and are an excellent place for the student as well as the new actor in town to get a start. Whatever your aspiration, you'll get the chance to get used to working on a set behind or in front of a camera. The job you fulfill or the roles you get may be larger, providing you with valuable experience and perhaps some good tape of your work. Since everyone involved is just getting started in the business, they are often more appreciative of your efforts, and the relationships you develop may last throughout your career. Some of these students actually do break through to the big time. There are many examples of successful people who brought along the people they worked with early in their careers.

The downside to student films is the likelihood of working on some real stinkers. The auditions can be silly, the director's direction bizarre, and the production chaotic. One actor related to us the experience of showing up for a 10:00 A.M. call and finally leaving the set at 4:00 A.M. the next morning, just as the crew was still setting up for the first shot. All this for no pay.

Many student films are advertised in *Dramalogue*, a weekly newspaper that contains some casting notices and other valuable information. You can also get casting information by calling and visiting the different schools.

One note of warning: Some student films are produced under union auspices and some are not. If you are a union member, you may get into trouble if you work on a non-union student film, though we will explain a way around that problem in chapter 9.

STAND-UP COMEDY

Seinfeld, Roseanne, Newhart, and Reiser. Becoming a successful stand-up is an obvious pathway for creative talent. Actors, writers, and other creative talent have long used this approach to break into the movie and TV business. The world of stand-up deserves a book of its own, though you can get some idea of what the life is like from the movie *Punchline*. This is one of the few professions you might be able to break into from your hometown, if your hometown is a major city. There are stand-up opportunities in most major cities, and most of them have amateur nights where you can try out your stuff.

INDUSTRIALS AND EDUCATIONAL FILMS

While not necessarily a stepping stone to the big time, many people learn something about the business doing films for private companies that are used to train people or to promote their company and products. In addition, there are companies that produce both short and longer films for the public school market at all grade levels.

The good news about these productions is that they are generally not union affiliated, so you don't have the problems getting work on them that we discuss in chapter 9. You can also get some experience, possibly even paid, working in front of or behind the camera. You can network and meet people who are

trying to break in or who have escaped the business. The work
is less sleazy and less dangerous than the porn industry, which
we discuss below, and as actors you can probably get work that
allows you to keep your clothes on.

THE PORN INDUSTRY

Sexually explicit films and periodicals are a big industry in Hollywood. Strip joints abound. High- and low-class prostitution is
an integral part of the fabric of big-city Los Angeles and the
entertainment industry. (The recent arrest of Heidi Fleiss for
running a prostitution ring that catered to the entertainment
industry was no occasion for shock or outrage for those who
work in this business.) The appetite of the porn industry isn't
confined to young women. There is also a significant gay porn
industry.

We won't deny anyone's freedom of choice, but we can
say unequivocally that an acting career in sexually explicit films
does not lead to other acting jobs. The two or three exceptions
to this rule only prove the point, and the most successful of porn
stars find themselves blocked when they try to find work in
Hollywood. It is only a little easier for directors, producers, and
writers who start out in porn. Generally a porn credit is considered worse than no credit at all, and you simply won't be able to
use it to get more legitimate work in most cases. For technical
people, the same caution does not necessarily apply, at least to
the same extent. These kinds of films are not ones you will want
to put on your resume, but the experience you get and contacts
you make can be helpful.

It is a fact that many actresses we know make their living
by dancing in strip joints, dance clubs, and mud-wrestling estab-
lishments. Women can make hundreds of dollars a night ca-
vorting in bikinis, G-strings, or nothing at all. Some may find

this work harmless in itself and a great way to support themselves while they pursue their acting careers. But more dangerous temptations await women who work in these places. Drugs and prostitution are only a step away, as well as other criminal activity.

We recently talked to an actress who worked in a dance club. She had resisted the step down into drugs and prostitution, but she was having a problem making her car payments. One of her steady customers suggested he could fix the problem by arranging for a couple of his "friends" to steal the vehicle. Another customer gave her an illegally obtained handgun to use for her protection. As long as she dances, this actress will have her moral balance tested by the types of people who are drawn to these places.

Some final warnings: Rumors abound that the porn industry is mob controlled. And the problem of becoming successful is doubled because it's not just about breaking into the legitimate industries. Sometimes it's about breaking out of the porn industry. The money seems easier there, and it's true that you may get a chance to direct a decade before you step on a Hollywood soundstage, but it's still not a good bet. Participate at your own risk.

SEX AND MONEY SCAMS

People who are new in town are the most vulnerable to the plethora of sex and money scams that permeate the industry. Actors, especially, are subject to this abuse, but there are naïve mistakes to be made by all kinds of creative talent. Half the young actors who come to town will tell you about being faced with one of these scams during their first few years. The business is full of flash and phonies who make promises they can't keep to hopefuls of all kinds.

These scams range from the criminal to the simply unethical. The bad are really bad. A SAG-franchised agent was recently convicted for sexually assaulting at least eleven women who interviewed with him. Another man ran a casting-call ad in the trades for over a year and a half, luring young women to a rundown warehouse in Ontario, California (more than an hour out of L.A.), where he badgered them into disrobing. The porn industry in particular, which we discussed above, feeds on new talent.

The money scams, although not always illegal, can sometimes be just as destructive. If you're in town long enough, you'll hear stories. We've heard about the woman who paid $1500 to get into an acting class in which she was taught that masturbating on stage was a good way to "free up her instrument," and the young man who was paying $375 a month for acting classes in which he spent his time learning the "correct" way to staple his headshot to his resume. These people were wasting their money and losing their dignity in the process.

It's not just actors who fall prey to these scams. There are those who routinely take advantage of creative-talent individuals: People who promise to read scripts for exorbitant fees; those who promise to get your project into some famous producer whom they know personally; or "fundraisers" who ask for seed money for a pet project. It's not always a phony trap—sometimes such requests do help first projects get made—but it's very rare for these gambles to pay off, even if they're legitimate. The scams seem endless. Throughout this book, we try to describe many of the sex and money scams we can think of, although our aims are outdistanced by the imagination of the slimy people who invent new ones every day. How can you keep up with the person who advertised a 900 number giving "six-minute seminars on how to make it in the business at just $3.95 a minute?"

Avoiding Scams

Advice to the Newcomer in Town

Network as quickly as possible. Take legitimate seminars and meet others who are starting out. Learn how the business works. Find out who the players are and how the game is played, so you'll be able to recognize a phony when you meet one. Of course, there are slimeballs who are actually players in the industry, so you have to exercise extreme caution when walking into situations that don't feel right.

Call before you go to a strange location. Ask for references. Check people out. Sometimes the union can be a good source of information about specific agents, managers, and lawyers. If you're asked to go to a meeting that doesn't sound like it's on the up-and-up, take along a friend. Avoid going to homes and apartments for meetings.

Never disrobe! *Refuse to do scenes and improvisations that call for you to "seduce" the acting teacher, director, or casting person. Be wary of acting teachers who won't let you audit or who insist you pay a large upfront sum to take the class.*

Avoid people who call themselves "consultants." Treat any invitation to dinner or for coffee to "discuss the project" as a date. If you don't want to date the person, don't go.

Last and most important of all, summon up your God-given common sense. If it seems like something's too good to be true, or if someone is asking you to do something you think is dangerous or suspicious, run the other way.

SPECIAL CONSIDERATIONS FOR ACTORS

THE BREAKDOWNS

Only in Hollywood could a system exist in which the person looking for jobs, the actor, is denied the basic information of what jobs are available. Sound pathetic? It is.

Here is how the system works. Many of the juicier roles in film and television never make it past the studios and more powerful talent agencies. To receive financing on a project, the studio or production company will negotiate with an agency to attach a "name," i.e., some actor or director who has star status. Since the project depends upon this star to get it rolling, the agency that represents the star can use this fact to demand a package deal. (We talked about packaging in chapter 4.)

The roles that are left over are cast through a casting director, who is given a list of the roles left to cast. The casting director will hold auditions and screen actors for the director and producers. After making calls to the creative talent or the agents with whom they are most familiar, the casting director will publicize the auditions by calling a private company called Breakdown Services. Breakdown Services prepares two lists of available roles, one for commercials and one for film, television, and some theater (referred to as legitimate) productions. These lists, the "breakdowns," are sent daily to the SAG-franchised agents and personal managers who subscribe, for a fee, to the service. Some 850 copies are sent out each day. Very rarely, the casting director or production company will also send this casting information to other publications, such as *Dramalogue*.

As you might have noticed, none of this casting information ever goes directly to the actor. Even if you wanted to subscribe to Breakdown Services, you can't unless you're a SAG-franchised agent or a personal manager. This is not a law, just a business decision made by Breakdown Services. Everyone but the agentless actor benefits from this system. The studios and production companies have a semi-efficient system for casting their projects. The more powerful agencies take their cut early on. The casting directors pare down the number of submissions they must process. The less powerful agencies keep their stable of actors in the dark and dependent upon them.

Predictably, a huge black market has developed for the breakdowns. In spite of threats of criminal prosecution by Breakdown Services, scores of actors each day get their desperate hands on the coveted breakdowns, and illegally copy them and distribute them at secret drop-off points or by fax to other actors. A bad spy novel could be written about all the shenanigans that take place because of this silly system. Everyone seems confounded by the problem of providing adequate access to the thousands of actors competing for the handful of jobs available. The actors' unions (SAG and AFTRA) have been able to do little to solve this problem. Gary Marsh, owner of Breakdown Services, asserts that he finds his business in a bit of a bind. If he were to make the breakdowns accessible to all actors, casting directors would be overwhelmed with submissions and stop using the service.

SHOULD I JOIN A THEATER GROUP?

There are many theater groups in L.A. It is said that more theater is being produced in Los Angeles than in any other city in America, including New York. Whether or not this assertion is true, the fact exists that a bundle of Equity-waiver theater productions are mounted each year in L.A. Many of these are produced by a myriad of theater groups in town, some in their own theater space and some at theaters rented on a production-by-production basis. A great number of productions, however, are independent. They are mounted by groups and individuals ranging from high-powered producers looking to find the next big hit (and to turn it into a very profitable movie), to a "name" looking for a star vehicle, to newer actors just looking to get some exposure, and to otherwise successful writers looking for a place to try out new material. Believe it or not, a few rare shows are produced by people just for the joy of it or because they are passionate about the play. Then there are showcases, which we will discuss shortly.

Actors' Equity Association is the union for actors that has jurisdiction over staged theatrical productions. This means that if you are a member of this union, you are restricted from acting in a play unless its producers comply with union regulations. We'll talk more about actors and other unions in chapter 9.

In Los Angeles, you will notice that most small theaters seat ninety-nine people maximum. This is because Actors' Equity has granted a special waiver to productions in Los Angeles operating in theaters of ninety-nine seats or less; hence the phrase *equity waiver production*. These productions are held to only minimal standards, certain safety regulations, and a meager provision for actors' salaries (as little as $5.00 a show). Nonetheless, we would suggest you become involved in these productions and join one or more of these theater groups. The theater is the best place to hone your craft; and yes, people in the industry will come to these shows, giving you a chance to show them your work. Perhaps you will even have the chance to experience the pure joy of living out a rich imaginary circumstance and moving the audience in the process, the joy that led many of you to give up hearth and home and pursue an acting career in the first place.

However, there is very bad news. A great majority of these productions are extremely amateurish and inept. That community theater back home is bringing more life to the stage with more professionalism than most productions in Los Angeles. Many of the theaters themselves are filthy. The plays that are presented are held together by profanity and shock value. The technical support can be nonexistent, the director a buffoon, and your fellow actors unable to act their way out of a paper bag. With this in mind, you will be forced to be very selective about the theater companies you join and the productions for which you audition. Your training as an actor will not be helped and can be harmed by participating in a bad show. You stand little chance of impressing the industry folks who see you in a bad play. It's hard to act in a vacuum.

Beware of theater companies that charge initiation fees and monthly dues to their members, and be sure to ask questions. You will want to find out how many shows a year the company presents, what kind of shows, whether or not new members are used frequently in the productions, the condition of the theater space, and the quality of the directors and other actors. Don't be afraid to ask questions and attend the shows the company is currently running. If you don't receive satisfactory answers to all these questions, don't hand over any money, lest it be used to subsidize the company owners' mortgage and the acting careers of other actors.

Finally, you need to be realistic about your own abilities. Stepping onto a stage will not magically transform you into a great actor. If you don't have the training to give a professional performance, seek that training first rather than embarrassing yourself and leaving a lasting impression of incompetence with any industry people who might witness your amateur efforts.

WORKING IN THE LARGER THEATERS

Several larger theaters in Southern California present a full slate of plays. These include the Civic Light Opera in San Bernardino; the Mark Taper Forum in downtown Los Angeles; the La Jolla Playhouse and the Old Globe Theatre, both near San Diego; the Pasadena Playhouse in Pasadena; and South Coast Repertory in Costa Mesa (near L.A.).

Since these theaters are governed by stricter rules with Actors' Equity, you will not be able to audition for productions there unless you are a member of that union or have received special permission from them. Call Actors' Equity to find out the rules you must follow to obtain special permission. There is extreme competition to get even an interview with these theaters, much less to be cast in one of their shows. A certain arrogance has also developed in some of these organizations, making the audition experience particularly unpleasant.

Most actors find the market for small parts in film and television to be more accessible to them than roles in the productions of these larger theaters. Finally, although the productions usually have a nice look, the acting and material can be just as awful as it is in the equity-waiver productions. Since we are in Hollywood, many of these theaters cast mostly "names" to beef up their box office. However, all these factors shouldn't deter you. In spite of the obstacles, some actors do succeed in obtaining work with these groups.

SHOWCASES

Let's get right to the point with *showcases*. Showcases are promotional tools to make connections and obtain work in film and television. The only thing they share in common with real theater is that they are both performed on a stage. Showcases are a selection of scenes performed by various actors to "showcase" their acting ability. They are usually organized and financed by the actors involved, who rent a theater for one or more nights, invite all the industry people they know with cutesy flyers, and serve really good food and refreshments to leave a lasting good impression. In the middle of all this some acting takes place.

You can't really call yourself a Hollywood actor until you've participated in one or more showcases. Despite the crass motive behind them and the absurd trappings that surround them, they actually may accomplish the purpose for which they are intended, i.e., making contacts and obtaining work. Since your sole purpose is to attract people in the industry and make an impression, you should consider whether or not to participate in a showcase from that perspective. Do the actors involved have the necessary connections to attract a significant number of industry people? Will the evening be produced in a first-class fashion? Is the theater space up to par and in a convenient and safe location? Are all the actors and the scenes they've selected first class? Are you ready to be seen? Is your scene partner good? Is the scene perfect for you, something you can understand and live out fully? Are you and your scene partner going to put in the rehearsal time necessary to make your scene outstanding? If the answer to any of the above questions is no, save your money for more worthwhile purposes. For all our criticisms of people in the industry, one trait they all seem to share is a good memory. Don't let their memory of you be a negative one.

Casting Workshops

Of all the scams in Hollywood, this has to be one of the more reprehensible and slimy ones. Here is how they typically operate: You go to some rundown theater in town. You're handed a scene you've never seen and assigned a scene partner you've never met. You're given twenty to thirty minutes to "prepare" the scene and then you perform it for a casting director. Then you sit there while the casting director "critiques" your performance. For this privilege you pay anywhere from five to forty dollars.

Everyone knows that the critique portion of the evening is a sham. The reason you are there is to meet the casting director and show her a sample of your work. The critique is added to give a veneer of respectability to an otherwise sordid affair. Plain and simple, you are paying a casting director for an audition. We believe it is doubtful you could ever positively impress a casting director under such conditions. Just the fact that you are lowering yourself to participate in these casting workshops will give the casting director a bad impression of you, to say nothing of your chances of giving a decent performance. In spite of our moral and practical condemnation of casting workshops, you may still choose to try one. Some actors swear by them. Some high-quality casting directors do participate in them, and some actors do get jobs from them. If you decide to try a casting workshop, we would advise you to choose carefully. Look for ones that allow you to pick your own scene partner and prepare your scene in advance. Check out the condition of the facilities. Get a list of which casting directors will be appearing which nights and pick ones who work regularly and have good reputations. Be careful to have the good sense to take any criticism you hear from the casting director with a grain of salt. Taking their critical remarks to heart will only undermine your confidence.

There is a variation of casting workshops that is important to mention. Many acting schools put on acting workshops and, at the end of several weeks of instruction, bring in casting directors and agents to see your work. Often these workshops are geared to specific genres—commercial acting, situation-comedy acting, acting on soaps, and voice-overs. These workshops cost several hundred dollars and the instruction is often poor at best. If you want to pursue workshops, check with people who've gone through them or sit in yourself to see if it's worth your time and money. Most likely, one of these classes might bring a return on your investment only if you are already well trained and are trying to break into a particular area of the business.

PREPARING FOR AND
NAILING THOSE FIRST AUDITIONS

We are reluctant to give much advice about audition techniques, since this subject is outside the scope of this book. Besides, there are no secrets that can be learned from a book about how to bring to life a bunch of words in a script. However, we cannot resist saying a few words about auditions. If you are well trained, you will have practiced hundreds of times, reading a script to get an understanding of the situation, knowing what you are doing, knowing how you feel about it, preparing emotionally before you enter the room, listening to your scene partner and allowing what he says to affect you, and treating the imaginary situation as a reality and living it out fully. There is no magic that you can learn by taking a "cold reading" workshop to help you nail the audition. This fact may come as a disappointment, but the craft of acting takes years of work and diligent effort. The longer you put in this hard work, the better you will get at auditions.

Is there anything you can do on your own time to improve your auditioning skills? Sure. First, read as many good plays as you can. Becoming familiar with this material will help you understand how a scene is constructed and what simple questions to ask yourself when you audition. What is the scene about? What are the people doing? Is it a fight? A confession? A proposal? How do the people feel about what they are talking about? How do the people feel when the scene begins? You might also try reading great literature, listening to rich classical music, and going to fine-art museums. A steady diet of hard rock, rap music, and trash novels can rob you of the sensitivity an actor needs to understand the nuances of feelings and human situations. An actor who cultivates this sensitivity will arrive at an audition with a distinct advantage. Finally, get solid training at a reputable acting school. We discuss how to find these schools in the next chapter.

Does this all sound tedious and time consuming? Well, so did Vince Lombardi's emphasis on the football fundamentals of blocking and tackling. His emphasis on the fundamentals resulted in the most successful team in professional football history. We've seen actors achieve similar amazing results when they avoided quick-fix cold-reading techniques and instead focused on developing the building blocks of their craft.

SHOULD I GET MY NOSE FIXED?

In their anxiety over whether they will ever get their next break, most actors will look for some fix, something they have control over. The feeling of helplessness is a chronic condition of most actors, and how well you manage this feeling will determine your chances for success. Many quick-fix attempts will only deplete your pocketbook. New headshots, a new tape on yourself, and weekend acting "intensives" may give you a feeling of doing something about your career and may do some good, but most actors engage in these expensive activities with far greater frequency than necessary. The most dangerous of these quick fixes is plastic surgery.

We saw a friend recently, an actress. There was something strange about her appearance. It wasn't the nose job she had last year. The surgery had been so minor, she still looked the same as before she borrowed thousands of dollars from her parents to get it "fixed." No, the difference was in her lips. It looked like she put on her lipstick while she was still half asleep and hung over from a wild night, or that she had had a fight with her boyfriend that had turned violent. Upon closer examination, we could see that she had had her lips injected with collagen, a current fad in which the substance is injected into the lips to make them look fuller. The effects wear off after a few weeks. Everyone she knew agreed this surgical procedure made her particularly unattractive and silly looking, but no one was willing to tell her that. What was frightening was that this was the second time she had done it. Although it was an obvious blight on her face to everyone else, to her it was an attractive feature that would surely lead to more acting jobs. It goes without saying that before the procedure the actress had gone a long time without a paying acting job and was desperate for work, and that after the procedure she remained just as unemployed.

What is instructive about this story is the degree to which this actress had lost touch with reality. Actors find their fantasy world to be a much more attractive place to inhabit than earth-bound reality. It's one of the primary reasons actors choose this career. But this propensity becomes dangerous when it involves mutilating your body.

If you are considering any of these quick fixes, it is probably a good time to take stock of your emotional life and determine what is leading you to such worthless, wasteful, and potentially dangerous actions. If someone on your team—your agent, manager, a casting director, director, or friend—is suggesting any of these fixes, you should begin to evaluate whether they should be a part of your trusted circle. There are plenty of roles for people who look just like you. If you are the best actor and you make the right contacts, you will get some of these roles. If you change your looks, you will still only succeed if you are the best actor and you make the right contacts. The real issues never change. So why should you? If you choose to ignore our advice and go under the knife, at least have the good sense to get a referral for a good plastic surgeon. This shouldn't be difficult, since you will meet plenty of actors in Hollywood with straight noses, perky large breasts, and puffy lips who can tell you where they got them.

PATHWAYS FOR DIRECTORS

In today's Hollywood, most directors have gone through film school, which we discuss in chapter 6. It's simply the best place to make connections, get some training on expensive equipment, and possibly come away with some decent film or tape of your work.

However, some people do manage to make it using another approach. Some are writers whose scripts are good enough to leverage into a directing shot; some do *music videos;* some start at an advertising agency as a director of commercials; some are successful actors; some have experience as an editor or director of photography; some have produced or directed industrial films for private corporations; and still others have found alternative pathways of ladder-climbing and jumping from other fields. There are even directors who come up through the theater, though it's a tough negotiation to convince anyone that theater directing makes you competent for film directing.

Of course, the directors who have started by financing their project through borrowing on their credit cards, family money, or loans from shopping-mall owners are legendary. It happens. (We talk more about film finance in chapter 20.) The first film doesn't have to be an expensive project, but it does have to be good enough to get the attention of the right people, perhaps through film festivals (see chapter 22).

PATHWAYS FOR PRODUCERS

Producers can literally come from anywhere, because you don't have to have any particular training to produce—at least at the dealmaking level as compared to line producing. (See chapter 2 on the distinctions between the two.) Many producers start out as someone's assistant. Many come from other disciplines in the industry, such as directing, managing, agenting, law, even acting. Or they start out with some family money they can put together; or they've been a manager for a rock group; or they just have a lot of nerve. Many fledgling producers also go to film school, which is a very important place to start networking.

Pathways for Agents

Believe it or not, the best place for an agent to start is the mailroom. Even if you've had a start as a "baby" executive or have a law degree, chances are you'll start in the mailroom. Agencies like to watch people operate from the lowliest position and then train them. Mailroom people get to know everyone in the building, and if they're savvy they make friends, learn the important names in town, and become befriended and mentored by senior agents. For agents, this is still the time-honored pathway.

Pathways for Lawyers

A good school helps but isn't absolutely critical. Cajoling or begging a studio to give you an internship helps (this is how Gail got started). Becoming a baby lawyer at an entertainment firm is a terrific way to get going. If you can't get into an entertainment firm, get into a very good firm and try to jump over to an entertainment firm. The farther out of the business you start, the harder it can be to get in. Connections help a lot, as does attending seminars and luncheons.

Pathways for Technical People

Technical people is, of course, an impossibly broad term, but we can make some general comments. People who do technical work have to actually know how to do something. Most often, skilled people get trained in film school, as we will discuss. Many people get started on the crew, or as gofers by networking and getting small jobs and then bigger ones. It's not too hard to get a job pulling cable on a super low-budget film or an industrial.

What you get in exchange for the terrible pay, long hours, and horrendous working conditions is some experience and some connections with other people who are also striving to build their careers. Others get their starts in local television, which they can do at home if they live near a reasonably big town. As always, many a career gets built by effective coattail riding.

While it's safe to say that an actor's most important contact is a director, for technical people it's the *unit production manager*, also called the *UPM*. He or she is usually responsible for hiring the crew for a shoot and will likely use the same reliable people over and over. Other good contacts for technical folks are the studio production executives, who are responsible for the nuts and bolts of a production.

CHAPTER SIX

Getting Trained

We discussed many career pathways in the preceding chapter. Many of them don't require specific training (such as starting in the mailroom for agents or starting as a model for actors). However, many people get their start with one kind of formal training or another. Training opportunities abound in Hollywood for just about any profession in the industry, so take advantage of them. Not only will the training put you ahead of your competition, but you will make valuable contacts as well. We will list many of the training opportunities here, but also remember that much of the training in Hollywood is done on the job or the old-fashioned way, through apprenticeships. So get out there and get to work.

ACTING TEACHERS AND COACHES

Here's the bad news. The quality of acting instruction in this city—as well as across the country—is abysmal. The rates that most acting teachers charge in Hollywood are scandalous. The abuses that actors are subjected to by their so-called teachers range from the insidious to the criminal. The good news is that a handful of good acting teachers do exist in Hollywood, giving perhaps the best instruction in the country. Several years of hard work with these teachers can help transform an inexperienced actor with a little raw talent into an accomplished performer.

One such program in Los Angeles is Playhouse West School and Repertory Theater. (Scott is on the staff at Playhouse West.) Like the other good acting schools, Playhouse West creates an atmosphere where young actors have a chance to develop their craft, one that takes years of diligent work to perfect. Every actor is well-advised to seek out one of these programs.

Anyone can hang a shingle and declare himself an acting teacher. You will see the ads in all the local trade papers and the schools that dot the L.A. landscape. The good ones charge fair rates, insist upon proper decorum in their classes, maintain clean and safe classrooms, study the craft of teaching from other good teachers, support their students with fair and honest criticism, offer training that provides a step-by-step discipline over several years, and accept only the most serious students. If a teacher meets this list of criteria, not only will he or she build a thriving business but will also do a great service to an industry that is sorely in need of well-trained actors.

APPRENTICESHIPS AND INTERNSHIPS

Although not as common as in the good old studio system days, apprenticeship and internship opportunities still exist for some careers. The formal ones, like the DGA Intern program or the set- and sign-painters apprenticeship program (administered by several studios in close consultation with the local union), allow beginners to get training and earn their necessary certification in a structured environment.

Other apprenticeships and internships are less formal but

generally acknowledged in the business as the way to get your start. As previously discussed, wanna-be big-time agents start in the mailrooms of the big agencies or as assistants in the smaller agencies. Would-be casting directors start as assistants to casting directors. Below we supply you with places for various training possibilities.

FILM SCHOOLS

There are several film schools in Los Angeles that provide training for budding directors, producers, screenwriters, and cinematographers. We won't speak here to the quality of the various schools, but we can tell you that they're all respected and will give you some worthwhile credentials when you're starting out. Perhaps the best service any of the schools provides is a place to meet people. Most people get jobs from their contacts and start their careers with at least a little help from their friends. Film-school friendships (and rivalries) can form the foundation of a career, and many of the programs offer some fine training as well.

The American Film Institute (AFI) is a private, independent school not affiliated with any university. The AFI offers a one-year program in directing, producing, writing, and cinematography. The students work in the medium of video. A select number of directors are asked back for a second year to produce short films. The AFI also has an Independent Filmmakers Program, which supports independent filmmakers and offers seminars and other training to the public.

The UCLA School of Theater, Film, and Television offers undergraduate and graduate degrees in directing, producing, screenwriting, and animation.

The USC School of Cinema-Television also offers undergraduate and graduate degrees in directing, producing, screenwriting, and animation.

Getting Trained

This is a book about Hollywood, but we would be remiss if we didn't mention New York University Film School. Having an NYU degree is a good credential in L.A., and there are enough successful graduates around to provide helpful networking for newcomers.

EXTENSION COURSES AND SEMINARS

An alternative or supplement to film school is taking extension courses. UCLA and USC in particular have developed wonderful and generally well-attended classes in all areas of the entertainment field, all of which are held on weeknights and weekends. They can be a terrific way to learn about the business and meet people. Typically, the teachers are working professionals, so you get an honest and accurate understanding of the area they're discussing. Because they work, chances are the teachers are connected or at least informed enough to set you in the right direction. Because many of the people who teach are on top in the business, they attract their colleagues and peers, who support and jeer them while they play academic. This gives you even more people to hit on to try to build your career.

Perhaps the greatest benefit of these courses or seminars is that you can use them as a way to meet others who are starting to network and create their own generation of people in the business. You can ask dumb questions before actually embarking on your career, after which you're expected to know something. You can practice your spin. You can start building up a clientele. In short, though the seminars can be costly, taking classes is a generally safe and savvy place to get started.

CHAPTER SEVEN

The People Who Represent You

If you want to be a producer, director, actor, or writer in Hollywood, you have to put together a team of professionals to find you work, hone your image, give you sage advice, and negotiate your contracts. Even the most successful composers, film editors, directors of photography, casting directors, and other creative talent need to have a solid group of representatives. Of course, it's easy to get great representatives when you're on the top. The trick is to know how to get good support when you're starting out, so you can maximize your chances of getting there.

You don't necessarily need all the people we mention below. For example, a beginning actor may have a manager but no agent or lawyer, or he may have all three. A very successful actor will probably have an agent or a lawyer, but not necessarily both (and probably no manager). Directors usually have agents and lawyers, but some of them only have lawyers. Writers may only have agents and no lawyers at first, but the most successful writers will have both or perhaps only a lawyer. Sometimes the lawyer backs up the agent or manager by reading a deal that's already negotiated, and sometimes the lawyer does the whole deal from the start.

Another representative, the publicist, may show up and be helpful at the beginning or the apex of a career, usually serving different functions at the various points during that career.

Most all successful creative talent will belong to a union, but the more successful their careers, the less they rely on the union to support and protect them. In a sense, the union isn't on your team; you're on its team. We describe in chapter 9 the hurdles beginners must overcome to earn the right to join one of the unions.

You'll figure out as you read this chapter that each of these categories of people and organizations has a different role, and they can all overlap. The important thing to know is what's available, and that you can be helped or hurt by the people you choose to be on your team.

AGENTS

YOUR FIRST AGENT

Here's the good news. Some folks arriving in town enjoy a "golden" period when everyone wants to get a look at them. This can be the case especially if you are still young, which in Hollywood has nothing to do with your real age but with how young you look. Some will even find agents and managers competing with each other to *sign* them, i.e., enter into an agreement to exclusively represent them. Here's the bad news. Even if you are one of these fortunate ones, you will find that your novelty wears off quickly. So don't get lulled into a false sense of security. Count on having to work hard at establishing your career. Remember to think long-term.

FINDING AN AGENT

We talked earlier about the Samuel French bookstores (one in the Valley on Ventura Blvd. and the other in Los Angeles on

Sunset Blvd.). Here you will find more books than you would ever want to buy about the business: plays, trade periodicals, handbooks, picture books, and on and on. These bookstores also carry several publications that list most of the agencies in town and information about the agencies.

A word of caution: We've yet to discover any publication that gives anything but glowing reports about each and every agency, which is far from the reality you will encounter. Your real challenge is to find agents who might be interested in representing you and, from this list, to discern which of these agents will do a good job getting you auditions and fighting to help you land jobs. The only system that has been developed to help you find that diamond in the rough, the good agent who is willing to take on new talent, is word of mouth. This is one of the first places where your organizational abilities, your networking skills, and your persistence will be tested. Everyone you meet is a resource, and one of the questions you should always be asking and keeping track of is, "Do you know any good agents?" And don't forget to evaluate the source of your information. The actor who told us he found his agent through the *Penny Saver*, a coupon magazine, certainly didn't think about his source.

A WORD ABOUT NETWORKING

Every person in the business should think of himself as a self-contained entrepreneur. As in any such business, one of the keys to creating new business is the quantity and quality of the contacts you make. There are a multitude of opportunities for making worthwhile contacts in the industry. We discuss some of them in this book. In addition to these, there are many others, such as screenings, seminars, charitable functions, churches and synagogues, personal growth seminars, and yes, even the dreaded Hollywood parties and clubs. We knew some Hollywood types who went psychic hopping to meet some of the *high-profile* Hollywood types, who were following the latest guru. Twelve-step programs like Alcoholics Anonymous were also a very fashionable social scene for a while.

The quality of these contacts, of course, depends upon the function you're attending, your role in it, how you conduct yourself, and how well you follow up on your contacts. It should be self-evident that you stand a better chance of making contacts that will pay off if, for example, you help organize a screening of a film at *IFP* (Independent Feature Projects, a support group for independent producers) than if you hang out in your sleaziest outfit drinking yourself silly at the latest Hollywood hotspot nightclub.

To illustrate how important networking is, we recently heard a well-established entertainment attorney gushing about a hot young actress and predicting how successful she would be. What impressed him was not the quality of her acting (which, by the way, is quite good because she has continued her training in spite of her success), but the fact that she remembered his name after being introduced to him only once. Imagine this one attorney and what he will say about this actress every time her name is mentioned. Then multiply this one attorney by the scores of other people who will do the same thing after meeting this actress, and you can see the power that effective networking can have.

COURTING AN AGENT

"OK," you might say, "I've bought *Agents and You: An Exhaustive Guidebook to Every Agent in the Northern Hemisphere* (just kidding). I've even got a couple of names of good agents from the checkout person at the local grocery. Now what do I do?"

Let us try to be as clear as possible about our opinion of attracting an agent's attention. Don't, don't, don't be lured into trying the countless silly schemes some actors and others invent to get an agent. Handing out toilet seat covers with your picture embossed on it, scratch and sniff headshots, or chocolate busts in the image of your face are only good for encouraging agents to treat you the way you're presenting yourself: as a joke. (Believe it or not, we know actors who actually tried each of those things.) Since you are drawn to acting, you are probably eccentric and original as it is. You don't need to take those qualities to the extreme, at least not off-camera.

What you must do to attract an agent is what people in every other business do. They send out calling cards (in an actor's case, a headshot and resume; in a director's, a short film). They make calls. They set up appointments. They get friends and associates to make referrals. They follow up. They become involved in trade organizations and community activities to expand their contacts. They exhibit examples of their best work. They continue to develop their skills so as to become more and more qualified. They do this day after day. Read a biography of almost any person in the industry you admire and you won't find many of them hiring a plane to write their name in the sky over Hollywood. You will read about them, throughout their careers, tirelessly doing all the things we just listed. You want a good agent? Get to work.

SIGNING WITH AN AGENT

Few agents in Hollywood will agree to represent you without signing you to an exclusive representation contract. The custom here is different from that in New York, where an actor might have several agencies working for him simultaneously. It is common, however, to sign with different agents who will represent you exclusively in a particular area of the business. Theatrical agents will represent you for film and television work, excluding commercials. (Ironically, very few of these "theatrical" agents will help you find work in the theater. In their view, not enough money is involved to make it worth their while.) Commercial agents will help you find work solely in commercials—television and industrials. Voice-over agents represent you in the very lucrative field of radio commercials and other voice-over work, such as cartoons.

Some agencies will have agents who work in each of these areas, but rarely will one agent work in more than one area, for reasons of efficiency, unless he works in one of the larger agencies. The agencies that do work in more than one area won't automatically represent you in each area; e.g., they won't take you on in their theatrical department just because they represent you for commercials. On the other hand, a well-established creative talent will use one agent for everything, someone who can provide full services.

Unions all have restrictions as to the terms a creative talent can accept. For example, if you're an actor and you sign with a SAG-franchised agency (God help the actor who doesn't), the agent is restricted in what he can and cannot put in the contract. SAG-franchised agencies have agreed with SAG, the Screen Actors Guild, to conduct business along certain guidelines. For instance, the agent can take no more than 10 percent of the money you generate in acting jobs in the area for which the agent provides representation, and the actor can terminate the relationship if the agent has not secured work for the actor in any 90-day period. These contracts, although quite standard (you can get a copy of one from SAG) and rarely open for negotiation, are not etched in stone. Percentages are negotiable, especially as you attain more clout in the industry.

Getting the Agent to Work for You

Here is where the real work begins. Most actors assume that once they have signed with an agent they can sit back and wait for the auditions and parts to roll in. Wrong.

Since agents make their money on commission, they will focus most of their efforts on their clients who are already working. However shortsighted this view may appear, it is the reality in most agencies. Your job, then, is to convince the agent that you are worth the investment of his or her precious time.

How do you do this?

First, don't expect someone else to be more passionate about your career than you are. You must become as aggressive about promoting your career as you want your agent to be. Are you continuing to develop your craft? Are you doing plays and student films and independent projects with quality people? Are you keeping abreast of what projects are being produced? Are you preparing fully for each audition? Are you systematically expanding your network? Are you asking friends and associates to help you get work and make contacts? The truth is that most work you get will be due to your own efforts and contacts, not those of your agent.

Second, make sure you communicate your efforts to your agent. It may give your agent a nice warm feeling to receive a birthday card, but what will fire the agent's enthusiasm about you is to send a flyer about the play you are doing or a note about the casting director you met at the show.

Third, enlist your agent in putting forth a similar effort. You are both after the same goal, so agree on some common strategies. For example, take your agent to lunch. Share the list of goals you have for your career for the year and what you will be doing in the next three months to achieve those goals. Get the agent's input and suggestions, then together draw up a list of what the agent will be doing in the next three months to help you achieve those goals. Make the list as specific as possible—this many auditions and general interviews a week, submitted for so many projects, and follow-up calls on each submission and audition. Then check in weekly to see how each of you is doing.

If you take charge of your career, communicate your efforts to your agent, and enlist your agent in a team effort, you stand a good chance of getting him or her to put forth a decent effort on your behalf. If you do all these things and you are met with lackadaisical indifference and a barrelful of excuses, it's time to move on to a new agent (discussed in chapter 13).

MANAGERS

DO I NEED A MANAGER?

Actors are generally the only people who use managers in Hollywood. If you read the above descriptions of managers and agents you will know that the two fulfill almost the same role, although the agent does it within some legal parameters, the manager often not. For example, in California, only licensed agents may procure and secure work for actors, including negotiation of the actor's contract. Do managers refrain from performing these tasks? We don't know any who do, although most managers are more comfortable when their actors also are represented by an agent.

If you are just beginning, it would be helpful to have someone—an agent or a manager—submit you for jobs, get you the audition, do the necessary follow-up to secure the job, and help you negotiate the contract. If you start with a manager, he or she will often also help you get an agent. Since managers typically represent fewer clients, they will often have more time to give you advice. Many actors, thinking it doubles their chances of obtaining work, have both an agent and a manager.

Managers probably aren't necessary if you already have an agent. With or without an agent, even a mediocre manager (the best you are likely to attract early in your career) might be worth the trouble. They can help you make some initial contacts with casting directors, agents, and others. They're able to provide you with some useful information about the business. They can help you structure and focus your efforts as well as give you a confidence boost that comes with the knowledge that at least one person in Hollywood believes in you.

As we've stated before, bad managers are really bad: They give bad advice, display unscrupulous behavior, and offer worthless help. Try to conduct your meetings with any manager in a neutral location. Be wary of those who make date after date with you without showing any results. Serious managers don't have time to meet with you that often. Watch out for private coaching sessions. This advice applies to men as well as women.

How Do I Find a Good Manager?

This is when your networking skills come in very handy. Ask for referrals from people with experience in the business. Sending out pictures and resumes to these people and requesting an interview is a low-percentage approach, but still one you might try. A better approach is to ask your contacts to make the call for you.

Sometimes a manager will approach you after seeing your work in a play or showcase. If the manager is legitimate, she may be a much better choice than one who expresses interest without knowing your work. A good manager will tell you the names of people they represent and offer proper references. Don't be afraid to make those calls. This is normal procedure in any business.

How Can I Tell if My Manager is Doing a Good Job?

A good manager should be able to produce some immediate results for you. Their contacts help get you in to see agents, casting directors, and others. A good manager will protect you from the unscrupulous people in the business. A good manager will help you keep on track. A good manager is accessible and works well in tandem with your agent. Because your manager should know your work and goals better than your busy agent, he should act as your advocate, encouraging your agent to get you out for bigger and better roles and ensuring that you get the best terms possible for each job. Obviously he should do this without alienating your agent.

WILL I ALWAYS HAVE TO SIGN A CONTRACT WITH AN AGENT OR MANAGER?

No. Sometimes you may wish to work out an informal arrangement so the two of you can determine whether or not it's a good match. No contract is signed, but the agent or manager will line up auditions for you and take an agreed-upon percentage if you get the job. This allows the agent or manager to see how well you do before making a commitment to sign you, while allowing you the opportunity to discover how much clout he has to get you into auditions. (SAG frowns upon such informal arrangements with an agent, but there's little evidence that the organization is doing anything concrete to combat them.)

Informal agreements with your representation might be worth trying at the beginning stages of your career; however, whatever your agreement, the key to determining whether you're being well served is how much your agent or manager is sending you out on auditions and interviews. Beware of countless one-on-one consulting sessions with your manager and of private parties and get-togethers with "important industry people." Talk is cheap unless it gets you into an office, sitting across from a casting director, and reading for a specific role. If your agent and/or manager can't deliver at least that, why waste your time with them?

ARE COMMISSION PERCENTAGES NEGOTIABLE?

You bet they are. You should never have to pay your manager or agent anything unless you get work. If they ask for money either up front or later to cover their "expenses," run as fast as you can. The standard arrangement is a contract giving the manager or agent 10 to 15 percent of all your gross earnings in the business, whether or not the manager or agent helps you get the work. The big agencies never ask for up-front money.

WHAT CHANGES CAN I NEGOTIATE IN AN AGREEMENT?

If the arrangements we've discussed so far seem unfair, they are. You should at least try to negotiate three changes. You'll find less flexibility in the big agencies, but you can always try. First, see if the manager or agent will take a smaller percentage for gross earnings up to a certain amount, say $50,000 a year. If you earn more than that in one year, then the higher percentage clicks in for amounts above that level. Second, try to exclude the manager or agent from deals they don't set up. For example, very few managers do anything for you in the commercial or voice-over areas of the business. They should not be entitled to a portion of this money. Third, try to eliminate the clause that entitles your manager or agent to a percentage of the money you earn on jobs even after you have severed your relationship. This often becomes a sticking point because your manager or agent may have negotiated the initial deal.

For example, say you audition for a TV pilot, *Star Tour, Another Deep Space Generation,* while the manager or agent is representing you. A few days later, your representation contract comes up for renewal and you decide not to re-sign with that representative. If you are cast in that pilot and the series is picked up and runs for seven years; and you make four spin-off *Star Tour* movies; additional money on the *Star Tour* comic books, coffee mugs, and placemats, together with appearances at *Star Tour* conventions in Ames, Iowa, and Fargo, North Dakota, guess who continues to take their cut? That's right—Ms. Manager or Mr. Agent, sitting in their homes in Malibu enjoying early retirement because of your hard-earned success.

The manager or agent will argue that since it was their hard work that got you that audition in the first place, he or she is entitled to some of the fruits of the deal. There is some validity to this argument. However, it would be most fair to set some outer limits.

As long as we are on the subject, let us suggest a few other clauses to check out. For instance, how long does the contract run? One or two years is normal; the shorter the better. We've yet to hear good reasons why a longer-term agreement is advantageous for the client. A representative usually agrees to make her best efforts to represent you, but you can guess how enforceable that is. You may have two more years on your agreement, but if your manager or agent has lost interest in you, the remaining time only inhibits you from seeking new representation. Further, does the agreement automatically renew unless you or the representative take some action before the renewal date to indicate your intention to terminate the relationship? If so, you should strike the automatic renewal clause and insist on renegotiation when the old agreement runs out.

Power of Attorney

Does the agreement contain a "power of attorney" clause? To give someone power of attorney means you are giving him the power to act legally on your behalf. This privilege can include the power to sign contracts for you, cash your checks, move your money around, and generally do anything that normally only you have the right to do. Does this sound reminiscent of those golden childhood years when Mom and Dad held absolute power over every facet of your life? It should. It's the power of attorney that most often leads creative talent into financial disaster.

Why is this clause necessary? Well, if you become a very busy creative talent you may want someone who has the authority to act in your name. While you are on location in Tibet, it might be helpful to have your representative back home conducting your affairs. He can approve which of your photographs will go on the billboard, line up studio time to cut your next record, and otherwise look out for your interests.

Until you have developed a relationship with someone you can trust as much as (or more than) your mother and father, this clause, superfluous at best, is a disaster waiting to happen. If the manager or agent won't eliminate this clause entirely, at least try to make it more specific and limited. A lawyer can help you redraft the language.

––––––––––

OK, now you've carefully read this section. You met with an attorney who has turned your three-page representation agreement into a novella written in bad Swahili, giving you every legal protection developed since the Magna Carta. You make an appointment with your manager-to-be at a safe location, like the lunchroom of the Hollywood station of the Los Angeles Police Department. You present the new document to your manager-to-be, politely but firmly reminding him that he is working for you and not vice versa. He gives you a long blank stare, excuses himself by mumbling something about a call he needs to make, and disappears, never to be seen again. Where did you go wrong?

The new person in Hollywood faces a severe power imbalance in almost every interaction. In order to make your way, you will need to give away more than you get. That doesn't mean you should roll over and concede at the slightest scent of power. You will, however, need to continually evaluate each demand and relationship in light of where you are in your career. Most people give away too much. But a few never get started because they can't stomach their low status in Hollywood. Our last bit of advice on this subject is to determine what's vital for your self-esteem and dignity and never compromise on those issues. Use the rest as bargaining chips, and never give them away unless you get something in return.

ATTORNEYS

WHEN DO I NEED AN ATTORNEY?

Throughout your career, you will, with luck, be negotiating, agreeing to, and signing scores of agreements: agency and manager agreements, day-player contracts, TV-series options contracts, and backend profit participation deals. All of the relationships you develop will have legal ramifications. The person who does not want to look back with bitterness, wondering where all the money went, will be wise to seek the services and advice of an attorney early on. How early? It's never too early to begin asking people you know in the business to recommend good attorneys and to keep a list of those names. If you happen to meet an entertainment lawyer, spend some time getting to know him. Size him up. Does he appear honest and open? Can he speak a form of English you understand?

The best time to meet formally with an attorney is when you anticipate forming a relationship with an agent or manager or when you are offered your first job, whichever comes first. Have a chat with an attorney. There are three good reasons why.

Three Good Reasons to Meet with an Attorney

First, *you should get in the habit of understanding all the ramifications of every relationship you enter. This will help you ease the sense of powerlessness you feel in this town. It will also start you on the way to making informed decisions that will become more and more critical as your career progresses. A good lawyer can help you understand these ramifications.*

Second, *even the most standard agreements leave room for negotiation. Maybe that manager won't budge from demanding 15 percent of all the money you earn until they put you in the grave, but what about that "power of attorney" clause? Perhaps he will back off from including an unlimited power of attorney clause. If you don't know what a power of attorney clause is, that's all the more reason to be sitting down with your trusted attorney. A good attorney can't save you from signing away your soul, but he can perhaps help you limit some of the more onerous terms in these agreements.*

Third, *if your career goes the way you dream it will, you will have the need for an attorney for many years to come. Learning to work with one early in your career—when less is at stake—gives you the chance to test the waters and find the right match. It will take time and experience to find just the shark who will serve your needs without devouring you in the process.*

HOW DO I GET A GOOD ATTORNEY?

In Hollywood there is a glut of people who call themselves entertainment lawyers, but very few have the real experience that will be helpful to you. You must shop carefully, but the good news is that you should be able to find many qualified attorneys who charge very reasonable rates in the beginning.

They know that if they serve you well early in your career, you are more likely to come back when you hit it big.

Law has become very specialized, and there are even sub-specialties within the entertainment business. So your hotshot cousin, who works primarily in real estate law, is not the wisest choice for negotiating an agency agreement. When shopping for a lawyer, you'll want to find out how much of an attorney's time is spent representing people like you and how long he or she has been doing it. You should also find out the depth and range of the other partners and associates in the firm. As mentioned above, referrals from people you trust in the business are a good start.

Part of your initial conversation with a lawyer should be about fees. How much you will be charged for this particular job? Don't be afraid to ask such questions, and don't be afraid to negotiate if the fee seems too high. Finally, don't hesitate to renegotiate if a job turns out to be simpler than everyone thought, or if you are not satisfied with the results. Some firms also will agree to take a percentage of your earnings as payment. It's all negotiable.

A good lawyer is someone who explains things in under-standable English, returns your phone calls in a timely fashion, has the respect of the studios, doesn't muck up a deal with extraneous or impossible demands, is very clear with you about fees, fights for you, and doesn't put his own or other clients' interests above yours.

One last note regarding fees. If you are paying a lawyer by the hour, watch those phone calls. Many attorneys we know bill you a quarter-hour for every phone call they get from you, even if the call only takes two minutes. We won't try to justify this practice except to explain that it's a cornerstone of a system lawyers use called "billable hours." If you associate this term with the phrases "hocus-pocus" and "rape and pillage," you'll get the picture.

CHAPTER EIGHT

The People Who Promote You

Most of these folks are employed primarily by actors, although directors and some high-profile below-the-line folks also use publicists. Certainly the studios and production companies will employ a small army of publicists to promote their projects. It is the thousands of actors in Hollywood who have created an entire cottage industry for people whose job it is to prepare and promote actors in an attempt to give them that necessary competitive edge.

PHOTOGRAPHERS

We mentioned above one kind of job a photographer does in Hollywood—that of taking publicity stills for a production. These are choice jobs in the business, but the bread-and-butter work of most photographers who do work in the business is taking headshots for actors.

Headshots are 8″ x 10″ photos of actors, usually of their face, though half- and three-quarter shots are increasing in popularity. They are an actor's calling card, often the means through which an actor will make the first contact with or impression on an agent or casting director. Since many agents and casting directors put so much undeserved emphasis on an actor's headshot, actors are under extreme pressure to produce a good picture of themselves. They will dole out hundreds of dollars trying to find that one photographer who can capture that elusive image of themselves that will captivate and entice the agent and casting director. These headshots must be updated every two to three years—or sooner if the actor changes his or her appearance noticeably.

There are many excellent photographers, most of whom know their value and charge accordingly. Some can even make their entire living at it. For the ones who don't, taking headshots can provide a healthy supplement to their incomes and fill in the gaps between other jobs.

PUBLICISTS AND PRESS AGENTS

Technically, publicists publicize the pictures and press agents publicize the individual creative talent, though the term *publicist* is commonly used to describe both breeds. The publicity part of the job is pretty self-explanatory. These folks use every device they can to gain attention for their clients in the media. Many a picture and many a star have languished for lack of good publicity.

Who needs a publicist? At the early stages of a career, a publicist is probably not necessary or particularly helpful. Until you have a body of work to promote, you have nothing for the publicist to publicize. No one is particularly impressed with a headshot without any credits attached. And publicists can be very expensive, since they usually charge a set monthly fee, $1500 a month or more for the really good ones.

There are publicists in town who work with theater groups to publicize their productions. If you are just getting started and find yourself in a great show, you might discuss pooling your resources with other members of your theater group and hiring a publicist to get the word out.

When Should You Add a Publicist to Your Team?

The appropriate time to think about adding a publicist to your team is when you get your first big break, for two reasons:

First, *the big break will give the publicist something to sink his or her teeth into.*

Second, *you'll be in a better position to afford the cost.*

Another part of a publicist's job is to shield his clients from unwanted attention. Once a creative talent reaches a certain level of fame, they need this protection. Without it, they would be deluged with interview requests that make it impossible to do their jobs. A good publicist knows his client's personality and needs and screens interview requests accordingly. Publicists also become the spokespeople to whom the press turns to confirm or deny the latest rumors about their clients, and they work to hide news their clients don't want published.

Studios still employ publicists, although the ranks have thinned somewhat since the golden days of the studio system, when the studios had the talent under contract and absolute control over their public images. Outside the studios themselves, several large public relations firms service the industry and offer opportunities for the fledgling publicist. In addition, a substantial number of publicists do freelance work or maintain their own small offices.

Publicity is a service profession that requires energy, a healthy unassuming ego, and finely tuned public relations skills.

PERSONAL TRAINERS

Have you noticed how "buffed" many actors look these days? Chances are they are using a personal trainer to acquire this well-toned physique. But actors aren't the only ones who need to have a good physical presentation, since so much of Hollywood is style. You'll find many a lawyer and studio executive spending time and money to make themselves fit the current image ideal.

Personal trainers in Hollywood operate no differently from those in other towns and cities. The only difference is the type of clientele they train and the money these clients are willing to pay. No other profession—with the possible exception of modeling—depends as much on physical appearance as film and television acting does. Actors know this, and they spend their money accordingly.

CHAPTER NINE

Unions

WHAT UNIONS ARE INVOLVED IN THE ENTERTAINMENT INDUSTRY?

SAG, AEA, AFTRA, SEG, DGA, WGA, IATSE, NABET, AFM, AGVA, AGMA, IBEW, Teamsters, and on and on.

Just about every segment of the entertainment industry is unionized. Most of the unions are based in Hollywood, but many of them also have branches in New York, and some, such as IATSE, have locals in many major cities where production occurs. Often individuals with the same job description will be covered by more than one union, depending on which union won which jurisdiction battle in the past.

Actors are so special that they have five unions, all of them happy to charge the actor a large initiation fee for joining and hefty union dues each year. They are the Screen Actors Guild (SAG), the American Federation of Television and Radio Artists (AFTRA), Actors' Equity Association (Equity or AEA), the American Guild of Variety Artists (AGVA), and the American Guild of Musical Artists (AGMA).

Here is our thumbnail sketch of some of the entertainment unions and what segment of the industry they cover. If you can't figure out what segment you belong to, look in chapters 2 and 3 for definitions. If all the names and initials make you woozy, skip ahead to read about how the unions will affect your career.

SCREEN ACTORS GUILD (SAG)
This union represents actors who do television or movie work that is shot on film. Recently, the Screen Extras Guild (SEG), whose members are extras, was merged with SAG.

AMERICAN FEDERATION OF TELEVISION AND RADIO ARTISTS (AFTRA)
This union represents actors who do radio work; voice-overs; voices for animation, phonograph records, non-broadcast material; and television work that is shot live or on videotape.

ACTORS' EQUITY ASSOCIATION (AEA OR EQUITY)
This union represents actors who do stage work.

AMERICAN GUILD OF VARIETY ARTISTS (AGVA)
This union protects the interests of performers who work in nightclubs, cabarets, theme parks, ice shows, and variety shows.

DIRECTORS GUILD OF AMERICA, INC. (DGA)
This union serves directors, assistant directors, unit production managers, and technical coordinators who work on either film or taped productions.

WRITERS GUILD OF AMERICA (WGA)
This union serves the interests of writers who write for radio, film, and television.

AMERICAN FEDERATION OF MUSICIANS (AFM)

Musicians, arrangers, orchestrators, and copyists belong to this union.

INTERNATIONAL ALLIANCE OF THEATRICAL STAGE EMPLOYEES (IATSE OR IA)

This is an umbrella union that represents many of the below-the-line workers in the industry. Some of the sub-unions, or *locals*, in IA are:

Motion Picture Studio Grips

Costume Designers Guild

Makeup Artists & Hair Stylists

Illustrators & Matte Artists

Motion Picture Set Painters

Script Supervisors

Story Analysts

Studio Electrical Technicians—The lighting folks

International Photographers Guild—Directors of photography, camera operators, film loaders, and still photographers

Motion Picture Screen Cartoonists—The animators

Motion Picture Editors Guild—The editors of film, sound, and music, plus the librarians

Motion Picture Studio Projectionists & Video Production Technicians

The Publicists Guild

Scenic & Title Artists—Those who produce the scenery and titles at the beginning of the film

Set Designers & Model Makers

Other IA locals include:

Affiliated Property Craftspersons

Film Technicians of Motion Picture Industries

International Sound/Cinetechnicians
Production Office Coordinators and Accountants' Guild
Motion Picture Crafts Service
Motion Picture Studio First Aid Employees
Society of Motion Picture and Television Art Directors
Motion Picture Studio Teachers & Welfare Workers

NATIONAL ALLIANCE OF BROADCAST ENGINEERS AND TECHNICIANS (NABET)

This union serves the people who operate the camera and equipment in television.

INTERNATIONAL BROTHERHOOD OF ELECTRICAL WORKERS (IBEW)

Sometimes the people who run the equipment in television at the local stations (as opposed to the network people) are governed by this union.

INTERNATIONAL BROTHERHOOD OF TEAMSTERS

Wherever there are trucks to be driven, you will find the Teamsters. As in just about every other industry, the Teamsters are a powerful union.

ASSOCIATIONS

As long as we are listing the unions, we should include the organizations that represent the business side of the industry; that is, the groups that bargain with the unions to set wages and working conditions in the industry.

ASSOCIATION OF MOTION PICTURE AND TELEVISION PRODUCERS, INC. (AMPTP) AND PRODUCERS GUILD OF AMERICA

As supervisors, producers are not considered employees in the classic sense, so these organizations operate more as associations rather than traditional unions that fight for better working conditions.

NATIONAL ASSOCIATION OF THEATER OWNERS

This is not a union representing individual theater owners as employees, but a trade association. It is very active in promoting and protecting the interests of movie-house owners and holds a star-studded, heavily attended annual trade show.

Other associations include the American Society of Cinematographers, the Association of Independent Commercial Producers, Inc. (AICP), and the Association of Talent Agents.

WHAT DO THE UNIONS HAVE TO DO WITH MY EARLY CAREER?

A whole lot.

Directors, cinematographers, music arrangers, grips, gaffers, and actors all have unions that negotiate their salaries, hours, pensions, health benefits, and other protections, often referred to as *working conditions*. The wages and benefits you receive and the health and safety rules that protect you are the result of years of hard work by these unions. Many non-union productions follow the standards set by the unions as people have become used to working within those standards. As a union member, you don't need to worry about many of the basics in any contract. Of course, the very existence of unions has created some restrictions in the work opportunities available, since not everyone can be a union member.

While some unions, such as AFTRA, have no restrictions for joining, most are what are called *closed shops*. Not just anyone can join. Since the major film and television producers are *union signatories* (meaning they agree to abide by union regulations), they cannot hire you if you are not a member of the appropriate union.

Once you have joined the unions (and paid several thousand dollars in initiation fees for this privilege), you are restricted from performing services in non-union projects. Union members who are caught doing so may be subject to fines and expulsion. As if getting started in this business wasn't already hard enough, this union foolishness will cause you to be shut out from working on many worthwhile projects. There are some exceptions to these rigid rules. We'll discuss one of them, *financial core*, below and discuss the ways studios get around working under union regulations in chapter 20.

On the up side, unions have steadily bargained for increased compensation, better safety regulations, broader health coverage, and larger pension contributions. The actors' unions have developed a system of franchising agents, which restricts the percentage an agent can take out of your paycheck, as well as giving you other protections. All of these efforts will benefit you once you are working.

Getting Your Union Card, That Elusive Catch-22

It's a joke, but an unfortunate reality, that you can't work on a union production without a union card, and with most unions you can't get a union card until you've worked on a union production. This catch-22 will test your persistence and creative abilities. Your job is to convince someone to make an exception for you. Friends come in handy here. You could turn to the casting director you met through your cousin to bring you in to audition and go to bat for you with the producers; or your college friend who is helping produce a low-budget feature; or a fellow waitress working as a lowly PA on a filmed TV show, who can get you work as an extra and then suggest you be given that throwaway line in the script, "Thank you, sir," which upgrades you to a speaking part; or your film school friend who gets a break on a low-budget film and puts you on the crew.

Think this process sounds complicated and overwhelming? Don't despair. You only have to face this problem once. Thousands before you have found a way to jump this first hurdle, and you can, too. The glitch in this procedure is that you are not required to join the union until you have your second union job. You get one freebie but you must join and pay that hefty initiation fee before accepting union job number two. Woe to the person who has not saved up enough money to pay his or her initiation fees. No card, no second job.

The Union Card Shuffle

As we've mentioned, some unions, such as AFTRA, have no requirements for joining beyond an exorbitant initiation fee. The majority of unions make you jump through some hoops to join their exclusive company.

The most straightforward way to gain entrance to the club is to be offered a job on a production which has an agreement with the particular union you wish to join. By law, the union must accept you as a member. In fact, they can force you to join before you take a second union job. The term used to describe this process is Taft-Hartley *(which refers to the law that governs union membership).*

Before you get very excited, you should know that the unions have usually made the production companies and studios agree that they will make every effort to hire union members before they take on a non-union employee, and sometimes the production company must pay the union a fee to sponsor you into the union.

Many of the IA locals maintain a roster system which lists every member in the union who is not working. The production company is required to hire from this list unless they can come up with a very good reason to hire you instead (such as your possession of some unique skill that is required for the job). So obviously the best chance you have of getting union work occurs when lots of productions are up and running and there is nobody left on the list.

Some unions will also maintain some other way to gain membership into their ranks. The Script Supervisors local, for instance, allows you to join if you work as a script supervisor for thirty days in any year in "qualified" non-union projects. SAG will let you join if you work as an extra in a certain number of union projects or if you belong to and do some work in one of the other actors' unions.

Call the union you're interested in to find out this year's rules for the union card shuffle.

WORKING NON-UNION

Sooner or later the issue of working on a non-union production arises for anyone whose career is covered by a union, i.e., all of the creative talent except for producers. At the beginning of your career, non-union productions may be the only work available to you. As your career develops, there will be opportunities you'd like to take on non-union productions. Even top talent may want to try something out of the mainstream now and then. In any case, it's likely that eventually you will be confronted with the issue of whether or not to take work in defiance of your union rules.

Sometimes the studios will help you get around this problem by setting up productions that are not governed by all of the unions. One way is to do productions overseas. Canada is hugely successful as a production center, because of the more favorable union situation there. A great deal of production is done in *right-to-work* states, where the union can't force the studios to hire all union talent. There's even a way to do a union-sanctioned, non-union production in the U.S. (See our discussion of Article 20 productions in chapter 20.)

Of course, there can be real problems working on non-union shoots. There's a reason people got together in the first place to enforce reasonable working conditions. Non-union productions are notorious for working people all hours, not feeding them on schedule, and sometimes putting cast and crew in danger because there's no one regulating activity on the set and no one to complain to if abuses are occurring.

Deciding to work on a non-union production when you're already a union member or trying to become one is a tough situation. The unions have different clout, and it's not that often that a union will picket a production if it feels its members are evading union coverage, but it does happen. Occasionally, too, you hear about a union retaliating against a member for working non-union, but not often. Most of the people we know who work non-union either do it with sanctions or very quietly. It's not a situation to be taken lightly, but neither is it a rare occurrence.

Financial Core

The Term Your Union Hopes You Never Learn

Until a few years ago, the rules were straightforward. If you belonged to a union, you could be punished by the union if you worked on a non-union production. However, because of a recent Supreme Court decision, a new category of union membership has been created called financial core.

Any union member can opt to become a financial-core member by simply writing to the union and declaring him- or herself to be a financial-core member from that day forward. What it means is that the member will no longer be restricted from working on non-union projects.

By law, the union cannot kick you out or discriminate against you in any way for becoming a financial-core member. You can still do union work, and you are still eligible for health and pension benefits. However, you will not be able to vote or run for union office, and the union may charge you another initiation fee if you reapply for regular membership.

Obviously, the financial-core option seriously undermines the power of the union over its membership and possibly in negotiations with producers for better wages and conditions. As a result, emotions run high with regard to this issue. But since it is the law, you should know about it. Something else you should know is that you must declare yourself financial core before you sign a contract or begin work on a non-union project. If you are contemplating this step, it's not a bad idea to consult a lawyer who specializes in labor law.

SECTION FOUR

Your First Real Job

If you have been spending your time working on your career rather than dreaming about it, chances are the happy day will soon arrive when you are offered your first real job in the industry.

WHAT IS A REAL JOB?

You've probably realized by now that there's no pathway set in stone in the entertainment industry. One good way to tell if you've got a real job is if you actually get paid for it. It can be one of the greatest sources of satisfaction to get paid for doing what you love to do. Even if the money is paltry, the fact that someone is willing to pay you is a good first step. Does it matter what the job is? Sure. We're not talking about getting a waitressing job in a studio commissary. You'll have your first real job when you're doing something directly related to some production.

Chances are your first real job will come with a contract. At the beginning you may not have your professional representatives in line, and you may be willing to sign anything. You will probably have very little negotiating power over the terms of your employment, but *even so there are a few things you should know about before you sign on the dotted line. Whether or not you've got hotshot representation, you have to be responsible for your own career. Therefore, you should know if someone is asking you to sign your life—or at least your career—away.*

This section describes some basic differences between motion picture and television contracts. We look at some of the basic terms in the various contracts you might encounter, discuss compensation for starting jobs, including union-scale deals, and hint at some of the goodies you might look forward to with greater success. Finally, we talk about what you do during the time between your first real job and your first big break. Sometimes that ladder of success seems awfully steep, but there are some things you can do to keep your hopes alive during the tough times.

CHAPTER TEN

Contractual Issues

THE DIFFERENCE BETWEEN MOVIE AND TELEVISION CONTRACTS

Though much of the dealmaking language is the same, and the deals are made in more or less the same offices and restaurants around town, there are some fundamental differences between movie and television deals.

Part of the differences occur because of tradition. The movie business has been building slowly over the past eighty years or so. If you look at contracts drafted in the 1940s, for example, you might be surprised to find that the deals resemble contemporary contracts fairly closely, apart from the reproduction technology. The carbon-copied contract from the old studio days is similar in shape and form to its laser-printed counterpart today, though the business terms have gotten progressively more complicated. (If you don't want to wait, skip ahead to chapter 17 to learn more about the hard-core, high-level issues that arise in the big motion-picture deals today.)

The TV business, on the other hand, has been growing only since the 1950s, and its roots began in radio. Many of the early TV stars had come from radio programs, and in some ways the structure of the new television medium more closely paralleled the early radio days than the movie business. Programming tended to be sponsored by advertisers and often featured radio talent such as Jack Benny and George Burns and Gracie Allen, for instance. Today's advertisers don't dominate television directly, although that may change with the explosion of technology. In their heyday, the networks didn't need to give advertisers name recognition or power, but things may change now that there are more players in the game.

Television contracts have many similarities to movie contracts, but they naturally require longer commitments from the creative talent for series productions. In the past, the stakes didn't seem as high as in the movie business, and contracts were somewhat simpler and more informal. Of course, until recently, a TV series was nowhere near as expensive as a movie. Today, each episode of a half-hour series can cost well over $1 million, and one-hour episodes over $1.5 million. The market has proven that television series can bring fortunes in reruns, so the stakes have grown much higher. Nevertheless, TV works on a somewhat less formal contractual basis, which we'll discuss below, than the motion picture end of the business.

BASIC MOTION PICTURE DEALS

We're going to assume at this point you're still working for scale, a term we'll discuss in detail below, and that you're not in a position to negotiate much more in your first contract. Nevertheless, you should understand the basic structure of the deals you'll make. Unless you get asked to sign a multiple-picture deal, which we'll go into in the next chapter, you usually sign up for just one movie at a time. Following are some basic components of motion picture deals.

START DATE

The *Start Date* is the date the studio anticipates beginning filming. It's an important concept for many reasons. Not only do you have to be there on that date, but the studio has to be ready for you, because your salary starts on the Start Date, whether or not the studio got it together to actually start production. Every type of creative talent is affected by the Start Date, since most contracts speak in terms of work and money commencing on the Start Date. If the production goes longer than expected, overtime kicks in and the production becomes much more expensive. In actors' deals especially, the definition of Start Date is a heavily negotiated point. Typically, at least in actors' deals, the Start Date is expressed as *on or about* a certain date. This cuts the studio some slack in terms of when they actually have to be ready to roll the camera. Usually the real starting date, or the date the cameras actually roll, is one week before or after the contractually appointed Start Date.

For example, if the Start Date is on or about September 15, and on or about means seven days before or after, then you may be called to work on a date any time between September 8 and September 22. If the studio calls the Start Date for September 15 and ends up delaying the start of production until September 30, your salary will kick in starting September 22.

Note that more powerful players get the studio to narrow the definition of on or about to a shorter range of days. For example, it might mean three days before and after the Start Date. The most successful creative talent have busy schedules, and the studio doesn't have the power to make them wait around with no additional compensation. A narrower Start Date window also works to kick in possible *overtime* provisions, which we discuss below.

PRE-PRODUCTION AND POST-PRODUCTION

Pre-production means the services you provide before the cameras roll, such as rehearsal and wardrobe fittings. *Post-production* means the time you must commit to finishing the film during editing, to dub your voice into the spots where it isn't audible, for instance, or to change words for the "PG" (Parental Guidance rating) version for TV broadcast. Typically, you only have to commit to five days of pre-production and two or so of post-production.

COMPENSATION STRUCTURE

Producers generally get a lump sum for a movie. They'll get a certain amount of development money if they brought in the idea (see chapter 2), a certain amount on the Start Date and during the weeks or months of production, and a small amount when the picture is delivered. Directors have a similar structure, meaning they get lump sums distributed at various stages of production. Casting directors get lump sums during pre-production and when all the actors are set. Directors of Photography get lump sums, usually with a provision for overtime. Most of these people will start earning overtime if shooting isn't finished within a certain time frame, based on the original production schedule. Just about everyone else gets a weekly salary.

Actors' contracts have developed a curious convention called *free weeks*. This is an invention designed to set the actors' rate of compensation at a higher level, in case the studio goes overbudget and has to keep the actor around longer than it intended. If the actors must stay past the agreed-upon period they will not be paid an additional fee because they've already been compensated by the higher salary rate. It also acknowledges that actors are not attached to the pre- and post-production as are directors and producers. Actors are free to go after they finish shooting while the others stay on the project until it's delivered, which can take six months or more.

A TYPICAL PRODUCTION SCHEDULE

Here's how it works. On a typical film you'll commit to five days of pre-production, ten weeks of shooting, two free weeks, and two days of post-production. Even though you have to work those two weeks after shooting if the film isn't completed within the original production schedule, they're referred to as "free," because when it comes to figuring what overtime is owed, those two weeks don't count. So, for example, if the studio goes into overtime, your daily rate is usually based on your entire salary divided by the number of days you got paid for (five days + ten weeks + two days). Since the free weeks don't count, your overtime compensation is more.

OVERTIME

Generally, every creative talent has some provision for overtime in their contract. It's really in everyone's best interest to get the project done efficiently and on time. The studio wants to stop the cash flow into the project as soon as it can, and the creative talent wants to get on to new projects. Delays are inevitable, and time is money in Hollywood.

Directors and top producers are expected to be around and working from pre-production until delivery of the completed film. This can take six months to a year or more, although overtime can factor into their agreements. Lower-level producers are often paid by the week, so overtime would kick in for them if the production takes longer than their contract allows. The amount they are paid for each week of overtime is calculated by dividing their salary by the number of weeks for which they were originally hired.

Actors and crew members enjoy the greatest benefits of overtime provisions. Actors get overtime as soon as the studio has used up the time allotted by the contract. Actors earning gigantic salaries are sometimes asked to waive overtime, but they usually don't, and the studio may find itself with an overtime payment of millions of dollars a week for its lead actor if the production falls behind schedule. For a star who gets $15 million for the production over a ten-week schedule, overtime would be $1.5 million. Like we said, it adds up fast.

Note that because of union protections overtime kicks in on an hourly basis as well as a daily or weekly basis. This has an impact on a production budget if the director holds the cast and crew on the set for too many hours in one day. It's not unusual for the studio to owe a $10 million actor an additional $1000 per day (a multiple of scale) for keeping him on the set for more than twelve hours at a time. The money may not mean much to the actor, but it works as a punitive measure intended to stop the studio from abusing the creative talent by working them too long each day. Unions don't allow crew people to waive overtime protection, so long days for the crew can cost a fortune in overtime.

Here's some sample language that will show you how these deals are set up. Assume for this example that the creative talent is an actor who is earning $100,000 for all services in the production.

SAMPLE CONTRACT LANGUAGE
(START DATE, FREE WEEKS, AND OVERAGE)

1. *START DATE:* On or about September 15, 1995 ("On or about" as used herein means a date occurring during the period commencing seven (7) days before the date stated and ending seven (7) days after the date stated, as Producer shall designate).

2. *SERVICES:* Creative Talent will report for the rendition of services in connection with pre-production and rehearsals for two (2) week(s) prior to the Start Date and for principal photography on said Start Date, and shall continue to render services after said Start Date for ten (10) consecutive weeks plus two (2) consecutive "free" weeks (the Guaranteed Period), and for such additional period or periods, if any, as shall be reasonably necessary to complete all services required of Creative Talent by Producer in connection with principal photography of the Picture. If Producer so requests, Creative Talent will render services in connection with post-production (e.g., retakes, looping and/or dubbing, added scenes) on three (3) consecutive free days following the conclusion of the Guaranteed Period.

3. *OVERAGE COMPENSATION:* An amount equal to $100,000 divided by the number of weeks in the scheduled period of principal photography for each full week of services rendered at Producer's request, in excess of the Guaranteed Period, travel days, "free" post-production days, prorated $1/5$ per day for services in Los Angeles or vicinity, or $1/6$ per day on location.

If you have a contract that more or less resembles the language we've included above, it's basically a typical deal.

TV DEALS

We had mentioned that TV contracts are sometimes done on a less formal basis. What does less formal mean? Take dealmaking. In movies, most studios try to work with the complete contract. It may be twenty pages or more (usually more) and dense, but the whole thing is sent out. Some studios like everything signed before anyone works—it's safer to have it all in print and signed than to rely on oral conversations or even letters.

In television, you are more likely to get a short-form *deal memo,* which is a memo laying out the essential points of your deal, such as money, credit, term, exclusivity (whether you can work for others). Once you sign this short form, you may get a longer-form agreement that is more densely worded with more legal gobbledygook (see chapter 18), but you may not see it before you've performed your services, and no one will expect you to hang around to negotiate it fully.

In addition to the length, the form of the contracts are also different from that of movie deals. Unless they're movies of the week (which are more likely to be set up like a movie), TV deals are expressed in terms of the series or production year, at least for actors and core directing and producing talent. If you have anything other than a one-episode commitment (which we discuss elsewhere in this chapter), your deal will be expressed in terms of a number of episodes out of the total in the series year. For example, you may get a commitment for seven out of thirteen episodes or ten out of thirteen. You will typically be giving a five- to seven-year commitment to the producer if you are cast as a series regular.

Of course, a hit series often creates an opportunity for you to renegotiate your contract. The way it works is that you negotiate one year and give the studio options to renew your services on a yearly basis for a number of years. The compensation and minimum-episode commitments are negotiated before you step on the set. We discuss these structures more when we discuss multiple-episode deals.

COMPENSATION FOR YOUR FIRST REAL JOB

Curious about the kind of money you can expect from your first job? Well, welcome to the wonderful world of scale. *Scale* refers to the minimum salary a production company or studio must pay you for union work. These salaries have been negotiated by the various unions and are readjusted each time the union contracts are renegotiated. As we've mentioned, producers don't belong to a union that is subject to a collective bargaining agreement, so they're more or less on their own for negotiating their own deals.

You shouldn't expect to receive more than scale for your first job, but then again, the scale rate for most jobs in the industry is pretty good. It should go without saying that if the job is a non-union one, you are left to your own devices to negotiate your salary. Worker beware!

You will sometimes hear the term, *scale plus ten*. Production companies and studios will routinely tack on 10 percent to your pay if you are represented by an agent. This way your agent can receive his commission and you will still make scale. (By the way, a SAG-franchised agent is prohibited from taking any amount that would cause you to earn less than scale. Contact your union if that happens.)

Payment

If you are working for a studio, network, or a large production company, you can probably rest assured you will be paid what is owed you. As long as they know where you live or who your agent is, the checks will arrive in the mail without your having to do anything.

By the way, most agents insist on the checks coming straight to them, so they can get their percentage before you even touch the check. Your agent will want to have the power to cash your check and cut you a new one minus 10 percent. Your manager will also want to get her 10 to 15 percent straight from your agent. This system should not pose a problem as long as you have a reputable agent. If you have any doubts, have the studio or production company send you a notice every time they send a check to your agent. Or simply call the production company and have them send the checks directly to you. Remember, though, that you are then responsible for paying your agent and manager their shares.

SCALE FOR ACTORS

EXTRA

If you are working as an extra on a SAG project in Los Angeles, you are guaranteed $72.00 a day, though this figure may go up soon. Stand-ins make $97.00 a day.

DAY PLAYER

If you are a *day player* with lines, hired for one or more days of work, it is customary to pay you scale plus ten, the union-negotiated minimum for that type of work plus 10 percent extra for your agent. You can look up these amounts in your SAG and AFTRA manuals, or call the union to find out what they are.

As we write, the minimum day rate for motion pictures and television under SAG jurisdiction is $522.00. For AFTRA, the minimum day rate for network television varies, depending upon type of program and program length, anywhere from $301.00 for a serial program under 15 minutes in length to $969.00 for a single non-dramatic program between 90 and 120 minutes. For commercial work, SAG's day rate is $443.00. AFTRA's is the same. If you don't know which union has jurisdiction over a given project, you can call your agent, the production company, or one of the unions to find out. As you work more, you may try to negotiate a better day rate. We will cover this issue later in the book.

THREE-DAY AND WEEKLY

If you are hired for a bigger job, there are three-day rates for SAG-governed television work, weekly rates for SAG-governed film and TV, and multiple-performance rates for AFTRA-governed work.

MAJOR ROLE

If your first job is a major role in a film or on a pilot, you should take extra time to determine whether you have been offered the best deal. You would be well advised to consult a knowledgeable entertainment attorney. Often that first small-time agent or manager you signed with will be overwhelmed by the complexity of the deal. We discuss this dilemma further in chapter 13.

We recently spoke with several members of the cast of a hugely successful TV series. They were in the sixth year of the show and still operating under the terms of contracts they had signed before they were even offered the roles six years before. They expressed regret and bitterness over their naïveté when they signed. Millions of dollars had been made off the show in reruns, foreign distribution, and merchandising. Needless to say, very little of that money had found its way to their pockets.

COMMERCIAL WORK

Commercial work, because it can be so lucrative, is also an area in which you might want to get additional help. We know an actor who was recently seen on every other billboard across the country advertising jeans. It was his first print job, and his agent negotiated a $1500 contract for him for a job that would usually pull in ten times that amount or more. By the way, most actors in town, especially in the beginning of their careers, seek commercial work. It's a great way to pay the rent and it carries no stigma; i.e., no one in film and television will hold it against you.

Today's commercial director is tomorrow's film director. Make an impact on him and he may cast you in his feature.

Why Actors Love Commercials

The reason commercial work can be so lucrative for actors is the payment of session fees, holding fees, *and* use fees.

First, the actor gets paid a session fee, *a set amount for each day he or she works on the commercial, just like the day-player rate we discussed above. The* holding fee *is money paid to the actor every thirteen weeks the commercial is running and is equal in amount to what the actor received as a session fee. So, for instance, if the actor worked one day on a commercial and received the SAG scale rate of $414.25, he or she is guaranteed an additional $414.25 every thirteen weeks for as long as the commercial runs.*

The first thirteen weeks start running on the date the actor begins performing any services. The idea behind a holding fee is that the advertiser doesn't want the actor to be appearing in a competitor's commercial, so the advertiser "holds" the actor by paying him a holding fee. During the fixed cycle of thirteen weeks, for instance, an actor on a McDonald's commercial cannot appear in a commercial for Burger King.

If session fees and holding fees sound good, use fees, *which are similar to residuals, are even better. The principle is that the advertiser must pay the actor a rate based on how often the commercial is shown. The way use fees are calculated is a subject reserved for people who have studied advanced calculus, but we can share some of the lingo. Terms like* program use, wild spots, hitch hikes, *and* cow catchers *are used to determine how much the actor gets paid. Cities get weighed and payments are determined by whether the commercial is broadcast via the large networks, individual stations, or cable; in how many cities the commercial appears; and how often the commercial runs. There's a specific formula that produces the agreed-upon payment.*

The important thing for the actor to know is that if he or she works on a commercial that is shown nationally for several months, he or she stands to make several-thousand dollars in use fees. All this money for only a day or two of work. Sound good? That's why actors love commercials.

SCALE FOR DIRECTORS AND WRITERS

SCALE FOR DIRECTORS IN FILM

Rates for directors depend on the budget of the project. For a low-budget film (up to $500,000), the directing scale rate is $5502 per week: The director is guaranteed eight weeks of employment, plus two weeks of preparation time and one week of editing time at the scale rate (the extra time only applies if the director is making double the scale rate or less). For a medium-budget film ($500,000 to $1.5 million) the scale rate is $6253 with ten weeks of employment guaranteed and the extra three weeks of preparation and editing time. For films over $1.5 million, the rate is $8755 for ten weeks, plus the three extra weeks.

SCALE FOR TV DIRECTORS

The going rate is $13,256 for a half-hour network prime-time show, which must be shot in four days with three extra days for preparation. A director is paid $22,511 for directing a one-hour network prime-time show, which must be shot in eight days with seven days for preparation. The rates go up if the show is one-and-a-half or two hours, and they go down if the show is non-network or non-prime time. Pilots, spinoff films, trailers, talent tests, promos, freelance shorts, and documentaries also have different rates, which the DGA can outline.

SCALE FOR FILM WRITERS

Writers are guaranteed different rates depending on the budget, the kind of production, what type of material they supply, and what type of service they perform. For example, if the writer supplies a first-draft screenplay for a low-budget film (under $2.5 million) the scale rate is $15,085. For the *rewrite* the writer is paid $12,569. For the *polish* $6287, and for the final draft $10,053. Polishes and rewrites are work done on an existing script, and the terms are open to interpretation, though a polish is considered to be more minor work than a rewrite. All the rates go up if the film budget is over $2.5 million. By the way, notice the difference between the definitions of "low budget" for directors and writers. Of course, a studio considers anything below $15 million low budget.

SCALE FOR TV WRITERS

The scale rate for a story and teleplay for TV is $15,172 for a 30-minute prime-time show, $22,315 for a 60-minute prime-time show. There are also rates for 15-minute, 45-minute, 90-minute, 120-minute, and over 120-minute prime-time shows, as well as different rates for high- and low-budget non-prime-time network shows.

TV writers also have weekly employment rates, and even a separate rate for writing in a new character. Writers retain some rights that the union has fought for over their stories and characters. Contact the WGA to learn more about the applicable rates and rights of writers.

One word of warning for writers: Much of your early work will probably be done for non-union productions, so you will have to negotiate your own wages. Even when it's a union production, producers are notorious for asking writers to perform additional services for less than scale. Although the WGA may not like to acknowledge it, a lot of writers do work under the table, i.e., under union minimums. Your agent or lawyer should be your guide in these matters.

SCALE FOR BELOW-THE-LINE PEOPLE

As for the other people we've discussed, the scale rate you'll get for a job will vary for a variety of reasons. For instance, work on commercials is often more lucrative than similar work in television. Here are some current numbers we got from a production company, so you'll have an idea of the minimum rates you'll be making when you get union work. It can also provide a guide for non-union work.

Unit Production Managers	$3291/week
1st AD	$3044/week
2nd AD	$2085/week
2nd 2nd AD	$1626/week
Director of Photography	$7500/week
Camera Operator	$37.78/hour
1st Asst. Camera	$32.80/hour
2nd Asst. Camera	$25.13/hour
Script Supervisor	$22.09/hour
Production Designer	$3750/week
Art Director	$2095.83/week
Asst. Art Director	$1568.71/week
Illustrator	$1466.97/week
Set Designer	$1212.13/week
Construction Coordinator	$1417.20/week
General Foreman	$26.57/hour
Carpenter Foreman	$26.57/hour
Gang Boss	$24.54/hour
Key Grip/Gaffer	$26.19/hour
Best Boy Grip/Gaffer	$23.69/hour
Grips/Lamps	$22.62/hour

Dolly Grip	$24.54/hour
Rigging Grip/Gaffer	$24.56/hour
Painter Foreman	$26.58/hour
Standby Painter	$27.42/hour
Craft Service	$21.59/hour
Propmaster	$26.19/hour
Asst. Propman	$23.13/hour
Set Decorator	$1608.20/week
Leadman	$22.63/hour
Swingman	$21.60/hour
Special Effects Coordinator	$26.57/hour
Asst. Effects	$24.54/hour
2nd Asst. Effects	$23.14/hour
Costume Designer	$1492.63/week
Asst. Costume Designer	$1218.79/week
Costume Supervisor	$24.15/hour
Set Costumer	$21.01/hour
Dept. Head Makeup/Hair	$33.29/hour
Extra/Key Makeup/Hair	$30.12/hour
Sound Mixer	$42.16/hour
Boom Man	$32.51/hour
Cable Man	$28.44/hour
Transportation Coordinator	$2200/week
Transportation Captain	$2000/week
Location Manager	$1808.68/week
Asst. Location Manager	$698.34/week
Video Assistant	$28.44/hour
Production Coordinator	$1300/week
Asst. Production Coordinator	$850/week

Some of the job categories, including technical jobs, remain tied to scale, even for the higher-level people. The numbers will be expressed as "double scale" or some multiple of scale.

Compensation for above-the-line jobs can go above scale as soon as you hit your first big break.

NON-UNION COMPENSATION

If you are working with a smaller production company, especially if the project is non-union, you should be extremely careful. An agent, manager, or attorney can provide you some protection. After all, if you don't receive any money, neither do they. We know many people who thought they were receiving a certain amount only to discover a much smaller paycheck in the mail, no paycheck at all, or that they were responsible for paying their own airfare to the location. The time to do all this checking is before you take the job, not afterwards.

RESIDUALS

In any union project, you are guaranteed *residuals*, extra money paid to you when the television show or theatrical motion picture is rerun, sold to cable or pay-TV, or shown in foreign markets. As the reruns multiply, you can receive quite a hefty sum if the show is popular. (Extra work does not entitle you to residuals.) These rates are usually based upon a percentage of the salary you originally made. Union members such as actors, writers, and directors who have worked on long-running series or successful movies can be the happy recipients of little bundles of money for years after their product has completed its initial run.

CREDIT

As silly as it may sound, credit can be just about as good as hard currency in Hollywood. Some of the biggest battles between agents and production companies and studios occur over credit.

We talk about credits in depth in chapters 13 and 17, because credit generally doesn't come into play until you've had your first big break.

As you move along in your career, credit will become a bigger issue, even for below-the-line folks. However, for your first job, credit will not be that complicated an issue. You'll want to check with your agent to make sure you're getting the best deal you can at this stage of your career. For instance, even if your part is three lines on an episodic television series, you might get listed in the credits as a "guest star," you might get individual billing, and you might even get listed in the opening credits rather than at the end after the last commercial break. It's often not the size of the part that determines who gets the best billing, but the power and push of your agent or manager. Still don't think credit is that important? Wait until you go to your first movie in Los Angeles and see how many people in the audience sit through the end credits looking at them more carefully than they watched the film. A substantial number are industry folks who want to know who the picture's cinematographer, costume designer, or even gaffer was.

IS THERE ANYTHING ELSE I CAN GET THIS TIME AROUND?

Well, no, maybe, and yes. If you've been struggling for a while, don't have a high-powered agent or publicist, don't have different studios bidding for your services, and are not dating anyone famous, then the answer is no. If you do have some of the things in this list, then the answer is maybe. If you have all of the things on this list, then the answer is probably yes. What kinds of things can you get? We've discussed previously some of the things you can expect or ask for. Anything you get above scale or beyond a normal first-timer deal will depend entirely upon the circumstances of your arrival and with whom you land. You might get some more money, better credit, the promise of the same dressing room as the second- or third-level stars, possibly an assistant if you're a producer or director, and maybe some extra travel. Since the real perks don't usually come until you've had at least one break, we've saved the icing on the cake for chapters 15 through 19.

CHAPTER ELEVEN

When Will I Work Again?

WHAT HAPPENS BETWEEN THE FIRST AND THE NEXT REAL JOB

As we've mentioned above, most people in Hollywood are hired from project to project. If you're not smart, you will finish your first job and find yourself back at square one. If you are smart, you will hustle your butt to take advantage of that first job so that the next one follows shortly after. Did you do your absolute professional best and learn everything you could? Did you take the time to get to know everyone on the set and get their phone numbers and addresses? Have you followed up with calls and cards thanking them for their help? Did you send a thank-you note to whoever helped you get the job? There is nothing more attractive in this town than someone who's working. It's like the dating world; if someone asks you out, everyone figures you must have something going for you. You will want to make sure everyone who might hire you or refer you for another job knows you are working.

SURVIVING THE HARD TIMES

Save, save, save. You must resist the temptation to rush out and spend your first paycheck on a new stereo system. Credit cards should be viewed as the devil's plaything. You will likely need every cent you earn to tide you over until your next job. The only reason you should spend this money is if you reinvest it in your career—spend it on training, tools, and publicity.

Your First Big Break

CHAPTER TWELVE

What Are the Breaks?

Breaks come in all shapes and sizes. Yours might be the first professional activity that gets you recognized while you're strolling the aisles at the supermarket. It might be a production credit that puts you on the list of directors the studio puts together when it's planning a new series. Perhaps it's the job or the deal that will get your phone call answered the first time you call the top studios or agencies in town. It might be getting a good table at the currently fashionable restaurant in town.

We can't say exactly what the big break looks like for any individual career, but here are some examples. For an actor, it might be getting a starring role in a film (maybe not the lead in the picture, but a featured role) or getting a part in a series pilot that has been picked up by the network. For a writer, it might be getting a script purchased *and* produced by a major studio, or being named co-producer on a TV series. For a director, it might mean winning the top prize at a prestigious film festival. For a technical person, it might mean getting a job on a big (e.g., high-budget or high-prestige) picture with a name director. For a composer, it might mean getting to write the theme to a new television series or game show.

Your First Big Break

Whether you're an overnight sensation or you've been working toward this break for a decade, once you've got a toe on that ladder to the stars, your chances of hanging on and moving up to the next rung will be greatly enhanced if you understand the implications of your good fortune. If you know what you're worth, you'll be much more likely to get it.

This section of the book is dedicated to getting the most out of the opportunity. If you know what you can get at this stage and what to avoid, you'll be ahead of the game.

CHAPTER THIRTEEN

Exploiting the Break

WHO SHOULD MAKE MY DEAL AND NEGOTIATE MY CONTRACT?

We assume you've figured out our bias by now, but it bears repeating in case you haven't gotten the message yet. If you don't already have your team assembled, and you have any reason to believe you may have a solid offer for work, get yourself an experienced professional representative now. Do not start your career by selling yourself down the river. Though it's true that bad representation can be worse than no representation at all, you owe it to yourself to be informed. *Do not attempt to swim with the sharks without having your own shark by your side.* Read the relevant parts of this book, especially the details in chapter 7 about how to put that team together. You'll never get the trappings of success unless you know how to ask for them.

Who should make your deal? It doesn't really matter if it's an agent or lawyer as long as they are competent, though it can help to have a better-known individual or law firm or agency on your side. If you have an agent, use him or her. Don't balk because you're not earning much yet and don't want to share your compensation. Even if it's a scale deal, chances are you'll get enough to pay your agent (scale plus ten, for instance, which we talked about above), and you'll have someone to call if someone suddenly asks you to drop your pants or you end up working overtime seven days a week. You may end up having to cooperate, but you'll get something for it, and the studio will know you're not a chump. If you had problems in the past getting an agent or lawyer, try again. Even if you were rejected before, if you have a solid job offer they will more than likely take a second look or recommend someone who will.

Educate yourself. No matter where you are in your career, you should consciously participate in the business side enough to be sure you're handling yourself or being handled properly. You don't have to understand the intricacies of net profits (only a handful of people do), but you should be well aware if you've given someone the right to put your face on a kewpie doll or signed away that great idea you had for the movie of the century. Whatever you do, you can start building your equity in your own creative talent now by protecting yourself.

SHOULD I CHANGE MY AGENT OR MANAGER?

Here is the sad reality. That first agent who took you on when no one else would when you were a nobody, who has come to see you in all those lousy equity-waiver plays, who hustled to get you those three lines on *Baywatch* so you could get your SAG card, who has become your confidante and best friend, may in fact not be the best agent for you when you get your first big break.

The business quickly becomes very complex and sophisticated when you work as a series regular or star in a miniseries or film. Lots of money and other benefits are up for grabs, so the studios and production companies will have their best people working overtime to make sure you get as little of it as possible.

A big break also provides the opportunity to make several strategic career moves that could ensure you bigger and better jobs for years to come, assuming you have someone on your team who knows what these moves are and has the connections to make them.

Chances are your first agent and manager will not be big-time players. They won't have the experience and expertise to help you get the best deal and exploit this wonderful opportunity. You will be forced to be very objective as you appraise whether they are the right people to move with you to the next level. One reason this appraisal is so important is the nature of the business. Talented actors and directors may get, at best, one or two windows of opportunity in their careers. If they fail to take advantage of these opportunities, their careers could be extremely short-lived.

For example, we know one actress who was cast as a regular in a critically acclaimed TV series. The series ran for only two or three seasons. During that time, all the series regulars except her were counseled by their agents and managers to hire publicists and get as much publicity as possible, so that when the series was canceled everyone around town would recognize their names. Predictably, all the regulars moved on to other acting jobs after the series except for our friend, who is back at square one in her career. The right agent or manager would never have let that happen.

How can you, the relative newcomer in town, determine whether you need to change your agent or manager? This is where all that reading and networking you have been doing will pay off. You can use your contacts' experience to inform your decision.

You should also take the time to sit down with your agent and manager and ask them to share with you their new plans for you now that you have this big break. They should be as excited about it as you are, and they should be brimming with ideas for how to exploit it. If they don't have a clear vision about how to take advantage of this opportunity and it's just business as usual, then it's probably time to look for new players for your team.

MAJOR DEAL POINTS FOR THE FIRST BIG BREAK

If you're stepping into the big leagues, chances are you're going to do better than a mere scale deal. Here's where your representatives can start having some fun. They're going to pitch you to the studio as the next Julia Roberts or Steven Spielberg. Simultaneously, the studio will do everything it can to hold back the force of hype. Though it may seem like a free-for-all much of the time, there are rules to the game. Typically, the studio will have some notion of what newcomer you most resemble in terms of your current value (and therefore how nice they have to be to you in the negotiation). They'll get information about your past deals either directly from your agent or through the grapevine. There aren't many secrets in the game. Like checkers, it's really a question of who's got the best moves.

We talk more about how production deals in motion pictures and television are structured in chapters 10, 20, and 21. Here we discuss how some of these issues play out in these first-break deals for creative talent.

COMPENSATION

You know your compensation will probably be above scale, but by how much? Start with the premise that the range varies dramatically once you reach the above-scale level. Also realize that compensation is like the stock market. It goes up and down with a whim or a rumor. There are, however, some things we can tell you.

The studio will find out how much you made before as well as how much people they consider comparable to you are making at their own and other studios. Though it might be considered rude if not downright invasive, studio people talk to each other all the time. They give each other information. They encourage each other to hold the fort against inflationary salaries and rights of approval. Does this practice sound a little monopolistic or smack of price fixing? Well, just remember that it doesn't necessarily mean you have to pay any attention or accept any particular offer without a fight. If you're hot and your agent is smart and tough, there are few limits on what compensation you can get, whether or not the market can bear it.

Knowing that rules are made to be broken, here are some current ballpark figures for first big breaks. Note that we're only talking cash compensation here. We discuss profit participations in chapter 17. Residuals (see chapter 10) also sweeten the pot, and they aren't accounted for here.

ACTORS

Series Regular (Television): $7500 to $12,500 per episode.

Motion Picture Featured Actor $150,000 to $400,000 for a featured role and a full schedule of photography.

WRITERS

Television: if under contract, $2500 to $5000 per week with a six- to fourteen-week minimum.

Features: $75,000 to $350,000 for all writing on a project that is produced, depending on how many writers end up on the project. (If the production doesn't get made, earnings are a fraction of these numbers.)

DIRECTORS

Television: $15,000 per episode on half-hour shows, $20,000 per episode on hour shows. Episodic directors always get scale, unless they're a "name."

Features: $250,000 to $500,000 if project is produced.

PRODUCERS

Television: $5000 to $15,000 per episode.

Features: $150,000 to $350,000 if project is produced.

CREDIT

This is the other area in which the first big break may give you some leverage. We also begin to see the significant role the unions play in negotiating credit. To start, you should know that the two main issues in credit are size and placement.

A Credit Primer

Placement: *Where does your credit appear on the picture and where is the credit relative to the other credits? There are deal conventions and there are union-driven rules in play here.*

It may be the first time you get main title *(i.e., before the picture starts) credit, as opposed to* end title *(i.e., after the picture is over) credit and maybe even credit in* paid advertising *(i.e., the promotional advertising the studio purchases in connection with the project). If it's a big enough project, a big enough break, and you have a big enough agent, you may get* above-the-title *credit (i.e., credit that appears before the title of the picture both onscreen and in paid advertising).*

Size: *How big is the credit? Is it bigger or smaller than someone else's? These sizes are measured in height, width, and sometimes thickness of type and length of time they remain on the film.*

Note that these days, credits are handled differently from how they were handled in the golden era of Hollywood moviemaking. Previously, the studios used to load most of the credits into the main titles (see the Credit Primer above), while the trend recently has been to reserve the main title credits for the players.

As a beginner you have limited power over the credits you'll receive, except that directing and writing credits are strictly regulated by the unions. We'll talk at length about credit negotiations in chapters 17 and 18.

DIRECTORS

By convention (and DGA rules), the director's credit (as in "Director" or "Directed by") is always the last before the start of the movie or television program. As for people down the line who are assisting the director, a lot depends on whether or not it's a DGA film, since credits are rigidly enforced by this union. If you're working on a movie, you may even get a *film by* credit (as in "A Film by"), which is one of the first credits you see above the title both on screen and in advertising, though the studios sometimes hold back on giving this credit to first timers with weak representation.

PRODUCERS

A producer credit can be almost anything, as we discussed in chapter 2. Probably the most prestigious credit is the simplest, as in "Producer" or "Produced by." If this is your first big break the studio may hold back this cherry, even if you've done all the work, and just give you Associate Producer, Executive Producer, Second Associate Producer, or whatever credit you negotiate. Naturally, the important producer credits appear in the main titles.

If you're lucky and the studio isn't too rigid, you'll get a *production credit,* as in "A Joe Blow Production," which always appears above the title in the main titles. Some studios resist giving this kind of credit to newcomers. Sometimes the studio will give you a production credit in your name, but not the name of your company. So you'll get "A Joe Blow Production," but not "A Joe Blow Company Production." The idea is that some of the studios want the only company name to appear in the main titles to be theirs, but this determination varies, depending on who's in charge of the studio that day.

WRITERS

Writer's credits are determined by the Writers Guild, and even if the picture isn't a union picture, WGA rules tend to apply anyway. Writing credits always appear just before the producing and directing credits in films. On a project produced by a WGA signatory, all scripts are submitted to the WGA, along with the studio recommendation for what the credit ought to be. The WGA reviews the recommendation and generally approves, unless there are many writers or one of the writers is protesting the script version or the credit the studio submitted.

Shared Writing Credit

Writing teams: *If a writing team gets a credit, there's an ampersand (&) between their names instead of the word* and. *For example, if A and B wrote together as a team, their credit would read "Written by A & B." If the WGA determined that the writing team of A and B should share credit with C, an individual writer, then the credit would read, "Written by A & B and C." Here are some more terms you should know.*

Written by *means the writer(s) came up with the story idea and also wrote the script.*

Story by *means the writer(s) came up with the story, but did not get credit for the final script.*

Screenplay by *means the writer(s) wrote the screenplay, but did not come up with the idea for the story.*

ACTORS

In movies, actors generally don't get special titles for their credits, such as *Starring, Featuring*. Lead actors are listed by name only, and the rest of the cast may be introduced with the term *Starring*. In television, you might see the credit *Guest Star* to distinguish an actor from regular cast members used. Acting credits are usually heavily negotiated. Placement and size are significant because they represent how important your role is and/or how important you are. The most important actors/roles get sole screen credit (not shared with anyone while the name is on the screen) and paid advertising credit (see chapter 17 for more on paid advertising). If the actor is among the featured players, sometimes his or her credit will share the screen with that of one or more actors, usually a negotiated number. Sometimes groups of actors are credited alphabetically. If the actor's credit appears alone, it is often referred to as *single card credit* as opposed to *shared card credit*.

One desirable form of special mention is credit at the end of all acting credits, preceded by *and*. An example would read, "Starring John Doe, Mary Roe, Tim Moe, *and* Larry Foe." An even more desirable mention includes the name of the character played. An example would read, "Starring John Doe, Mary Roe, Tim Moe, and Larry Foe *as George*." The method chosen has to do with the relative strengths of the actors and the current policies of the studio about giving out these credits. (More about important language pertaining to actors' credits in chapters 17 and 18.)

MULTIPLE PICTURE AND EPISODE DEALS

The good news is that the studio wants the right to use you again. The bad news is that you may find yourself exclusively committed to doing additional movies or years of a television series with people you may or may not want to work with for compensation lower than you're probably worth, now that you've had your first big break. This scenario presents itself often with actors but can also occur with first-time directors.

The studio often insists that newcomers sign multiple-commitment deals. After all, it's logical. If the studio is taking a chance on an unknown commodity, it wants to earn some dividends from that risk. If you are skillful, appealing, or otherwise desirable, the studio may want you around for continuity of your character or because you're cheaper than someone else with a track record.

On the other hand, a multiple-commitment deal may also represent an investment in you that forces the studio to focus more attention on your work. Since studio heads know they've got you around, they may decide to use you over someone else with whom they'd have to negotiate a whole deal with, start to finish.

What do you need to know about multiple deals? The first thing you need to know is the *seven-year rule*. If you're working in the state of California or working for a company based in California, chances are you'll be protected by the seven-year rule. The rule is a state law that protects people from being stuck under one contract for more than a seven-year period.

Why a Seven-Year Rule?

The origin of this rule, which applies to all professions in the state, was actually in Hollywood. The studios used to have many of their creative talent under long-term contracts that lasted for years. Many people tied to these contracts became unhappy with the management, the work offered them, or the compensation. When Bette Davis was under contract to Warner, she struggled to limit the studio's right to use her to only four films per year. She didn't have the right to choose which roles she had to take. In retaliation, Davis and others refused to do the movies assigned to them. In turn, the studios would punish them by suspending them and extending their contracts still further.

The result was that the creative talent stopped earning money and were prevented from working for anyone else. Worst of all, the contracts they hated so much ended up restricting them even longer. Some of the early rebels, including Davis, went to court to defeat these contracts, and the seven-year rule was the outcome.

What does the seven-year rule have to do with multiple deals? If the studio has the right to put you in three additional movies after the first, they can really tie up your career. Since it usually takes at least nine months to plan, shoot, and release a picture after the script is written, it can take over a year to get the next sequel going, even if everyone is rushing. If you've signed up for more than one picture, you can see how one studio may monopolize your time during your peak career years.

If you sign a multiple-episode deal, you can't be forced to commit to the entire run of a series if it goes beyond seven years. Most studio people are aware of this rule, but don't expect every independent to be respectful of the law. The best way to protect yourself is to avoid signing any deal that ties you up exclusively for an unlimited term. However, if you find yourself in such a predicament, you may be able to get out of it because of the seven-year rule.

MULTIPLE-PICTURE DEALS

Often in features when a newcomer is signed, the studio will get a commitment for two or three optional pictures. The option, of course, belongs to the studio, as these options are usually one-sided. This is especially true in cases where the project is one that might spawn a sequel or two. If you're a hit in the first picture, the studio will be under enormous pressure to have you back as that same character in the sequel. What can you do to make the most of a multiple-picture deal (assuming you don't have the clout to avoid it)?

First, try to limit the option. If you're an actor, make sure the commitment is only for the same character in the series. That is, you will only agree to play the same character in a sequel or remake—they don't have the right to slap you into any role in any project. If you're a director, make sure you can only be forced to direct in the series. The same thinking applies for producers. Also, try to make it a one-picture, instead of a two- or three-picture deal.

Second, try to get yourself in a *Most Favored Nations* position on a number of key points. Now is as good a time as any to explain this helpful little phrase.

Most Favored Nations

This phrase traces its origins to the realm of foreign diplomacy. The concept is that you enjoy the status that our best allies get. Sounds nice, right? It is if you can get it. Try to include in the negotiation a clause stating that if anyone else does better than you on a particular point—be it money, profit participation, credit, dressing room— the studio matches the conditions for you, point by point.

Needless to say, most studios hate this provision and refuse to give it, or they will avoid it or narrow it so much it's not meaningful. Nevertheless, it's worth asking for. Sometimes, for instance, you can get yourself put in a certain class. For example, you might be an actor in a featured—but not starring—role. You might be able to get the studio to agree that if any person other than the lead actors gets his or her name in advertising, you will, too; or if any actor other than the lead actors is given a profit participation, you will, too; or if the director gets a Winnebago while on location, you will, too.

Like we said, it's nice if you can get it.

Third, ask for escalations on key points, based on the performance of the first movie. For example, if the first movie made more than $50 million at the box office (we'll explain how this works in chapter 17), ask that your salary goes up an additional $100,000 for the second picture. If you get a leading part in your second movie, ask that your credit be placed no lower than third. You and your representatives should always look toward contingencies that could sweeten your deal.

PREEMPTION

Always a battleground in multiple-picture deals, the *preemption clause* refers to the studio's ability to call the creative talent back to work to fulfill commitments for additional pictures. As you can imagine, it can put a roadblock in your professional plans if the studio has the right to yank you out of whatever you're doing to start a picture. It can make it impossible to enter into other deals, let alone plan a vacation with the family. There are a number of ways these provisions can be limited, however. You might limit the amount of time the studio has to get the next picture ready for shooting, the length of the new shooting schedule, and the number of days the creative talent has to be available for reshooting. You can also expand the periods of time during which the creative talent is free to work for others.

The following gives you an idea of the language of multiple motion-picture deals with preemptions. As you might guess, such language gives lawyers headaches, so it's important that someone in your camp is knowledgeable and can handle this section of the negotiation. If you signed this agreement without enlisting your lawyer to negotiate more favorable conditions, you will almost certainly regret it.

Multiple Pictures with Preemptions

Optional Projects: In consideration of the engagement of Creative Talent for the Project, Creative Talent hereby grants to Producer the following exclusive, irrevocable options for Creative Talent's services in three Optional Projects (which may or may not be sequels). With respect to each optional Project, the terms and conditions shall be the same as those relating to the Project (except as detailed below):

A. Compensation:
    1. First optional Project: $
    2. Second optional Project: $
    3. Third optional Project: $

B. Option Exercise Periods: Option for first optional Project to be exercised, if at all, by notice in writing not later than the earlier of (i) one (1) year after the date of initial general release of the first Project or (ii) eighteen (18) months after completion of photography of the first Project. Options for subsequent optional Projects to be exercised, if at all, by notice in writing not later than the earlier of (i) one (1) year after the date of initial general release of the prior optional Project or (ii) eighteen (18) months after completion of principal photography of the prior optional Project. If a particular option is exercised and principal photography of the applicable optional Project has not commenced within "Start Period" (as defined below), the next option must be exercised, if at all, prior to the expiration of Start Period. If Producer fails to exercise any option hereunder, Producer shall not have the right to exercise any subsequent options.

C. Start Dates/Start Periods: Producer to designate date for principal photography to start ("Start Date") not later than one (1) year after the date on which the option is exercised ("Start Period"). Creative Talent to receive no less than fifteen (15) days prior written notice of Start Date for the applicable optional Project. If no Start Date is set within Start Period, then compensation for applicable optional Project is payable in twelve (12) weekly installments commencing thirty (30) days after expiration of Start Period.

D. Outside Rights: After completion of services of a Project produced hereunder, Creative Talent may render services in an "Outside Engagement" (as defined below) until Producer exercises the next option hereunder (if ever) subject to the following: At all times hereunder Creative Talent must give not less than thirty (30) days, but no more than sixty (60) days, prior to the start of principal photography of an Outside Engagement, notice of intention to render services in an Outside Engagement. Upon receipt of such notice, Producer has ten (10) business days to preempt. If Producer preempts, Creative Talent may not render services in such Outside Engagement and Producer must designate Start Date for next optional Project not later than sixty (60) days after proposed start date of such Outside Engagement. "Outside Engagement" shall mean bona fide legally binding commitments to perform in any television, stage, and/or theatrical motion picture Project engagement, television pilot, series, and/or variety show. Any proposed long-term or multiple theatrical motion picture Project or television engagement shall, for the purpose of this Agreement, be deemed to consist of separate engagements, each for one theatrical or television motion picture Project, as the case may be.

E. Extensions: Each Option Exercise Period may be extended by a period equal to time in which Creative Talent is unavailable to Producer because of outside engagements and/or because of Creative Talent's breach or disability and/or by a period in which a force majeure event exists.

―――――――

MULTIPLE EPISODE AND SERIES TELEVISION DEALS

As we've discussed, television series deals must be structured to support a series that could be in production for years. Since the series' lead actors, the key producers, and directors must be available for the run of the series, deals which provide for longer commitments (usually five to seven years) are much more common in television than in motion pictures. In motion pictures, you see multiple deals mostly for newcomers and established people only when sequels are anticipated. The opposite is true for series television. Here, the key creative talent are always signed for multiple-year deals before the series is set up. It makes good business sense. You can't have "Roseanne" without Roseanne.

The question here is, in how many of the episodes will the studio use you in a particular year, and how much will you be paid for each episode? As you can imagine, the Most Favored Nations clause comes up a great deal in these negotiations. If you haven't already, see our discussion of this point in the prior section. Creative talent want the assurance of a Most Favored Nations clause. The last thing they want is to find themselves stuck in a series commitment and have newcomers come in and top their contract provisions.

Of course, for the highest-level creative talent, especially the actors, contracts seem to get renegotiated every year, even if the actor signed a so-called airtight contract at the beginning of the series. When someone's hot, he or she gets a lot of bargaining power. It's not unusual to hear of someone threatening to walk off the set if he doesn't get what he wants. The law states that you can't force anyone to work if he doesn't want to—ever heard of the Fourteenth Amendment to the Constitution? There's no slavery in this country, and no one can force you onto a set.

A studio or production company can hurt you, though, if you don't want to comply with your contract. If the studio doesn't want to release you, it can sue you for damages caused by your failure to perform. They can stop you from working for others by getting an injunction. However, studios don't like to operate this way, since it won't get you where they want you, which is on the set and happy. That's why every year there are contract free-for-alls on some successful series.

HIATUS

The *hiatus* is the period of time when a series is not in production. A major issue that comes up for television people is what they are allowed to do during their hiatus. Whether the studio is motivated by its need to protect its image or whether it's simply a control issue, it may want to limit what the creative talent can do on their time off. The studio usually has approval over the shooting schedule the actor can agree to during a hiatus. The way it works is when a movie producer wants to use a series star for a lead in a movie, the producer has to go to the television producer and confirm that the actor is indeed available for the period of time the actor's services are required. This can create enormous scheduling problems, not to mention power wars, but it happens all the time.

If you get nothing else from this book, please take our best advice: Get professional help before entering into any deal as complicated as the ones we're describing. It's tempting to sign anything when someone wants you at last or when you're getting something you've really wanted. The beginning of your career is an especially good time to establish that you take yourself seriously. Consider it your social security.

SHOULD I INCORPORATE?

Should you form a personal corporation (called a loanout corporation) at this stage of your career? There's a short answer and a longer answer to this question, but first, a short explanation.

What is a *loanout corporation?* Since we're not tax attorneys or accountants, we'll just describe this term generally. People often form corporations for the same reasons they create corporations when they start a business. Corporations enjoy certain privileges people don't, such as tax advantages, and creative talent form their own one-person corporations to take advantage of these same privileges.

Why Do They Call It a Loanout?

The concept is that the corporation loans its employee, the creative talent, to the producer. There's some Hollywood history to the development of this term. In the old studio-system days, when the studios had dozens of actors and directors under long-term contract, they would "loan out" their creative talent to other studios. It was a tremendous source of income to the studios, especially when it came to stars like Clark Gable, who was loaned out for Gone With the Wind.

How does incorporation work? Since the corporate tax rate is lower than the individual tax rate, the money that goes into a corporation is taxed at this lower rate, and the corporation can decide when and how much to pay its sole employee. If a great deal of money comes into the corporation in a lump sum in one year, the corporation may not pay all or any of the money to its employees until the next year, thereby putting the creative talent in a lower tax category and easing the tax burden.

For example, you make $150,000 this year and put it into your corporation. You make $10,000 the next year. The corporation can spread the first year's money over two years, say $80,000 a year ($150,000 plus $10,000, divided by two). With a generous helping of business expenses, you theoretically pay fewer individual taxes. What constitutes business expenses? Corporations are businesses, so they get to deduct many expenses incurred in setting up or running the business. They can purchase insurance and equipment and other things that can be written off.

Now for those short and long answers to the question should I incorporate? The short answer, and the correct one, is to consult your accountant or your tax attorney, or both. He or she is the only one who can tell you what's right for you at this stage of your career.

The longer answer is to consult your accountant and consider the following. You or your professional adviser should analyze your income and determine whether it's necessary or even helpful for you to become a corporation at this time. There are pitfalls in incorporating. You have to follow certain formalities to do it correctly, such as filing *Articles of Incorporation*, usually with the Secretary of State. This costs some money. The government allows individuals to incorporate so long as they don't abuse the attendant privileges.

For example, there are only so many write-offs that are appropriate: You may be able to write off your secretary as a business expense, maybe even your Winnebago, but a yacht is probably a stretch. You also can't use a corporation to defraud someone. If the government or any court thinks you've abused your privileges, it can do something called "lifting the corporate veil," which means you lose all protection gained from initial incorporation, and you may have more trouble to deal with than back taxes.

CHAPTER FOURTEEN

Avoid Being Exploited

LOCATION FEVER

You've heard about the movie star who meets another actor during the production of a picture and falls in love, only to have that relationship break up when the movie is completed. Next time you read about that star, he or she is going around town with someone who was on the set of his or her latest production.

Movie star stories are fun, at least for the rest of us to read, but don't think temptations begin and end with actors. Location fever is a phenomenon that touches everyone on a set. People who live basically gypsy lives find themselves thrown together for short, intense periods of time. They work long hours together in a high energy, sometimes stressful situation. They tend to spend their free time together, especially when on some distant location where people on the set might be the only ones they know. Romance kindles, then flames. Then it's on to the next project, and the fever cools down. This scenario may sound romantic and certainly can be, but it can also be a real problem for people who try to maintain relationships while they work in the entertainment business. We guess you could say it's a way people exploit each other.

Don't Get Caught Paying Double

We've mentioned this in other contexts (see chapter 13), but it bears repeating here. If you switch agents or pick up another manager, you may find yourself owing a percentage of your compensation to more than one person. This can happen even if you've dropped one agent for another. These matters must be handled with clarity and on paper. Your lawyer can tell you where you stand. Do yourself a favor and find out before you make any changes or additions to your representation.

The Ego Problem

As you know, certain careers in the business bring with them the extra opportunity and burdens of fame and fortune. Successful actors and even some directors, agents, and studio executives will experience that giddy feeling usually reserved for sports stars and lotto winners, as they watch their cash reserves explode and receive the adulation of adoring fans and newfound friends.

We call it a burden because your character will be sorely tested by this success. Anyone who has seen a tabloid or watched one of the talk shows knows that there's a price to fame: the pressures of big-money productions, the long hours, the gypsy life, the egos, and the loss of privacy. You become vulnerable to being worshipped for the person you portray, your connections, or the money that often comes with success.

Hollywood is littered with stories of people whose egos grew at the same pace as their phenomenal careers, mostly with disastrous results. The legacy these people leave is tainted by drug abuse, temper tantrums, broken marriages, hollow personal lives, and embittered old age. Even though there are plenty of people ready to exploit the newly famous, the irony is that these people are most often betrayed and exploited by their most trusted ally, themselves. Of course, anyone with the requisite hunger to make it in the entertainment business is probably going to say "gimme some." You almost have to erect blinders to the pitfalls of success to strive for that golden ring.

While some people seem to thrive in the spotlight, obviously in control of the situation and delighting in the attention, others wither, behave badly, or kill themselves with drugs or other indulgences. We can only raise the issues, but as you read this chapter, think about who you are and how you'll do when the fickle finger of fate points favorably at you.

With some degree of luck, you'll achieve all the success you deserve. We encourage you to build a character which allows you and your loved ones to truly and deeply enjoy this success. Go back and read section one if you need to be reminded of what we mean by character, or read some of the biographies and other books we suggest in our reading list. Finally, make friends with some people whose character you admire. There is nothing like a circle of good people to elevate and inspire you to the kind of character you will need to survive in this town.

WHAT PRICE FAME?

Kiss privacy and a settled lifestyle good-bye. We all know we live in a celebrity-driven society. However, the depth of people's identification with celebrities is still shocking, as anyone knows who watched on TV the thousands of people who flocked to get a glimpse of O.J. Simpson as he and his friend were spotted on an L.A. freeway.

The stalking of celebrities by disturbed fans is a common occurrence. Less dangerous, though perhaps more intrusive, is the daily stream of admirers who can't resist interrupting the celebrity as he eats dinner in a restaurant, shops in the supermarket, goes to the movies, exercises at the health club, or walks on the beach. Many of us harbor a secret desire to be recognized and acclaimed; but like too much of your favorite dessert, excessive acclaim can leave you feeling sick to your stomach. If privacy is one of your most prized possessions, avoid those careers in the business that are sure to rob you of it should you succeed as fully as you desire.

The lack of a settled lifestyle, however, is a problem for most any successful person in the business. Most entertainment careers demand that you spend weeks and even months away from home while on location. You will rise before dawn and work late into the night much of the time. Lawyers have a saying that "law is a jealous mistress," and that characterization is just as appropriate when speaking about the entertainment industry. We talked about this problem when we spoke about the different careers in chapter 3, but it's worth bringing up again. If you plan almost any career in the business, you better enjoy living a much different lifestyle from most other folks. You better make sure your family, your parents, your siblings, your spouse, and your kids enjoy it, too, because it will profoundly affect their lives.

"PLEASE TAKE OFF YOUR CLOTHES"

Perhaps only Congress and a few religious cults outdo Hollywood in the breadth and severity of sexual harassment. Put any mixed-gender group of actors who have been in Hollywood for a year in a room, and we would bet that seven out of ten will have a story of sexual exploitation. Put any group of studio executives or producers together, and you might hear some stories about their own or their colleagues' bad behavior in this area. Anyone who tells you the casting couch is a thing of the past is a liar or a fool. Here are examples of what we're talking about.

Sexual Harassment
Some of the Milder Stories We've Heard Recently

An actress meets with a manager and is told point blank he will represent her if she gives him a blow job.

An agent tells an actress she will never make it in this town because she is not pretty enough and has no personality. That afternoon he calls her and suggests she come over to his house for dinner to discuss ways she might correct these deficiencies.

An actress goes in for a general (a meeting in which the actor is not auditioning for a specific part) with a casting director. The casting director tells her to take off her shirt. When she asks why, he says, "I want to see your boobs." When she hesitates, he leans across his desk and screams, "Let me see your tits!"

A writer calls an actress who just finished auditioning for his film. He suggests they go out for dinner that night. When she declines, he mentions that he is about to join the producers and director who are in the process of deciding who will play the role she auditioned for. He asks her if she might change her mind about dinner.

An acting coach calls a student into his office for a private session, tells her that her main problem is how inhibited she is, and suggests she do an improvisation with him in which she tries to seduce him.

An actress goes in for her first audition with a female casting director and an assistant who is running a video camera. The actress is told to strip, even though she's auditioning for a part that does not call for nudity.

An actor auditions for a TV show produced by a major studio. A casting director from another major studio calls the actor's manager and tells her if the actor will sleep with the casting director of the TV show the actor will get the role.

An actor meets with a manager to rehearse for an audition, and the manager suggests they improvise the scene in which the two men wrestle together. He suggests the actor will get more out of it if they strip to their underwear.

The star of a film invites a young actress who just got her first role to his trailer to rehearse. He assaults her. She resists. The next day she is called by the producer and told she won't be needed on the film anymore.

A producer gives his card to a waitress and invites her to audition for a role in his next movie. She brings a male friend to his office and the producer throws her out, berating her for having so little trust in him that she brought the male friend. The next day, the producer's secretary calls and tells the actress to return, but this time to read for a smaller role. She goes by herself this time. The producer turns on a videotape camera and suggests she improvise a scene with him in which (surprise!) she is trying to seduce him on his couch. She does the best she can, until he grabs her and begins fondling her. She breaks away. He locks the door and tells her he will have his way with her, whether she struggles or not. He says if she reports him, he has the videotape proving she came on to him.

The stories go on and on. It's not just the lowlifes in Hollywood who prey on actors and, of course, it's not just actors who get approached. Secretaries, production assistants, and others are vulnerable to this behavior as well. Many of the predators in the stories mentioned above are well-respected names in the industry and horny young men and women in low- to mid-level studio positions. The great disparity in power between the individuals involved seems to breed this sick behavior. A producer we know brags that he sometimes beds three actresses a day while he is casting a new project.

Where can the young person turn for help when confronted with this abuse? Unfortunately, almost nowhere. The unions have established sexual-abuse committees and regulations, but these serve primarily as window dressing to convince the membership that the unions are addressing the problem. In a recent case, several courageous women reported to the local district attorney's office that they had been sexually assaulted by an agent. He was brought up for criminal charges. It was discovered that a thick file of complaints against him was collecting dust at one of the union offices.

The sexual politics in Hollywood are deeply entrenched and anyone who challenges this setup is sure to suffer consequences. Hollywood is a town that presents an illusion of liberal open-mindedness and concern, but generally operates with reactionary fervor against anyone who rocks the boat by complaining or seeking help. There is an exception to this closing of the ranks to protect the predators. Sometimes an executive will have made enemies; and when someone complains, the studio walks away and lets them be charged. The complaint can also be used as an excuse to summarily fire some fairly powerful people. This scenario has happened to more than one executive in the past few years. The point is that they made too many enemies. Even in the cases in which sexual harassment has come out, however, it rarely has a positive impact on the careers of the accusers.

Some people do receive protection from the better agents and managers. One of the ways to judge your agent or manager is by how well he or she protects you against the abuses mentioned above.

––––––––

The Production-in-Progress Scam

One final sexual scam is worth mentioning, since it happens with such regularity. That is the production-in-progress scam. You will soon discover that everyone in Hollywood is working on a film or TV project that is sure to begin production any day now. For every thousand of these projects only one will actually be produced.

Young actors are frequently approached by someone, claiming to be involved in these projects, who guarantees them a role in the project. Often the person offering this great chance has never seen the actor act. He just knows she is perfect for the part. What follows is a series of lunch dates, parties, and dinners. The actor, delighted to be included and fearful of losing her role, will suffer through these meetings.

There are two usual outcomes: The actor will refuse to become sexually involved and the producer/director/writer will lose interest in her and stop calling her; or the actor will become sexually involved, and after a few sordid sessions, the producer/director/writer will lose interest in her and stop calling her.

To avoid such scams, you should know that the normal time for an actor to become involved in a production is when the money is already in place, the shooting schedule is set, and a casting director has been hired to screen the actors.

———

This does not mean you should isolate yourself from the rest of the entertainment community. You need all the contacts you can get. If you're single, we are not advising you to become a nun or a priest. Many wonderful romances spring out of this business. Trust your instincts. If it smells funny, it's probably rotten.

SEX, RACE, SEXUAL ORIENTATION, AND AGE DISCRIMINATION

Like anywhere else, there is discrimination in Hollywood. We're not talking about who will try to get you in bed, but who will ignore your job application. Having raised the topic, we could and perhaps should write volumes. Instead, we'll have to content ourselves with a few comments, probably overgeneralized and certainly opinionated, but useful, we hope.

To start, it shouldn't surprise you that Hollywood reflects our larger society. Like most business environments in this country, Hollywood was and is dominated by white males; and particularly when it comes to careers off camera, issues of sex, race, and age certainly come into play.

Women are slowly and often painfully working their way into the ranks of directors, producers, studio executives, and lawyers. For example, while you saw only a handful of women lawyers in the business ten years ago, the studios and law firms are now filled with women, at least in the lower ranks. It's not so much that the powers that be don't think women can do it, though you sometimes hear stereotypical grousing in executive circles about corny stuff like women being too emotional.

When Gail sought her first job in the industry, she was warned by a supposedly friendly mentor, "[In the entertainment business] you'll have to deny your femininity right up front." Later on, upon starting a new job as a lawyer at a studio, the first day her new bosses took her to lunch and instructed her never to cry in front of the guys, and they meant it.

People of color are certainly represented in the industry in growing numbers, but insofar as behind-the-camera careers go we don't think the industry has been a particularly welcoming environment. You probably won't see a proportionate representation of people of color in the industry now, but here again doors are slowly being pried open.

Age is a funny game in Hollywood. Being older and wiser isn't a particularly valuable quality in the game. Everyone seems to be young at the studios, meaning in their twenties and thirties. If you haven't attained a certain status in town by your mid-thirties, it's assumed you're past your prime. Studios are legendary for using people up and then discarding them, at least in the higher ranks.

On a lighter note, the entertainment industry has always provided a fairly good working environment for homosexuals. Individual hatred has probably been the cause of pain for more than a few people, but we believe the general industry standard is that talent is valuable. Very few people seem to care who you sleep with away from the office, so long as the work gets done.

Of course, all is not progressive. Few of the employers have altered their insurance programs to provide coverage for same-sex partners, and some HIV-positive people have encountered career obstacles. Although the entertainment community has popularized those red ribbons that signify sympathy with the fight against AIDS and donated money to the AIDS cause, on an individual level more than one actor has felt it was necessary to hide his status in order to keep working.

Where do you look for help if you feel you're the victim of discrimination? In our opinion, the unions haven't been much help. There are organizations for women, people of color, and gays and lesbians in Hollywood. People of age, however, aren't represented by a larger group as far as we can tell. Of course, if you can prove you're a member of a protected class and you've been discriminated against, you may have the law behind you. Talk to a lawyer before pursuing any legal maneuvers.

AFFIRMATIVE ACTION

Don't count on it. Hollywood is no better than the rest of the country on this issue. Although there are individuals still trying to make the world a better place through social programs, there aren't many formal programs with teeth for recruiting and helping protected classes, especially since the recent limits on affirmative-action programs. On the other hand, there are still some remnants here and there, though often only token programs. If you can fit into one of those slots you might want to go for it, but don't expect affirmative action to make your career in Hollywood.

We may be cockeyed optimists, but we believe that hard work and talent can go a long way. You probably won't be able to escape all discrimination, but try to avoid the jerks if you can.

Protecting and Selling Your Creative Works

CHAPTER FIFTEEN

The Value of Creative Ideas

Hollywood is fueled by creative ideas. Some get sold. Some get copied, with or without permission. Others are thrown around as bargaining chips or used to tease money out of reluctant investors. Many ideas are stolen outright. In fact, most ideas in themselves belong to everyone, no matter how unique you think they are, unless they're developed in some tangible way. What you need to know is that you may be able to protect some ideas if you know what you're doing.

WHO NEEDS TO PROTECT THEIR CREATIVE WORK?

Most creative talent have something they need to protect. Writers have spec scripts, screenplays, or novels. Producers have the rights to other people's screenplays, personal agreements with actors, ideas for creative talent packages they can put together, and financing that they can bring to the table. Actors may have characters they've created or material they've worked up in connection with their auditions. Costume designers have sketches.

Set designers have artwork. A director might have prepared some material in connection with a true story. Whatever you have, it's best to give some thought to how to protect it before throwing it to the marketplace.

Don't I Own All the Work I Create?

Not necessarily. Unless you're entitled to one of the basic protections we discuss below, you may not own your own creations. For example, if your work was done as a work for hire, *you may have sold all your rights, subject perhaps to certain rights to buy back the material or to get it in* turnaround, *both terms which we discuss at the end of this chapter.*

THE BASIC PROTECTIONS

If you've got some creative work, in whatever form, there are a number of ways you may be protected against others taking it and exploiting it without giving you any compensation.

First, you may have a work that would qualify for copyright protection and therefore cannot be copied without your permission.

Second, even without copyright protection, you may have some rights under contract law, if you've entered into some form of a contract with the party exploiting the work.

Third, you may be able to acquire some protection from registering the work with the Writers Guild of America.

Fourth, you may be able to use your agent or other representatives to protect your work.

Fifth, you may have certain rights under the WGA or pursuant to a turnaround provision.

COPYRIGHT PROTECTION

We can't tell you all you need to know about copyright law in this book, but we can tell you some of the basics. For works written under U.S. law, *any original work of authorship written in this country since January 1, 1978, is automatically protected under U.S. copyright when it is fixed in a tangible medium of expression.* This is a mouthful, so let's take it a term at a time.

ORIGINALITY

Originality under copyright law doesn't mean it has to be totally new. It means it must be written by you and be something more than just an idea. Ideas, even great ideas, in themselves are not copyrightable. It's the *expression* of the idea which can be protected by copyright under our laws.

Here's an example: "Boy meets girl, boy loses girl, boy gets girl" has been the theme of hundreds of plays and movies since the beginning of time. In and of itself, it is not protected. However, if you flesh out the story and add enough details that make it unique *and* you write the story down or record it in some fashion, you might make it something that can be protected. What makes your work unique, at least as far as copyright is concerned, is the way you've expressed your story and what you've added to make it a unique work—not the idea behind it. So your boy-meets-girl story may not be anything new, but if you place it in outer space in the Zoka galaxy and come up with all kinds of interplanetary impediments to their love, you may have something you can protect. Merely listing ideas or facts is not enough.

COPYRIGHTABLE WORK

A work can be a literary work (such as a book, article, screenplay), movie, television show (or other audiovisual work), musical work, sound recording, sheet music, dramatic work, choreographic work, photograph, sculpture, pictorial or graphic work of art, or a piece of computer software.

THE COPYRIGHT ACT

On January 1, 1978, the Copyright Act of 1976 took effect. If you wrote your work after that date, and it would otherwise qualify for protection (i.e., it's an original work), your work will be protected for your entire life, plus fifty years after your death. Note that there's a movement here and abroad to extend the term to life plus seventy years. The law provides that only you (or your heirs during that fifty-year term) can sell it, and only you can profit from exploiting the material. Note that for works created between 1978 and 1989, a copyright notice (©) had to be affixed to the work to receive the benefits of protection. This rule was relaxed (meaning it's not strictly required) since 1989, when the U.S. joined the Berne Convention, an agreement between the affiliated countries regarding their copyright laws.

If your work was written before 1978 and is less than seventy-five years old, it might be entitled to copyright protection, but only if it was a qualifying work and the proper formalities had been followed (such as properly affixed notice, registration in the Copyright Office, and proper renewal). If you have a question about an older work, you should consult an attorney to find out its status, since the old law had different rules about the term of protection that can make it tricky to know what kind of protection you've got. If your work is not protected, it's in the *public domain*, which means anyone can do anything they want with it.

TANGIBLE MEDIUM OF EXPRESSION

Your work must be written down, tape recorded, drawn, or in some other manner expressed in some tangible, fixed medium.

The Value of Creative Ideas

Let's say you go to a party and tell someone in detail about your great idea for a love story. Six months later, to your chagrin, you notice that almost your entire story has been copied in a movie of the week. Here's the rub: Even if your story was very detailed, you won't get copyright protection if it was stolen (although there may be other remedies, which we'll discuss below). How could you have protected yourself? If you had written the story down with dialogue, settings, and plot twists and given it to that person to read, and they literally copied a significant amount of the way you expressed your idea (such as exact dialogue), you may have a case.

COPYRIGHTS OUTSIDE THE U.S.

Each country has its own copyright law, though many countries have agreed to honor each other's laws. The U.S. has joined in a number of agreements with other countries to provide some continuity and protection across borders (we mentioned one of them, the Berne Convention, earlier). We can tell you that the term of protection is life plus fifty years, at least (and more likely seventy), depending on the country. International laws are complicated, and figuring out how the laws of one country apply to the laws of another can give you a headache. If you need to know whether your work is protected outside the U.S., or if your non-U.S. work is protected here, you'll have to get an expert to do the analysis. We discuss so-called *moral rights*, one of the other key differences between U.S. and non-U.S. copyright law, in chapter 18.

Registration

Should you register your work? Note that under the old law, which we discussed above, the rules of registration were elaborate and fraught with hazards. One scheme developed to comply with the old law was sending your material to yourself by registered mail to prove the date of creation (of course, you couldn't open the sealed envelope). Those tricks are basically relics of the old law, though it doesn't hurt to be able to prove you wrote something first. There are a few copyright mavens in Hollywood who specialize in figuring out if works written under the old laws were properly registered and renewed. Once in a while they get to trump someone's rights by proving that the formalities weren't properly followed, and they spend considerable time trying to figure out who the heirs are to a particular estate.

Strictly speaking, you don't have to officially register a work to be protected under the new law, but it makes it a lot easier to sue if you have properly registered it, and you'll get a broader scope of protection. It's fairly easy to register a work with the Copyright Office. Just call them or a local federal government information line in your area. They'll send you the forms with an explanation of how to register your work.

We've told you only the bare basics about copyright here. But realize that you don't want to be in the position in which you have to sue somebody over stealing your work. It can be incredibly costly, since you'll have to find a copyright expert to represent you effectively. The better route is to do some of the things we've listed below to protect your work.

What If You Think Your Work Was Stolen?

First, ask yourself if you might be entitled to copyright protection based on what we've already told you.

Second, ask yourself if the person you think stole it had access to it, and if there's substantial similarity between your work and the one you think is a rip-off.

If you can answer these questions affirmatively, you may have enough to consult a lawyer. Just remember, the law is changing constantly, and litigation is expensive and painful. Better to inform yourself and protect what you've got, which we discuss below.

ADAPTATIONS

Be very careful when writing material based upon someone else's work, since copyright law prohibits you from copying someone else's work without their permission. If you bring a property to a studio or a producer and it's based on a book, play, or someone's life story, our advice is to tell them. It complicates matters, but it's much better to take care of rights issues up front. If you can't deliver clean rights to your work, you'll risk undermining yourself and the people you're trying to do business with. More than one production has been killed by a studio's legal department because the writer of the adaptation didn't bring in proper rights. Once a project is ready for production, it can become very tricky and expensive to clear these problems up.

LIFE-STORY RIGHTS AND
ISSUES OF PRIVACY, PUBLICITY, AND DEFAMATION

Let's say you want to do a biography of Napoleon. The mere facts of someone's life story are not protected under copyright. However, if those facts are compiled in a book, presumably with some narrative, the biography or autobiography can acquire copyright protection. From a copyright standpoint, it may be difficult to stop someone else doing a life story you've developed, even if you thought of it first. If the subject of the life story is alive or if there are enough heirs around, the best way to handle this problem is to get them under contract. You'll have more access to information, and your competitors will be cut off. We talk more below about making contractual arrangements to protect your rights.

A few words of warning about life-story rights. First, this can be a complex area of the law, and if you seriously want to tell the life story of a contemporary person, you should get some legal advice. You may be able to use the facts of someone's life story without regard to copyright protection, but there are other rights that might kick in. Here are some general guidelines.

People have rights under the laws of certain states that give them some rights of privacy. They may also have some rights to control the use of their name and likeness, depending on how well-known they are.

If someone is a private individual and still alive, then he or she has *rights of privacy* (the right to be left alone and not exposed to public scrutiny) under the First Amendment to the Constitution. A living public figure has fewer rights of privacy, depending on the kind of private facts you want to expose.

You can't freely *defame* (hold up to public ridicule by statements that are not true) living people without exposing yourself to legal trouble. However, you can give your opinion about someone, though it's not always clear what's an opinion and what's a statement of a fact. You can generally say more about public figures than private ones without getting into trouble, so long as you're not maliciously disregarding the truth. You can say just about anything you want about deceased people.

Generally, a studio hesitates to buy any life-story rights of a living person unless he or she is very "public" or you have a contract allowing you to tell the story. Even if they are very public, certain public figures, such as movie stars and celebrities, have a *right of publicity*. This is the right to exploit their own name and likeness because they've developed themselves into a commodity that's literally their business.

There are some issues covered by the First Amendment that support the writer or producer over famous people. The courts have been reluctant to stop biographical productions, but they have also stopped producers from certain kinds of exploitation of celebrities, such as merchandising. You may see a biography of Elizabeth Taylor without her permission, for example, but you won't see Elizabeth Taylor dolls unless she wants you to. This right is descendible: that is, it survives the death of the celebrity and is controlled by his or her estate.

The major example of this distinction can be found in the selling of Elvis Presley. Elvis is obviously still a major source of revenue, which his estate controls through the legal principle of right of publicity (which, in fact, his estate was instrumental in establishing in this country). Other active estates are those of James Dean and Marilyn Monroe, among others.

A Few Rules of Thumb about Life-Story Rights

If you have permission from the living people you want to portray, you'll have an easier time selling the project to a studio and less breath holding as the product gets released. If they're alive, sign them up together with any other living people you'll need to tell their story, especially if you plan to fictionalize any part of it. If you can't sign these supporting individuals, you may end up having to fictionalize them. Once you fictionalize, you risk creating a character so different from the real person that an average person wouldn't recognize the portrayal. As you can imagine, this can be tricky to do, and it may take the guts out of your story.

Let's say you have signed up the main character, but her spouse is a critical element in the story and you want to use his name and actual details about his life. If you didn't get his permission, you'll be more vulnerable to claims such as defamation or invasion of privacy. If he's a living, private person not involved in any public events, you may have to fictionalize him significantly enough so he's not recognizable.

If the subject is a living, private person involved in public events (say, the civil-rights movement), you can probably do a story based on that person's involvement in the public event, so long as you do your research and know the facts. Similarly, politicians may be okay, but when dealing with living or deceased movie stars or celebrities such as sports figures, you're treading dangerous waters. You should think twice about presenting private lives or merchandising images.

What if you can't get permission? It's a catch-22. The problem is, if you've asked for permission and your subject has refused it, you've put that person on alert and you'll have to be even more careful, if not because the law demands it, then because the studio is nervous. As usual, it's best to get professional advice on this.

PUBLIC DOMAIN

One solution to copyright problems is to use something in the *public domain*, or no longer under copyright protection. In this country, any work that is less than seventy-five years old should be checked for copyright protection. With European works, if the author is alive or has been deceased for less than seventy years, you may have to clear copyright before using the work. If the work you want to base yours upon still enjoys copyright protection you'll have to approach the owner (who may or may not be the original author) and ask permission to use the work. The work you do based on someone else's work is referred to as a *derivative work*.

Note that every country has its own copyright law, and a work protected in one country may not be protected in another. We can't explain international copyright in depth here, but there is an issue of moral rights (discussed in chapter 18) to consider, which gives artists more rights than they have under U.S. copyright law.

CONTRACT

Another way you can protect yourself without necessarily relying on a successful copyright lawsuit is to have a contract with someone. It's a pretty simple concept. If you have an agreement with someone regarding your material—be it a script you wrote, a character you created, or sets you designed—you have a chance of proving that person owes you something if he exploits it.

If possible, an agreement should be entered into before you show someone your material or perform your services. Of course, a written contract is always better than an oral agreement.

You may have heard of the case of Art Buchwald suing Paramount Pictures over the film *Coming to America*. When Buchwald sued, it wasn't because the studio had copied his work, which would be the claim under a copyright infringement suit. Instead, Buchwald and his partner had entered into an agreement with the studio for their idea about an African prince who comes to America to seek a bride. The actual stories, other than the basic idea we just stated, apparently weren't so similar. However, the agreement said that if the studio made a picture based upon their work, it would pay them a percentage of the profits of the picture (we'll discuss profit participation in chapter 17). Because there was a contract, the judge in this case determined that the studio had used Buchwald's idea as a basis for the work. Because of the contract, the court didn't have to resort to the kind of scrutiny that would be required by a copyright case (such as substantial similarity), even though the expression was different.

Buchwald won on a contract claim, as opposed to a copyright claim, because he had a contract, with the studio.

Work for Hire

If you are hired by someone to do some creative work, it's more than likely the contract will state that all of your creative work is deemed a work for hire or a work made for hire pursuant to copyright law. This means the studio (or whoever paid you) owns the rights to the work. You probably can't walk away with the material you've created when you have completed your work (though you may have some union protections, which we discuss below). This is true for people who act as well as people who do technical or design work under contract.

If you bring in the project already written, you may enter into a contract in which you're hired to further develop the work. Note that everything you do for the studio will usually be deemed a work for hire, meaning the studio owns it. Even if the studio doesn't pick up the option, you will not own the additional material you wrote or had written while under contract, though you should own what you came in with initially.

Contracts take many forms, and we don't intend to go into too much detail here. You should understand that if you enter into a working relationship and sign a piece of paper saying that your work is a work made for hire, then whoever hired you will own that work. If it's a union project, you may have the right to buy back the work if it's not exploited (which we'll discuss when we talk about unions), but the basic right to use the work and sell it to others will belong to the person or studio who hired you.

WRITERS GUILD REGISTRATION

Anyone can write up a short description of their work (sometimes referred to as a *treatment*) and register it or the entire work with the Writers Guild. It doesn't amount to copyright registration and doesn't offer legal recourse if something goes wrong, but it does show that you submitted a work at a certain time, which can be very helpful in proving you wrote something first. It's a fairly simple and inexpensive process, and you don't have to qualify for membership in the WGA to use this service. We discuss the protection the WGA can provide for its members when we discuss reacquiring your rights later in this chapter.

YOUR AGENTS AND REPRESENTATIVES

If you've tried to submit something to the studios, you are probably already aware that very few of them will accept an idea unless it's submitted by a registered agent. A work given to the studio that is not specifically requested is referred to as an *unsolicited submission*, and the studios and major producers will generally not accept it. If they do accept it, it's usually under the condition that you sign a waiver of your rights in case they don't buy it and end up doing a similar or perhaps the same story later.

Why the seeming paranoia? Because in the 1950s a studio (Paramount again) actually got sued by someone who claimed that the famous director Billy Wilder used his idea in a movie. Wilder and the studio claimed they had no idea that the plaintiff had called Wilder's secretary and pitched his idea for a movie plot. In fact, the allegedly submitted story was based on a real story that had been published in the newspaper. However, the court found that the secretary listening to the story created an *implied contract* that the plaintiff would be paid if Wilder used the material. Ever since then, studios generally do not accept unsolicited submissions, which means that most works have to be submitted through an agent or lawyer so there's no appearance of impropriety. Using your team this way not only protects you, it also makes it more likely that your material gets read. We talk about choosing your agent or lawyer in other chapters in this book. The point to make here is to avoid getting so desperate for work that you give your creative ideas away or so sloppy that they can be taken from you.

SELLING YOUR RIGHTS AND GETTING THEM BACK

The best way to maintain control over your rights, once you've thrown them into the ring for sale, is to be careful about the way you sell them. You should know the difference between optioning and selling your rights and how to get them back, either by buying them back or through *reversion*. Your lawyer will probably be more concerned about the issues of licensing versus assigning your material, which is a different concern. As in all things, the more you understand, the more strength you'll have when your deals are being negotiated.

OPTIONING VS. SELLING

We're speaking here about what you need to know once you've got someone interested in buying your work. (If you're interested in learning how producers and writers get someone interested, check out chapter 2.)

If you've already written something or have access to someone else's original work, there are at least two ways you can broker it to the studio. If you sell your rights, you may get a cash lump sum and perhaps a profit participation (see chapter

17). You don't get your property back if the project never gets made, because the studio owns it.

However, you might decide to option your property instead. It's a very typical business practice for both sides. It gives you back the rights to your material after a period of time, and it saves the studio money. It's usually more expensive to buy a property than to merely option it for a year or two. Typically, if you enter into an option agreement, you'll give the studio the right to develop the property for a period of time for a specified amount of money. If the studio doesn't *exercise the option* (*buy* the property from you after a certain period of time), the property reverts to you.

Whatever you do, you should know that an agreement must be in writing whenever there is copyrighted material being transferred. There are no such things as verbal options, and especially if you're the buyer, you should *get it in writing*. The agreement will include a provision for how much money it will cost the studio to buy the property if it decides to exercise the option. A typical option period for a script is one to two years, often with a right to renew for another year. The studio may pay you nothing (or a nominal sum of money, say $5000 to $25,000) for the first year.

Should You Give Someone a Free Option?

Sometimes producers who are starting out will ask for a free option. It's not unusual for people without a track record to give a producer a free option to try to get someone to buy the project, or at least option it from them for later development.

The free option is not always the greatest idea, however, if you let too many people shop the project around town. If everyone knows it's been rejected, you may never have your shot at having the material looked at by the right people, and you won't have made a nickel. In any case, if they don't exercise the option (referred to as pick up the option*) during the agreed-upon period, your original material becomes your property again, free and clear. The material prepared at the studio remains the property of the studio, though it may go into turnaround, which we discuss below.*

If you give anyone a free option, do it only for a short period (say, one to six months) and make sure it's not automatically renewable unless you get the renewal in writing.

Here's some sample language that will show you how these options are set out in a contract. Note that this is for an assignment, but you can option a license or just about any rights. These are just the introductory paragraphs. Of course, you should consult your attorney or at least get some good form books if you need an actual contract. We've listed some sources for form contract books in the Appendix.

LANGUAGE FOR AN OPTION AGREEMENT

AGREEMENT dated _____ between _____ ("Owner") and _____ ("Purchaser") in connection with the _____ project presently entitled "_____" (the "Project").

I. Assignment of Rights: Owner hereby irrevocably conveys, grants and assigns to Purchaser the sole and exclusive _____ rights, in and to the following material: the _____ written by _____ entitled _____.

II. Consideration: Purchaser agrees to pay and Owner agrees to accept as full consideration for the rights herein granted and for Owner's warranties and agreements herein contained:

A. Basic Consideration:

   (a) For the option period(s) hereinafter provided, the following sums:

      (i) $ _____ upon execution hereof. Upon such payment, the rights granted hereunder shall be for a period ("Initial Option Period") commencing as of the date hereof and expiring _____.

      (ii) If Purchaser, in its sole discretion, elects to extend the Initial Option Period, Purchaser shall give written notice along with payment in the amount of $_____ on or before the expiration of the Initial Option Period. Upon such payment and notice, the rights granted hereunder shall be for a further period ("Second Option Period") expiring _____.

If Purchaser elects not to extend or exercise its said option, then the rights granted hereunder in and to the Work shall expire automatically at the end of the final day of the applicable option period.

   (b) If Purchaser, in its sole discretion, elects to exercise its exclusive option, Purchaser shall pay Owner the sum of $_____ less the sum(s) paid above, together with written notice of such election.

License vs. Assignment

Sometimes you will be asked to license your rights, and other times you will be asked to give an assignment of all of your interest in a work. A *license* is the right you give someone to borrow your work for a period of time for certain uses. When you license your property to another party, there is the implication that you still own it, even though someone else has certain rights to exploit it for certain purposes.

In contrast, an *assignment* consists of selling off your rights, and therefore giving up your power to further exploit the material. You can assign all of your rights, which literally means you give away all current and future rights in all media in perpetuity. Or you can assign only certain rights, such as motion picture rights (which leaves you with such rights as publishing, theater, multimedia, and perhaps some forms of television).

There are some arguments about when a license becomes an assignment, but we think it's most helpful just to be aware that with a license you still basically own some rights to the property, and with an assignment you probably don't.

A license is like renting a house you own to someone else, and an assignment is like selling it to someone. As an example, a completed television show that has already run on a network will most likely be licensed into syndication rather than sold outright through an assignment. A script that hasn't been produced yet is more likely to be assigned.

A license isn't necessarily better than an assignment. Your power to control the rights to your material will, like everything else in the game, depend on your clout and smarts. You can license virtually all useful rights and yet assign almost none of them. Just make sure you and your representatives are clear about what you've given away.

TURNAROUND

There is another way you can get the material back after you've sold or optioned it to a studio. *Turnaround* basically refers to the situation in which a studio has decided not to put any more money into a property but is willing to let someone else try to develop your material. The idea is that the producer (or sometimes the writer) who developed the material will enter into an agreement with the studio which states that they have the right to *shop* (try to sell) the material to someone else with the hope that it can be *set up* elsewhere. Why would the studio let something go into turnaround to you? For money, of course. If they let you take it, they get paid back their expenses plus interest, and usually you'll owe them a percentage of your profits if the project makes any money.

WGA RIGHTS

There's another way writers can get back their material from a studio to which they have assigned their rights, though it can be a costly proposition. Even a writer who has written a script under a work-for-hire provision of a contract (see above) has certain rights to purchase back the unproduced material from the studio. If the studio hasn't produced the material within a certain period of time, the writer can inform the studio he or she wants to buy back the rights. The studio must sell them back to the writer as long as the writer can come up with the money.

When You've Become a Working Professional

What is a working professional? *There is no precise definition for this term. Roughly speaking, however, we are talking about people who have more or less supported themselves for two or three years on their earnings from the business. They may have actually had some of their work produced and distributed and have other work commitments lined up. They may not be well-known or in the money, but they're not waiting tables for a living anymore, either.*

If you've reached it, this period could be the best time of your life. You are making a living doing what you love. You have separated yourself from the pack and considerably increased your chances of fashioning a lifelong career filled with great rewards.

Unfortunately, we see many people in this stage of their careers who have only succeeded in changing the nature of the anxiety and fear they feel. Now, instead of fearing they will never make it, they live their days wondering if they're getting the right deal, making the right career moves, holding out for the right projects, or being treated like a player. Of course, there's always the big question: Will I ever work again? If you've set it up right, you will be reaping the rewards and be more in control at this stage of the game. If not, you just might miss those carefree days when you were waiting on tables.

The following chapters outline some of the new challenges you will face. We'll take time to discuss some of the more complex contract and work issues with which you will need to become familiar. It wouldn't hurt, however, to review some of the basics we covered in the earlier chapters. If you take care of the basics, most of these new challenges will be easier to confront.

CHAPTER SIXTEEN

Top-Level Contract Issues

So what do you get when you find that elusive pot of gold at the end of the rainbow? If you're what is considered "bankable" in Hollywood, there can be extraordinary money and power available to you. We'll talk about the dollars and explain the mysterious world of profit participations. There's also perhaps a greater aphrodisiac to consider, which is the clout to control your creative destiny. Who gets these goodies? Mostly the above-the-line people we discussed in chapter 2, but high-level directors of photography and editors must also understand these issues.

Power in Hollywood starts with the deal, and the deal is usually memorialized in a contract. You might be surprised at the level of detail that goes into contracts at the top level. One explanation is that the stakes are too high to leave anything to chance. The studio doesn't want to risk unbudgeted demands that become impossibly expensive. The creative talent wants to be sure they'll have the resources necessary to create an optimum working environment.

Top creative talent negotiate for, and often get, the entire pie in the sky. That pie may include top dollars, credits, personal production companies, and all the trappings that make someone a true player in the business. For many people who have dedicated themselves to making it in the movie and television business, the ultimate reward is working, particularly on good projects, because it's the love of the craft that got them there in the first place.

The most successful creative talent can get some golden opportunities to control the creative process, and the smartest players negotiate for the power and goodies that help them work at their creative best. Of course, many others simply take the money and run. Note that we're really talking about creative-talent deals here. The people with regular jobs, such as studio executives and the other regular employees we discussed as studio overhead in chapter 3, generally don't have as many different kinds of contract issues as creative talent. Studio people fight over their titles (everyone wants to be some kind of vice president); money; office decorations; and if they're at a high enough level, stock options. But it's mostly the creative talent who need to deal with the glamour-puss contract issues.

With regard to these issues, you have to decide what's important to you. Every person has individual quirks and beliefs about what is going to make them work at their best, whether it's having the power to approve who rewrites the script, the right to choose co-stars, or—and this happens—having a contractual right to have a dozen bottles of a particular brand of bottled water delivered each day to the set to wash your hair. Everything goes into a negotiation. Only you can determine whether your quirks are necessary for the right creative environment or are just candy to feed your swollen ego.

Once someone at a studio decides they must have you, almost anything goes, and we've provided a checklist of what issues will come up in contract negotiations once you're really in the game.

Do I Really Need to Know All This Stuff?

It depends on where you are in the game.

If you just like to know enough to have some juicy party chatter, then skip the profit-participation section and the boilerplate discussion and go right to the section on perquisites in which you can learn about some of the silly and outrageous requests prima donnas ask for and often get in their contracts.

If you want to be taken seriously, educate yourself on how the money and power side of the business works. Baby executives, lawyers, producers, and top-level creative talent are much more effective when they know what the lingo means. There are a lot of people who never learned the nuts and bolts of the business who are trying to play the game, and the serious players see them coming a mile away.

CHAPTER SEVENTEEN

Now That You've Got the Power to Negotiate

The entertainment business is made up of equal drives of art and money, and there's no question that negotiating is an art in Hollywood. Once you've attained a certain level of success in the business, your deals become more sophisticated. Yet they don't often work out. Many creative talent find themselves put through a revolving door on a deal only to end up with nothing besides lawyer bills. Why does this happen?

Why Do Deals Fall Through?

Deals fail for a multitude of reasons, but here are a few that occur most often.

1. The creative talent's team, whether its agent, manager, and/or lawyer, seriously misgauged their client's value and what the studio was willing to pay. When they held out too long, the studio walked.

2. The representatives are engaged in some kind of a guerrilla warfare with a particular studio (or each other). They are using the creative talent as a pawn in that war, whether or not they had anything to do with the original problem.

3. The studio is angry at the agency or lawyer for always demanding too much or for lying, so the studio wants to teach the representative a lesson by being especially inflexible.

4. Someone at the studio changed his or her mind, and the business affairs executive has to make it look like the creative talent or its representation was unreasonable.

In this chapter, we'll review the main points that will come up in any higher-level deal.

MONEY ISSUES

CASH

We talked in chapter 13 about how the studio business-affairs people try to hold the line in terms of compensation paid to top creative talent. Salaries are leaked (and lied about) in almost every negotiation. Generally, the studio will try to pay the creative talent something based on their last salary, the importance of their last job, the state of their career at the moment, and their value to the production.

Leveraging points in a salary negotiation can include questions such as: Can someone else do it? Is that other person available? Are you tied to the project by holding some rights or attachment to another creative talent? If you're in a healthy but not spectacular stage of your career, the cash will be partly determined by the salary level of someone else the studio finds comparable to you, with some extra money thrown in if you have a top agent or lawyer. However, if you're very hot now, you own the rights, or the director is in love with you artistically or personally, the sky can be the limit here.

Getting money up front is usually a good idea, as opposed to taking less money and some form of profit participation, since profits are a mighty relative term in Hollywood. If you should be above scale due to the status of your career, and someone wants you to work for scale against the profits, beware. Only people who really believe in a project *and* don't need the money —or desperate people—agree to do work for virtually nothing with the promise of profits.

If you have a choice, you'd generally take the cash, unless the project is superhot and the profit definition is very favorable. Sometimes you get just cash. If you're a more significant player, you'll get cash plus net profits or gross profits (see our discussion of these concepts below). Generally, the performer's cash fee is actually an advance against profits, meaning you get the money now, and profits, too, but only after enough money has come in (after deductions) to equal the amount of money you were paid up front. For example, if the performer's fee is $20 million as an advance against 20 percent of the gross receipts, the film must earn $100 million before the performer earns any additional money. Some contracts will provide an *escalator clause,* which provides for bumps up in cash compensation if the picture is a hit. If a picture makes $40 million at the box office, for example, you might get an additional $100,000. In TV, people with clout get advances against profits tied to a particular number of episodes produced.

The variations are endless, limited only by the creativity (and greed) of the players. While you should understand these terms, every movie is a crapshoot, so get the best team of advisers you can, and rely on them when the offers come in.

PAY OR PLAY

Pay or play is a concept developed to allow the studio to decide not to use you so long as they pay you. It really protects both sides. The studio gets to make the decision that you're not right for the job. They can get rid of you by paying you all the cash compensation they would have owed you had you completed the work. And you benefit because you get paid whether you do the work or not. Profits are generally not payable to people who have been "pay or played" off a production. However, sometimes (though rarely) the highest-level creative talent get the studio to agree to pay a pro-rata share of the profits that would have been due them if the work had been completed. For example, if you had a pro-rata provision in your contract and you got half way through the production obligation when the studio dumped you, you'd be entitled to one-half of the profits you would have been entitled to if you'd stayed and finished.

If you get a pay-or-play provision in your contract, the pay-or-play commitment generally begins on the Start Date (which we discussed when we described the basic structure of compensation packages in chapter 10). Once that date is passed, you're owed all your compensation, whether or not you start or complete your services, so long as you aren't fired for cause, which we'll talk about in the Boilerplate section of this chapter. The studio wants you to be ready when they're ready to shoot. This could result in you being held up for the extended periods of time it takes the studio to get the project together (and prohibits you from taking other work). Powerful creative talent can narrow down the amount of time the studio has to start production. This narrowing kicks in overtime and allows actors to schedule themselves optimally while they're hot.

If you are really hot as in blazing, you might get a *pay-and-play* deal. In this case, the studio has to pay you *and* use you, too. They can't change their minds and drop you for other creative talent. This clause is exceedingly rare, however, even for the top-level performers, though sometimes actors' representatives bring it up. It's usually laughed off the table as an amateur shot, and there are too many variables and too much money at stake for the studio to risk this promise. You could become ill or get fat or crazy; or a studio executive could get replaced by someone who doesn't like you.

Sometimes, instead of a pay-and-play deal, you'll see commitments in contracts that allow producers and directors to buy back the material they brought in if things don't work out. That way the studio doesn't have to use you, but you haven't totally lost control of the material. As we mentioned in chapter 15, writers have certain rights to reacquire their material under the Writers Guild agreement.

TAX INDEMNITY

When creative talent work outside the U.S, they are at risk of getting hit with a tremendous tax bill, both from the U.S. and from the foreign country in which they're working. One way around this is to get the studio to reimburse you for any additional taxes you may incur if you're shooting on a foreign location. Because foreign taxes are complicated and expensive, the studios do it only for their more important creative talent. If your representatives don't know about foreign taxes, find some who do. You could find yourself paying double or triple taxes without proper precautions.

PROFIT PARTICIPATION

If you've heard any dealmaking lingo at all, you've heard the words net profits, and maybe you've heard about gross participation, cash breakeven, actual breakeven, and even rolling breakeven.

Since profits are an elusive and misrepresented concept in Hollywood, you may notice that profit sharing is also referred to as *contingent compensation* because your getting any money is contingent on a number of events occurring. The current trend is to remove the word *profit* entirely and replace it with *proceeds*. The studios took quite a beating on the phrase net profits, especially since James Garner and Art Buchwald exposed studio accounting methods in their litigations against their respective studios. If you can get yourself to read the explanation of how profits are defined, you'll understand why there's almost never a profit in Hollywood after the accountants are done counting. All of these terms, and the ones we list in this section, represent the relatively complicated and often creative ways studios do their accounting to avoid paying additional money to anyone if a production is a success. It's a joke around Hollywood that the really creative executives are the business-affairs people and accountants who come up with these schemes. In any case, we promised we'd explain the fascinating world of profit participations, so hold onto your hats as we go on the tour.

THE BASIC CONCEPT

The basic idea is that the participant (you) gets to share or participate in the profits, i.e., the excess money left after the studio has paid itself for certain costs of the production. This concept is simple, until you look back at the ways these deals are calculated. The first and most important concept to understand is that studios do not like to give anyone any money over and above cash compensation. Typically, because of the structure of profit deals, they don't have to unless the picture is an immediate blockbuster hit. This is because the studio layers on additional costs, such as fees and interest, that make it practically impossible to show a profit, at least on paper. Most studios have virtually the same ways of calculating participations, which shouldn't surprise you at this point in the book. The second concept to understand is that even though the studios calculate these participations in roughly the same way, every person's definition of contingent compensation can vary widely. It depends on how powerful the person is and how savvy his or her representatives are. Each definition has a unique way of defining what goes into the pot and what comes out, and those definitions can make the difference between hitting a gusher and coming up dry.

History of Movie Profit Participation

The idea of a creative talent participating in the studio profits on a picture didn't come into common practice until the 1950s. From the earliest days of silent films until the collapse of the studio star system, most actors were under contract to the major studios, getting a salary but no cut of the profits.

In the old studio system (from the beginning until the late 40s, more or less), creative talent had to rely on their agents to get the cash up front, mostly in the form of their weekly salaries, with occasional signing bonuses. That is, they'd get a lump sum of money just for signing the contract. The only exceptions to this rule were stars like Mary Pickford or Chaplin, who started their own production companies and thus maintained creative and financial control. A few stars like Bette Davis set up their own production companies while still under contract to a studio in the early 40s, thus taking on some of the risk in exchange for creative control and a chance at the profits.

Most actors were not able or willing to carry the risk of running their own companies, so the contract system persisted; and the studios, which produced hundreds of films each year, kept dozens of stars under contract at a set weekly salary. Many of the studios made huge amounts of money loaning their contract players to other studios (we touched upon this in the section on loanout corporations in chapter 13). This system changed after World War II, partially because some actors such as Bette Davis, Olivia De Havilland, and Don

Ameche bucked the system to wrest away more control over their careers.

The system changed primarily because studio production shrank with the advent of television competition, and the studios no longer needed to have a stable of actors under contract. At that point, more independent producers started producing films on their own, sometimes with studio financing, usually using studio distribution systems, but no longer tied to shooting on the studio lots or using studio personnel.

Creative talent suddenly found themselves free agents to negotiate their own deals. Out of this new way of doing business, some creative talent began sharing some of the risk of production by taking a smaller fee up front in exchange for a share of the profits of the movie. Some actors and other players such as writers made some good money in the early days. Of course, the team with the most lawyers and accountants—the studios—soon figured out a way to let the creative talent take the added risk and only give the impression that the creative talent were sharing in the profits.

———

Films still make money, of course, but rarely do they turn a profit, at least as defined by the studios, especially when it comes to very expensive productions with lots of heavyweight creative talent taking the first money that comes in. The concept is more applicable in television, at least when a series hits syndication, which we'll talk about in chapter 21.

HOW IT WORKS

What follows is not always logical. Just remember, the studios have gone to great lengths to make sure every film does not show a profit, no matter how much money the picture takes in. Remember Art Buchwald, who sued Paramount over *Coming to America?* (See chapter 15.) When the court ruled that Buchwald should share in the profits of the movie, the studio denied that he was entitled to any profits, even though the picture made over $100 million at the box office. Stay tuned, and we'll show you how the studio can pare $100 million down to nothing when it comes to sharing profits with creative people. If you're not interested in the nitty gritty, just look over the following box for basic definitions, so you'll know what people are talking about when it comes to profit participations.

———

The Hierarchy of Participation Deals

If you're not interested in reading this admittedly difficult material and just want to cut to the chase, here's the bottom line: participation from the top down. Just remember, these terms are all made up by creative lawyers and accountants, and they vary from deal to deal.

Gross Participation *generally means that the person who gets this kind of deal gets a percentage of the actual distribution take after some off-the-top deductions. They don't have to wait until the studio earns back all of the production and distribution money it spent.*

Net Participation *means the participant has to wait until the studio has earned back every cent it spent on the production and distribution of the film, including interest and overhead on what it spent. It rarely pays off.*

Breakeven *falls generally somewhere between gross and net. Instead of being stuck with waiting for the studio to earn back all the costs, the participant starts earning money sooner. It's sometimes called a* nice net, *and breaks down into specific types, including the* rolling breakeven.

Deferment *means the participant will generally get a lump of money (as opposed to a percentage) at some point along the way between gross and net.*

If you want to see how all of these participations are figured, keep reading.

———

NET PROFITS

Most participants such as writers, featured (but not lead) actors, and less successful directors and producers negotiate contracts that provide some share of the net profits, let's say 2 to 10 percent of net profits, or 2 to 10 *points*. *Net profits* are defined as the money left over after the studio has made all of its deductions to consider itself repaid for all the money it has put out in connection with the production. This process is called *recoupment*. The structure is basically similar for motion pictures and television, though there are some differences. If you can't stand the detail (and few can), check out the chart below, which summarizes the process. If you're a glutton for punishment, we follow the chart with all the gruesome detail.

Summary of How Profits are Calculated

Here's the short form of the calculation for movies. For television, the income comes from licensing fees received from the broadcast of the product (as opposed to box office gross), but the calculations are basically similar. If you want to know what these terms mean in detail, read the long form below.

The basic concept is that the studio will give you a percentage of what is left over from the money it receives from the box office (gross receipts) *after it deducts the items listed below:*

Exhibitor's cut What the theater owner takes out

Off the tops Fees and dues, checking, conversion, collections, residuals, licenses and duties, taxes, reissue, theater-level advertising

Distribution fees A percentage subtracted from the remaining box-office money

Distribution costs Actual costs of distributing the product

Interest Interest added to what the studio has spent on the product

Negative costs What it cost to shoot the film

Gross participants Money paid to players who don't have to wait for the studio to earn back its money before paying out some of the box-office receipts that have come in

Overhead A percentage the studio adds to the negative cost for its expenses, such as its studio staff and money paid to gross participants

Deferments Money paid to people who get cash before net participants, but usually after gross participants

What's left, if anything, is net profits or proceeds. As you can tell, it's quite a feat for a film to be successful enough to pay anything to people who've made these kinds of participation deals.

If you want to know more, read on!

—————

Following is a detailed explanation of how profits are calculated, starting with *gross receipts*. Gross receipts are what come into the studio after the theaters or broadcasters of a program have taken their cut. The gross receipts are often referred to as the *pot*.

EXHIBITORS CUT

This is relevant to motion pictures only. Distributors and exhibitors cut deals on each picture that's released, and the split on the take will depend on the heat the picture generates.

For example, for a picture everyone expects to be a big money maker, the studio will start with 90 percent of the box office. The movie theater that exhibits the film will usually take a 10 percent share of all box office in the first weeks of exhibition. For a tepid picture, the split may start out 50/50, and the theater will take a greater share the longer the picture lasts in the theater. For every dollar that comes in, at most only $.90 leaves the theater, and the average is probably closer to $.50. Of course, theater owners make their real money from selling you $3.00 boxes of popcorn—they get to keep *all* that money.

OFF THE TOPS

Also relevant to motion pictures, these are fees charged virtually to every participant, no matter how powerful. There are about eight of them, such as:

Fees and dues The studio always gets back the money it puts out for associations such as the Motion Picture Association of America, Inc. (MPAA), which charges basic dues and assessments on all products based on all sources of revenue. Other associations are the Motion Picture Export Association of America, Inc. (MPEAA) and the Association of Motion Picture and Television Producers, Inc. (AMPTP).

Checking is the expense the studio incurs when it actually sends people to the theaters to see if the theater owners are cheating the studio out of box-office receipts.

Conversion is the cost of changing foreign receipts into dollars.

Collections refers to the costs of chasing after exhibition revenues that weren't paid over to the studio.

Residuals means the kind we talked about in the discussion about unions.

Licenses and duties are the costs of doing business in foreign countries.

Taxes Yes, Virginia, even movie studios pay taxes.

Reissue is distribution after the initial release.

Theater-level advertising The studio makes deals with the exhibitors to offset the cost of local advertising.

If you have enough gross receipts (after you've deducted the off-the-tops), you continue subtracting the following items in the specified order. The idea is that you only get to profits if you have sufficient gross receipts to initially recoup the studio's distribution fees plus distribution, production, and other costs; interest, and overhead;—all of which we'll explain below.

DISTRIBUTION FEES

The studio takes a percentage of the gross receipts, which varies with the medium and the channel of distribution, from 10 to 50 percent. The fee is usually 30 percent of U.S. box office for movies, 40 percent for foreign theatrical, 25 percent for network distribution of television shows, and 35 percent for syndication.

Though the distribution fee is a huge chunk of change, the fee is never broken down or explained by the studio, unbelievable as that may seem. It's for the studio's distribution system, whoever and whatever that is. It's also a set percentage that presumably covers everything the studio can't get listed in the other categories. After reading what else the studio deducts, you'll be hard pressed to explain exactly what this category covers. However, it's not hard to figure out what happens to the pot. If the studio gets $.50 on the box office dollar, it subtracts its off-the-tops (say $.05), then takes 40 percent of the remaining $.45. Needless to say, the so-called profits are continuously whittled down to nothing, even on pictures or television series that performed phenomenally.

DISTRIBUTION COSTS

Yes, this is a separate charge from the distribution fee. The studio deducts its actual costs of distributing the picture, from preparing the advertising to buying television time. (Don't try to make sense of why these costs aren't covered under the distribution fee.) By the way, this is usually defined as *costs paid or incurred,* which means this sum is added to your costs and accruing interest (discussed below), even if the studio hasn't actually had to pay anything yet. These costs are actually deducted as they are incurred, so they can vary each accounting period. Since distributing a movie can cost an amount equal to one-third or more of the cost of shooting the movie, distribution costs can add up, especially when the film is first released and the media blitz for the film is the heaviest. Let's say for the sake of discussion we have a moderate studio film, which at today's rates might have cost $20 million to shoot. Because there are so many fixed costs, these costs on a cheaper film are a greater percentage of the negative cost than those of a bigger film. Therefore, on a cheaper film, the costs are probably higher than one-third. Figure the studio will spend another $8 million for distribution costs, and these costs will be deducted from the gross receipts. The studio isn't nearly recouped yet. We still have more costs to deduct!

INTEREST ON NEGATIVE COST
(125 PERCENT OF PRIME RATE)

Traditionally, studios have financed their own productions through their affiliated banks. This tradition has been modified recently as the studios have found themselves cash poor after the intensive mergers and acquisitions of the 80s and 90s. Even though the studio might have used its own money to produce the project, it charges interest to the film budget for having, in effect, loaned itself the money. (We discuss negative cost in chapter 20.) This includes interest on all expenses to build the sets, pay the creative talent, and other fees and costs. If this sounds absurd, it is. Welcome to Hollywood. The interest runs from the time the money is spent or incurred (see previous paragraph) until it is recouped. Let's say the studio spent $20 million to shoot the film. Every accounting period interest (say,

8 percent) is figured on that portion of the $20 million that is not yet recouped, and the interest is deducted from any money that comes in.

If a picture doesn't pull in a lot of money in the first few weeks of production, interest costs will add up and compound. No matter how much money the film eventually makes, it can't repay all that interest (think of your credit cards right after Christmas). There's no profit on paper, even though the studio continues to make money. That is how $100 million becomes $0 in profits.

NEGATIVE COSTS

We are finally at an item which makes sense—well, almost. Negative costs refers to the actual cost of making a picture, up to the point when the film is ready to go to the laboratory for copies (or prints) to be made from the negative. In our earlier example, that $20 million figure we were throwing around would represent negative costs. Note that these are costs paid or incurred.

GROSS PARTICIPANTS

In case you were thinking that the studios were your only competition for this money, let us introduce you to gross participants. These are people or companies who have enough clout to climb higher on the food chain than net participants. They start getting money before the studio has finished taking its share, almost always before negative cost is recouped and sometimes much earlier in the process. That means if you have any big time players involved in your production, you have even less of a chance of collecting net profits or any kind of contingent compensation.

A gross participant can be defined in so many ways it even taxes the creativity of a lawyer to define what kind of gross participation the client will have. One of the simpler kinds of gross participation is a "deferral," which means the participant gets a chunk of money when the film grosses a set amount. (We discuss deferrals below.) Other gross participants start taking a share of the gross receipts before some or all of the costs are recovered. The ones with the most clout, and there aren't many, may be in a *first dollar gross* position. They start collecting almost at the same time the studio does. Even the highest-level gross participants start collecting after some breakeven event, which we describe below.

OVERHEAD

Here's a wrinkle. The studio tacks on an additional 15 percent to the negative-cost figure (which in this case includes direct production costs *and* gross participations) to cover overhead. This mysterious 15 percent fee is never explained or accounted for. In our example, if the studio spent $20 million on negative costs, it doesn't have to give any money to anyone until it gets its off-the-tops, then its distribution fee, then all the distribution costs, then the interest on the negative cost and any money given to gross participants, then 15 percent overhead, and finally, the cost of actually making the movie.

As you can now see, the studio gets to keep much more money than the cost of production before it has to declare a profit and give some of that money to net participants. There are more favorable positions for participants, which basically serve to put them closer to the spigot of the income stream before the interest and other added costs make any participation impossible.

DEFERMENTS
(ACCRUED BEFORE ACTUAL BREAKEVEN)

This term describes money given to creative talent at certain points of recoupment. For example, writers typically get only net profits, so they don't see profits unless a production is a major hit. The studio may concede the point of giving a cash bonus of $50,000 or $100,000, usually at a point at which the studio has made enough back to cover some of its costs. The participant who accrues a deferment does it before one of the *breakeven points* described below. Because these people get paid cash, the net participants get pushed back, since the studio has to recoup deferments plus interest plus overhead before netters can share in the pot.

BREAKEVEN

This term is technically defined as the point when the balance of what has been or will be paid out equals what's come in. It's also the point after which the participants may start getting some money. It sounds simple, but it gives lawyers and accountants some of the biggest challenges in the game.

INITIAL BREAKEVEN OR INITIAL ACTUAL BREAKEVEN

This is the first point in time at which the studio goes from a loss to a profit position. If you can get a deferment or a gross points participation after an initial breakeven—or better yet a cash breakeven (see below)—you're better off because the studio can't delay your position by adding further interest and costs. Otherwise, in each subsequent accounting period, the studio keeps adding its costs, such as further distribution fees, distribution costs, and deferments; and a picture could go from initial breakeven back to a loss position, meaning you get no money.

CASH BREAKEVEN

This is the best breakeven situation, because the studio doesn't add in all incurred or anticipated expenses. It actually assumes that the studio is no longer in a loss position, or that it is in less of a loss position because it more or less arbitrarily decides that its distribution fee will be reduced from the standard 30 or 40 percent. The idea is that once cash breakeven is achieved, no further distribution costs are charged to the participants.

ROLLING BREAKEVEN

This term may sound kind of good, but it really doesn't get you anything much better than regular net profits. Instead of the studio taking a fee on all further revenue, it takes a fee only on its further distribution expenses, and it almost always occurs after initial actual breakeven has been reached. This is a complicated and generally meaningless way of figuring out at exactly what point in time (based on averages and other clever math manipulations) the studio has continued to hit breakeven. Since it is never the same point in time, it rolls. (Net profits roll, too, but no one ever mentions that.) Frankly, an agreement based on a rolling breakeven doesn't get you too far. Go for a deferment at cash breakeven, if you can.

HARD AND SOFT FLOORS

Haven't had enough yet? The scheme of "hard and soft floors" was developed to make producers fuller participants in the participation process. How does it work? The studio makes a deal with the producer that his or her profit participation will be determined by how many points are given to others. It's a way a producer can take more from the pot, if there aren't a lot of gross participants. The producer will be given a net profit participation of perhaps 50 percent, reduced by participations given to other participants to a soft floor of 15 percent, which can be reduced to no lower than a hard floor of 10 percent. Say that again? Well, essentially the producer gets $.50

out of every dollar of net profits reduced by every penny given to other profit participants until all that is left to give to the producer is $.15. If deducting any more money would take the producer below $.15, the studio recalculates what's left over and makes it off the top, reducing the original dollar to say, $.95, meaning it will only reduce the producer's share further by essentially 15 percent of the extra amount, and then only until the producer is reduced to 10 percent. The hard floor guarantees the producer will get at least 10 percent of the net profits. Whew!

Here are some examples of the type of language used in participation deals. In the wake of the Buchwald case (see chapter 15), some of the studios have used euphemisms for net profits, such as contingent compensation or net proceeds, but they add up to the same thing.

NET PROFIT PARTICIPATION
An amount equal to ___% of 100% of the "Net Profits" of the Project, if any. "Net Profits" shall be defined, computed, and accounted for in accordance with Producers Net Profits definition (including, without limitation, its 15% overhead charge on negative costs).

Of course, the producer's definition of net profits is fifty pages of detailed language, but we've described above how it basically works.

GROSS FROM FIRST DOLLAR
(i)   An amount equal to ___% of "Adjusted Gross Receipts" of the Picture commencing from the first dollar of Adjusted Gross Receipts.

Typically, the first dollar grossers will also have been given a hefty advance against the gross receipts.

PARTICIPATIONS ESCALATING AT DIFFERENT BREAK POINTS

(i)   An amount equal to ___% of the "Adjusted Gross Receipts," if any, of the Picture after "Initial Cash Breakeven" until "Initial Breakeven."

"Initial Breakeven" shall mean when "Net Profits" are first available for distribution.

"Initial Cash Breakeven" shall mean when "Net Profits" are first available for distribution, except that the distribution fees shall be 12 ¹/₂% in lieu of the fees set forth therein.

(Note that this would be a very high-level deal, almost up there with the first-dollar gross players.)

ROLLING BREAKEVEN

"Rolling Breakeven" shall mean the amount of Gross Receipts when "Net Profits" are first available for distribution ("Initial Breakeven") plus the amount of Gross Receipts required to:

Recoup distribution costs and the contingent payments accrued after Initial Breakeven; and

Deduct and retain distribution fees on an amount of Gross Receipts, which amount of Gross Receipts is sufficient, after deduction of said fees, to recoup the items set forth in (i) above.

Don't ask us to explain the preceding language; we did warn you it's complicated. As far as we can tell, this last item falls into the category of *nice net,* which means the studio has made it a little easier, and we mean just a very little easier, to collect your money. The key problem is you don't get anything until the picture has reached Initial Actual Breakeven, which occurs the day after never.

SOFT FLOOR

An amount equal to ___% of 100% of the Net Profits of the Picture, if any, reducible to a soft floor of ___% of 100% of Net Profits by all participations granted to third parties in accordance with the following reduction formula. First, all net profit participations shall be deducted from creative talent's net profits on a point-for-point basis. Second, all gross participations accruing after breakeven shall be deducted on a dollar-for-dollar basis. If creative talent's participation has been reduced to its floor, all gross participations accruing after breakeven (or any portion thereof) which have not been applied in effecting such reduction shall be an "off the top" deduction in computing creative talent's net profits under this Agreement. Gross participations accruing prior to breakeven shall constitute a charge included in the negative cost of the Picture. No net or gross participations or deferments may be granted by Producer or creative talent without Producer's prior written approval.

Sometimes there's a "hard floor" built into these things, meaning that whatever happens, your cut doesn't go below a certain equivalency point, but you get the gist. Again, a bigger cut of net profits doesn't help much unless, of course, you get some of the net profits in something with no big stars. Once you add a big player into one of these participation schemes, netters don't do very well.

MERCHANDISING

On certain properties, the studio may make a fortune exploiting your name and likeness in the role. We'll talk more in the approvals section about controlling that exploitation, but there's a financial twist you should know about as well. Generally the profits from merchandising are included in gross receipts as part of the pot. If you've got a merchandisable production that may generate posters, lunch boxes, dolls, or other items that can be sold separately, have your representative negotiate a separate pot for merchandising. Typically, the studio will agree to 5 percent of the merchandising pot. We've heard of 7 to 10 percent pots, too. The money in this can be enormous, and it shouldn't be overlooked as a deal point in your negotiations if the property looks like it's exploitable. Rumor has it that some of the *Batman* performers made more money than the studio, based on their participation in the merchandising money pot.

If none of this detail about participations makes any sense to you, don't worry. It takes several years for attorneys in the business to figure out this subject, if ever, and the important thing is that you find someone who does understand the game to handle this part of your negotiation.

———————

Tips for Negotiating Your Profit Participation

Tip one: *Never be impressed with someone offering you net profits in a project, unless they are willing to radically alter the traditional way net profits are figured.*

Tip two: *If you have enough clout, insist that your agent and lawyer get some sort of gross participation deal for you, even if it's after a breakeven point.*

Tip three: *Ask for a Most Favored Nations clause in your contract, which guarantees your net profits will be calculated to the same level as for any other net participant. See our discussion of this provision in chapter 13.*

Tip four: *If you really are counting on a profit-participation deal to bring in some money, have your agent or lawyer negotiate a clause with some clout. Get the right to audit the production company's books if you become suspicious about its bookkeeping. Everyone has a right to audit, but you can make it more clear and forceful. The big boys and girls get clauses like this. Why shouldn't you?*

Tip five: *We subscribe to that old proverb, "A bird in the hand is worth two in the bush." Get as much cash as you can up front.*

CREDIT/NAME AND LIKENESS

Credit is often the most fought-over issue in a negotiation, because credit represents a number of the juiciest points to win: Ego, power, and fame are all tied up in where your name appears on screen or in advertising. Because of the importance of credits, and because of the incredibly complicated language that has developed over credit provisions, this section of a contract can take up pages and pages.

We touched on the issue of credits in chapter 10, but there are a few points we can add when you've achieved star power. This is the one area in which many studios are willing to grant a form of Most Favored Nations provision (see chapter 13), though they may still resist using that term.

Depending on your clout, you want to be the first credit, the largest credit, and the most often mentioned credit of anyone connected with the picture. In any advertising, it's your name that gets mentioned and—if you're an actor—your picture that gets shown, your voice that gets heard, and your film clip that gets played.

ABOVE THE TITLE

Above the title is probably the biggest distinction between the players and the wanna-bes. The title is the title of the picture. Generally, the producer's production company ("A John Doe Production"), the director's *film by* credit ("A Jane Doe Film"), and the lead actor(s) will get an above-the-title credit. Often this is expressed as "above or before" the title because in print advertising and on posters they have a *billing block,* which includes all the credits. Because there is usually artwork in posters and ads, the studio likes to keep everyone's name in the billing block except for well-known actors and maybe directors like Steven Spielberg.

PAID ADVERTISING

Paid advertising is what the studio buys to advertise the picture during its release. You've seen ads in newspapers, but this also includes the billing block that appears on screen with trailers. Ever notice that the billing block is usually projected with such speed that you can't really make out anyone's name? That's because these credits became a battleground long ago and have lost most of their useful purpose. The studio resists these credit "gives" because it's more complicated to create advertising if you have to use names and faces in every ad; more complicated means less creativity and more room for mistakes, all of which are expensive and troublesome in this sensitive area. We supply more information about paid advertising credit in rather excruciating detail in chapter 18.

Through the years so many categories of creative talent have gotten paid-advertising credit that the billing blocks have become smaller and smaller. Sometimes there are so many names in the billing block that they have to do two billing blocks and you still can't read any names. Nevertheless, paid ads are hard won, and they extend not only to names in print, but the issues of oral mentions and—for actors—*likeness* as well. How do you get parity of oral mentions in advertising? Ask that if any other actor's name is mentioned, such as in trailers or on radio ads, yours will be, too.

What about your likeness? Generally, advertising includes artwork that may be based on a photograph, a frame of film, or an artist's rendering of an actor in his or her role. Issues regarding likeness include whether or not your likeness must be used and how big it must be in comparison to that of other players (ideally, no one's likeness should be bigger than yours). We are treading the line that borders approval issues, which we'll discuss later.

Finally, what if you don't want credit? Yes, this issue comes into play in negotiations as well. One scenario in which someone wouldn't want credit occurs when a well-known actor is doing a small part, usually referred to as a *cameo*, often as a favor to the other creative talent or because the role is interesting. Often the actor will limit the studio's right to use his or her name in advertising or perhaps even on screen. This prevents the studio from falsely advertising the product by making it seem the actor has a big role and, of course, protects the actor's *right of publicity*, which we discussed in chapter 14. The idea is, if anyone exploits the fame of the performer, it'll be the performer. If the studio wants to do it, it must pay for the privilege.

Here are some sample credit provisions. Notice that all credit provisions are subject to significant boilerplate limits, which we talk about in chapter 18.

Sample Credit Provisions
Basic Credit for an Actor

Actors' credits tend to be the most complicated, since there is almost always more than one actor competing for size or placement.

Provided that Performer appears recognizably in the role Performer was engaged for in the final released Project, Performer shall be accorded credit, on screen, in the main titles (if any), on a separate card, in not less than _____ position of the entire cast, in a size of type not less than the average size of type used to display the largest credit accorded to any other Performer other than the performer playing the role of "_____". All other matters pertaining to such credit shall be determined by Producer in its sole discretion. Performer shall not be entitled to receive any credit in paid advertising.

Basic Plus Paid Ads Only Where Someone Else Gets Paid-Ad Credit

Usually if an actor gets any paid credit, it's only when someone else also gets the credit. Also known as being "tied to" another actor.

(a) *On Screen:* In the main titles (if any), on a separate card, in not less than _____ position of the entire cast, in a size of type not less than the average size of type used to display the largest credit accorded to any other actor other than the actor playing the role of "_____".

(b) *In paid advertising* in which credit is accorded to _____: in not less than _____ position of the entire cast, in a size of type not less than the average size of type used to display the largest credit accorded to any actor other than the actor playing the role of "_____".

Basic Credit Plus All Paid Ads

In this example, the actor gets paid advertising credit anytime any actor gets it. A truly high-level actor will get paid-ad credit when any other person gets it.

(b) *In Paid Advertising:* In not less than _____ position of the entire cast, in a size of type not less than the average size of type used to display the largest credit accorded to any actor other than the actor playing the role of "_____".

Regular Title vs. Artwork Title for Any Creative Talent
Higher-level talent will negotiate the size of their credit in the billing block as well as in the artwork titles. See chapter 18 for a description of these two terms.

In a size of type not less than the greater of (i) 100% of the average size of type used to display the "regular" title, (ii) _____% of the average size of type used to display the "artwork" title or (iii) the average size of type used to display the largest credit accorded to any other creative talent.

Credit Above the Title for Any Creative Talent

Creative talent's credit shall be accorded above or before the "regular" title in paid advertising in which credit is accorded to any other creative talent.

(A better credit would be above the "artwork title".)

The above is only a start. As you can imagine, the possibilities are endless when it comes to actors' credits, and producers and directors generally get the same treatment.

The other group that will often negotiate the right to limit or refuse the use of their names in connection with a project is writers. There is at least one screenwriter who insists on the right to take her name off the credits. Why? Well, as we've discussed, writers have the least creative control over their material, and more often than not, the final version of the script they've written horrifies them. Naturally, they don't want the studio to give them credit, especially if they have some sort of reputation to uphold, real or imagined. Therefore some writers ask for and receive the right to take their name off the credits and replace it with a pseudonym. This request is rarely granted without a struggle, because the studio is often paying for the name as well as the words. Note that in cases in which it does allow for this, the studio will usually ask to pre-approve the pseudonym so as not to be stuck with a nightmare situation, such as an angry writer insisting the pseudonym be Frank N. Stein. You'd be amazed.

PERQUISITES

Perquisites, also known as *perks* or *perqs,* provide one of the most outrageous areas for dealmaking in Hollywood. This is the area in which the agents and lawyers go to town, because the sky's the limit in terms of the material greed and ego gratification available to those who've made it into the world of high-level negotiation. Giving great perks to someone is also a way of avoiding or granting the cash or profit participation they've asked for.

When studio executives hire a so-called A-List creative talent, they know that in addition to big money and profit participation, they'll have to budget a huge chunk of money to suit the particular ego or creative genius. This chunk of money is often referred to as *star baggage,* and it's grudgingly considered a part of the cost of doing business with top creative talent. Typically, a major creative talent will cost at least $150,000 in added perks, and it's not just actors.

There's no way of predicting what any particular creative talent will require when they come on board a production, but here are some of the standard and more extreme examples of perks.

TRAVEL

Every creative talent contract which requires travel to a location will provide for travel, generally first class for the higher-level people. If you're a high-level creative talent, extra tickets are often thrown in for companions and friends (we discuss some of these people below). Transportation is also generally provided between the airport and hotel, and hotel and set.

If you rate, you'll get a car while on location, and if you really rate, you'll get a car and your own driver waiting for you, perhaps even day and night. A top talent may ask for and get a Mercedes with the portable phone. If you're very strong indeed, no one will be allowed to use the car and driver but you and your guests, even if that means the car and driver sit all day while others have to walk. Sometimes the studio will give a high-end car to the creative talent, but this kind of gift is usually only inspired by a hit movie.

PRIVATE AIRPLANES

Normally, creative talent agree not to fly anything but commercial airlines during production. This is presumably for safety reasons. Once production is going, the studio doesn't want anyone taking risks, at least off the set. But some creative talent we know get permission to fly their own planes during production, all at the studio's expense. One of them gets the studio to hire his private plane with crew every time he goes on a job (of course, the crew must also be paid, housed, and fed). If you haven't bought your own jet, there's always that corporate jet the studio executives buzz around in, which they might lend you if you're on the current hot list.

LODGING

Typically, the studio will rent a block of rooms in a hotel or whatever accommodation is available at the location. Of course, this is only the starting point for high-level creative talent. Generally a suite of rooms is contractually agreed to, and we've known cases in which the suite had to include connecting rooms for a secretary, nanny, personal trainer, and even free weights for working out. A list of possibilities of what might be provided in your suite and dressing room or trailer could include shower, television, cellular phone, fax machine, pizza flown in from your favorite New York pizzeria, special water for washing your hair, or just about anything imaginable.

TRAILERS

Whether or not a project is shot on location, each performer—and usually the director and producer—will have a trailer of some sort to use between shots. The smallest of these is a *honeywagon*, a euphemism for something that is little more than a covered toilet. Most top creative talent negotiate for the latest model Winnebago (in addition to their hotel room), which offers all the comforts of home, and follows them from location to location. One star couple owns the biggest Winnebago around; and, of course, the studio must rent it, along with their driver, every time one of them performs. Never mind that the studio has its own fleet of these mobile homes, and forget about the obligation to hire union drivers, whether or not there's anything for them to drive.

EXPENSES

Expenses can rise to fairly high levels. Often creative talent will get cash for expenses over and above the hotel room, referred to as *per diem*. This cash is nonreturnable, even if it's $5000 a week for expenses and the location is in the middle of the rainforest where you can't possibly spend a dime. It's just another way of adding cash to the deal. Note that virtually all creative talent, including crew members, who are asked to go to a distant location (defined as more than 50 miles from home), will get a per diem. It's one of the consolation prizes for living a gypsy life.

STAFF
Personal assistant, nanny, masseuse, personal trainer, acting coach, therapist. If you're a big enough name, no one at the studio will question why your regular personal staff shouldn't go on the studio payroll for the duration of the production. The studio will even give your staff connecting rooms to your suite and have your gym equipment sent to you every time you travel.

WARDROBE
While many actors have enough status to be allowed to buy their wardrobe at cost, some get the studio to give them their wardrobe at no charge.

PREMIERES
If you are a popular performer or one of the few name directors, it's in the studio's best interest to get you to the premiere. It's free publicity and shows the world you are willing to promote the project. The studio especially likes creative talent to get to the U.S. premiere, but picking up the tab for everyone to go to international premieres can get fairly expensive, especially if the name isn't that big. Of course, major creative talent have their people negotiate the right to refuse to show up at these events. When they do travel, the studio picks up the tab for them and their entire entourage. The studios also entice creative talent to show up at premieres to promote their favorite charities.

SPAS, TOUPEES, AND PLASTIC SURGERY
Some stars begin to feel they need a little augmentation to get themselves camera ready. The studio will buy them a couple of sets of "rugs" after they've been sent to the spa to knock off those extra pounds. And more than one star has been allowed (if

not required by the studio), at studio expense, to undergo plastic surgery in preparation for a part.

PARTIES

Everyone likes to be popular, and the studios regularly throw big bashes for cast and crew, especially if they think major talent will show up. Generally these affairs aren't negotiated in advance. Every film has a budget for parties, sometimes buried under the heading "miscellaneous." This is another opportunity to get the studio to do a benefit of some kind for a favorite charity.

The most offensive party we've seen was when some then-hot producers flew a planeload of "starlets" (who weren't even featured in the film) across the country to decorate and entertain for a party at the end of one shoot. The studio picked up the tab and looked the other way. Anything for the creative talent.

UMBRELLA PERSON

No, we're not kidding. This is the person one studio had to pay for the express purpose of waiting by a star's dressing room door in order to escort the star around the set with an umbrella to minimize the star's exposure to the sun. Don't want to tarnish that porcelain complexion!

APPROVAL POWER

Having approvals is a great way for you to gain some control over the creative process; to give agents, managers, and attorneys free rein to be inventive; and to drive studio executives insane. Here are some ideas to get you started.

SCRIPT

Generally creative talent have to take the script as the studio likes it. But the highest-level players have a lot of say about scripts, especially top-level producers and directors. Writers rarely have any say in their scripts. Actors usually have less clout unless they're at the highest level.

Most A-List actors (and many directors) negotiate clauses that give them script approval up to a certain point, as defined in their agreement. That point might be the number of weeks left before the Start Date. For example, they can drop out of the project up to six weeks before the start, but after that date they're committed, even if they don't like the subsequent revisions. Some script-approval provisions allow the creative talent to request changes on the first or second set of revisions, but not thereafter. Although rarely, some provisions state that the creative talent is not required to walk on the set if the script isn't ready for them. Of course, studios hate to give in on this point, since it can drastically delay a production and either kill the project or cost a ton of money.

Another approach to script approval is to require that all the script changes are run past the talent for approval. The studio will try to contain that discretion by allowing only "reasonable" approval. Other script approvals will be narrowed by time limits on their obligation or by limiting the kind of changes that can trigger the approval clause. Specific approvals might be available only when there are significant changes to the character, for example, or changes that would cause the production to go over budget by more than 5 percent.

Script approval takes on great significance in Hollywood, where it's not unusual for an actor to step on the soundstage and be handed a script that's been through half a dozen writers and bears no resemblance to the script the actor originally agreed to perform. Most writers have to steel themselves to see the final version of their project, since it's often totally different from what they wrote in the first place.

CREATIVE TALENT

Of course, a powerful producer or director will get to work in tandem with the studio to choose the major creative talent (and the line producer will generally choose the crew and below-the-line staff). Highest-level actors also get some form of approval of the people they work with. Sometimes it's merely a consultation about performers, directors, editors, and others. Sometimes it's actual approval, though the studio tries to limit these rights in the same way that script approvals are limited—by time or stage of production. You can imagine the complexity that competing approvals can cause in a production, so creative-talent approvals are given sparingly. The show must go on, and it can't if everyone gets a vote.

ACTORS

Approvals in this area usually go only to director and producer and perhaps the lead actors, but it depends entirely on the clout of the person with the approval. Do you want to approve only the second lead, or does your creative vision require approval rights which extend to giving the nay or yea to everyone, including walk-ons? Sometimes the studio limits the scope of these approvals by agreeing only to grant individual approval on a list of mutually agreed-upon choices, so the studio maintains some flexibility in terms of negotiating its deal. It's not very practical to say only this one creative talent can direct, produce, or star in this picture, but it does happen. After all, what would *Gone With the Wind* have been without Clark Gable as Rhett Butler?

DIRECTOR

Lead actors in particular like to have the right to approve the director. It helps a lot to be the one with the power to chose (or fire) the person who will wield the most power on the set. If the director is your hand-picked choice, it's bound to be a happier set, at least for you.

EDITOR AND DIRECTOR OF PHOTOGRAPHY

These two categories of creative talent are as crucial to the look of a production as any. Generally the director and producer get consulting rights, but of course those with clout get actual approvals, as do actors. One reason for this is that it's very important to trust the eye of the editor or DP. Another is that sometimes either the picture or the performers have to have a certain look. This issue can be especially critical to a performer who has to be shot a certain way (like only from one side or angle), so he or she may demand approval on hiring these individuals.

SECRETARY / MAKEUP / HAIRDRESSER / WARDROBE / DRIVER

Secretaries are generally personal secretaries who get put on the payroll for the duration of the project. Makeup artists, hairdressers, and other personal-service people can often become a significant part of the negotiation. The studio wants to accommodate performers, but they also want the service personnel to work for more than just the stars. When certain performers want exclusive rights to these individuals, it poses a problem. Most directors and many stars employ the same staff of people in film after film. One particular star even gets the right to have her makeup person go to screenings of the dailies to make sure the performer looks the way she wants to on the silver screen. Of course, when too many people have approval rights, the studio gets a huge headache trying to accommodate everyone's choices.

NUDITY

By SAG rules, all actors have the absolute right to approve what is done with their bodies on the screen. No one has to shoot a nude scene if he or she doesn't want to, and if the actor consents to do a nude scene, specific separate waivers must be negotiated and signed prior to the scene being shot. Many a lawyer and agent have negotiated exactly which body parts can be shot, because it can get very specific.

For example, it's typical that you can shoot buttocks but not genitalia, and breasts but no nipples. These details are actually negotiated in writing. Actors also get the same approval right even if they don't actually shoot the scene themselves; they get to approve both the studio's choice to use a *body double* and the body double who will be used. Hate your thighs? Insist on a body double. Don't want to get in bed with your co-star? Get a body double. There are people out there working as specialty extras who body double for a living.

In spite of all this, sometimes it doesn't seem to matter how much you negotiate. One star found that the carefully controlled nudity she did for the theatrical version became all-too-revealing in the home-video version, which uses slightly different dimensions of the original film simply by nature of the format. It was totally inadvertent on the studio's part, but this performer is now permanently showing more goods than she expected in living rooms across America.

STUNTS

Actors often get to approve their *stunt doubles,* the people who step in when it's time to fall off that cliff and do other dangerous stunts. This way you can make sure the stunt double is built like you or is built the way you would like to be built. The good part is that it's the stunt people who get the bumps and bruises —not you.

PUBLICITY

Mostly these approvals have to do with actors, since there are only a handful of directors who are known by name. Because it can really help a picture to have the performers appear on all sixteen late-night talk shows, the studios have made publicity requirements part of every contract. Naturally, not all big stars want to hit the road to publicize the picture, especially if they're not particularly proud of their work or of the completed project. Still, these obligations are negotiated so that the actor can do this work on his own terms, or not at all. One actor we know found himself in New York City on the opening day of his film riding the escalator of Macy's dressed in his medieval costume from the picture.

PHOTOGRAPHS AND LIKENESSES

These approvals are a great way to drive the marketing department of a studio crazy. A photo/likeness approval can require the studio to submit at least 500 stills for approval, of which the talent may only have to approve 250. Other times, the star may not even have to approve one shot. Of course, a studio will try very hard to put time limits on the decision making. It's the same thing for any likenesses, such as drawings. The goal is to get approval of all purposes likenesses might be used for, so you get to approve every ad, photo, and commercial.

MERCHANDISING

Unless the talent demands control of this area, the studio assumes it can do anything it wants with an actor's name, image, and voice. Most players want to have a say about the use of these personal traits in every possible venue. It's not just a money issue for many people. Unless there is some control in this area, a talent might find his or her face on a toy gun or attached to someone else's body on the poster. Approval prevents such potential calamities. Some people don't care about the extra cash and tell the studio it can't use their image, name, or voice in any merchandise. Still other people like the money, or maybe they're just curious about how they look at eight inches tall, as long as they have control over what the doll looks like.

REAL POWER

There's no doubt that gaining any of the approvals we've discussed above constitutes some degree of power in Hollywood. However, there's a level of power that comes with success that gives what to many is the greatest win of all—the power to control the creative process. Here are some ways real power is given and exercised in Hollywood.

CREATIVE CONTROL

This is the ultimate and therefore perhaps rarest of "gives," and the one that gives the studio the biggest headaches. Generally given only to top directors, creative control is a powerhouse provision. The contractual language may vary, but basically a relevant clause is a relatively simple statement saying that in creative matters (as opposed to budget matters) the director exercises ultimate control. What it means is that as long as it doesn't cost the studio any additional money, the director can cast his daughter in a lead role, whether or not she has any acting experience or talent, for that matter. Having creative control goes beyond having a lot of say, which contracts and union agreements usually provide, to actually having the right to make final decisions, no matter what anyone else thinks. Of course, surrendering creative control makes the studio very nervous, even though it may not have any better ideas than the person making the decisions.

CUTTING RIGHTS

The people who get to say that the picture is ready for distribution are among the most powerful in Hollywood. The director gets a cut (called, logically, the *director's cut*), but the studio is mighty reluctant to agree to give up rights to the final cut. Of course, they do have to yield to the players. Top directors routinely negotiate *final cut* provisions, which allow them to fashion the film until it meets their vision. Sometimes, though pretty rarely, performers get some rights regarding the cutting of the picture. As you might expect, these rights are highly prized. Cutting rights are limited as much as possible. The studio often makes the rights conditional, based on whether the director stays on schedule and under budget. It might also limit how many cuts the director can make. Since films are recut for international distribution (each country has its own rules about sex and violence), the cutting rights may be limited to the U.S. theatrical release. The studio may additionally grant specific cutting rights for the network TV or video versions. Each possibility is tortuously discussed in these provisions.

Every once in a while you'll see the re-release of a film, and it will be advertised as the director's cut. Usually that means the studio took the film and ruined it, at least according to the director, and this version represents the way the director intended it to turn out.

PRODUCTION COMPANY

Anyone can start a production company. All you have to do is give yourself a name and print up some cards. However, if you can get someone else to pay for or back your production company, give you a pot of money to play with, and promise that your projects will be submitted to the right people at the studio, you've got real power in Hollywood. Sometimes production companies are started by bringing competent producers onto a lot and setting them up to find material for the studio. It's a cyclical thing—sometimes the studios think production deals are a great idea and sometimes they don't, depending on the success or failure rate of the production companies they've supported recently.

When a movie star has a production company, more often than not it's part of a package the studio has put together to entice the actor into starring in a project or two for the studio. For example, the studio may know Cowboy Bob is perfect for the new cowboy movie they want to do. Bob is bored with cowboy movies, so in order to get him back in the saddle again, the studio sets up a production company for him so he can plan his Shakespearean debut. Will the studio actually make that Shakespeare movie with Bob? Probably not, but they'll hire him a secretary or two, a reader to evaluate scripts that come in, and give him a suite of offices on the lot and maybe even a parking space (sometimes the biggest "give" in a studio deal, because reserved parking can be the equivalent of an executive bathroom). For reasons you can probably figure out by now, such production companies are often called *vanity companies*.

First-Look Deals

A variation on the production company is the *first-look deal*, which may or may not involve the studio fully financing a production company. In a first look deal, for an exchange of money, the studio gets the right to be the first one to look at any projects the talent might be interested in producing. These agreements can be fairly complex documents, but the basic idea is fairly simple: The studio sees a project first, and if it doesn't like it, you can take it elsewhere. Sometimes the studio has a right to match any offer someone else makes, since it's a well-known concept that it doesn't want what's offered until someone else wants it first. The underlying assumption in these deals is that movie stars like to have offices with their names on them, but generally they're no real threat when it comes to developing properties. Of course, many stars take real advantage of the studio's resources and develop properties that actually get made, whether or not they star in them. It's an effective way to segue from an onscreen to a behind-the-camera career.

MULTIPLE ROLES

Also known as multiple hats, multiple roles are yet another variation on the same theme. The goal is to get the studio to acknowledge your clout by naming you a *hyphenate,* a term whose definition will become obvious. The most common type of hyphenate is probably director/producer, the term used when a director also assumes a producing role. Sometimes, but far less often, producers decide they want to become directors. Unless the title is merely window dressing, it means that the designated individual can have creative and financial control over a project. Actors enter the hyphenate arena with more and more frequency. Many actors trade on their bankability as performers to negotiate producing or directing credits.

CHAPTER EIGHTEEN

So What *Is* in That Boilerplate?

We've got to warn you. This chapter is pretty much for lawyers, really careful agents, and contract nerds. Though everyone seems to complain about this stuff when it appears in contracts, hardly anyone ever reads these provisions—and even fewer understand what they mean. It doesn't even make for good party chatter. It's just too much of a bore. Still, it doesn't hurt for creative talent to understand these provisions. More than one creative talent has gotten snagged on a provision that neither they nor their representatives bothered to examine closely; and more than one creative talent has overpaid his or her lawyer for negotiating points that basically don't make any difference.

Just about every contract in Hollywood, especially the higher-level agreements, have pages and pages of densely written, almost incomprehensible language attached to the body of the agreement. *Boilerplate* is the term used to describe the language that goes along with and anchors every contract. Generally these documents are referred to as *schedules* or *exhibits* or sometimes simply *the contract*, while the additionally negotiated points are often referred to as an *addendum*. Boilerplate refers to the language that the studio wants to apply to everyone, generally to ensure that it retains the rights to go forward with or stop production and distribute the product.

Most of the boilerplate clauses run on for pages and pages, even though they are almost never discussed by the agents and studio business-affairs people who make the deal. An alternative that has been developed to save negotiation time is to make certain changes available without haggling. The number of changes available depends on the clout of the creative talent, but each studio trains its lawyers in gives. They have a list of low- and high-level gives that they routinely insert into contracts. These points are usually relatively inconsequential, but they foster goodwill by making the creative talent feel like the studio is being generous. Sometimes the lawyers from both sides can spend hours and hours negotiating over these gives although most of them cover events that never occur.

To understand why these clauses are included, you must remember that the cardinal sin for a lawyer is to fail to account for any potential problem, no matter how remote. This explains why the clause that allows the studio to use your image in the film covers not only use throughout the world but throughout the universe in perpetuity. Hey, that space colony on Mars in the next, next century is sure to want cable. As silly as this sounds, it does make some sense. Millions of dollars were gained and lost by the failure to anticipate the advent of videotape technology. A lot of lawyers were left with egg on their faces, and their angry clients were left with much less. Seemingly insignificant clauses may include such stipulations as the performer can't gain too much weight or be arrested for a felony. Although these are things most of us would never think of negotiating, they could turn into a big expense, inconvenience—or worse—a studio embarrassment during the course of production.

How much should you worry about this legal gobbledygook? Well, some. If you have a good attorney you may sleep easier at nights. You are paying your lawyer all that money precisely so he or she takes the time to decipher this stuff. However, your attorney should always be willing to translate it into understandable English for you. An attorney must also have a common-sense approach to what is important and what is not, so you don't end up paying a fortune in legal fees over a clause that is virtually meaningless.

One last point. Just because it's boilerplate and looks like it's been in the studio contract forever (and it probably has) doesn't mean it's not negotiable. Maybe you want to keep the rights to your image for the solar system beyond earth. If you have enough clout our attitude is, why not?

RIGHTS AND MORAL RIGHTS

We touched on this issue in the introductory paragraph to this section. Most contracts will have something which states that all results and proceeds of the creative talent's services shall be deemed a work made for hire (discussed in chapter 15). The consequence of this statement, which is usually explicitly stated, is that the studio will be the sole and exclusive owner of the production for all purposes in all media and by all means now known or hereafter devised throughout the universe in perpetuity. This ownership covers all creative talent, from actors to directors of photography and set designers. There's some controversy in legal circles over whether or not such language is sufficient to protect the studio against changes in new technology (such as on-line services), but for now it's what the studios rely on.

Another issue that might come up in contract negotiation is a waiver of the *moral rights of authors* or *droit moral*. The studio will specifically state that the creative talent waives these rights under U.S. or foreign laws, even though it's not entirely clear you can waive these rights outside the U.S.

A (Very) Short Primer on Moral Rights

What are these rights? Moral rights, also referred to as the right of patrimony, is a concept of international copyright law. Stated generally, it basically gives the creator of a work the right to stop other people from copying it, changing it, or using their name in connection with the work without the permission of the creator.

Under current U.S. copyright law, only the owner of the work has this right. Since most work done for studios is done as work for hire, the studios have avoided granting these rights, which are given to artists in virtually every other country in the world.

In the rest of the world, no matter who paid for the production, the artists who work on it (such as the writers, producers, directors, even editors, photographers, and performers) might have the right to prevent or at least limit the studio from exploiting the rights to the property. Naturally, the idea of having to ask the creative talent permission to sell or change the work horrifies U.S. producers, who have so far been successful in lobbying Congress against including moral rights in the law.

Another point specified in the boilerplate is the studio's right to use the creative talent's name and likeness and *biographical* data in connection with the distribution, exhibition, advertising, and exploitation of the product. This is a point that deserves some attention. You really don't want to give the studio total carte blanche for any kind of exploitation. You may want to retain the right to pre-approve any biographical information used or to limit the use of such information to uses only in direct connection with your role in the production.

So What *Is* in That Boilerplate?

Often a creative talent may limit use of his name in endorsements, so that he doesn't suddenly see his name used to plug a product he doesn't believe in, just because the studio has an advertising arrangement (also called a *commercial tie-in*). In these cases, the studio enters into an agreement with a consumer-product company in which the company advertises the film in return for the use of elements from the production. If you don't want to see your face on a plastic cup at your local fast-food joint, ask your attorney to negotiate some control over image/likeness exploitation.

Actors have special boilerplate provisions about the use of their performances on records, which would include cassettes and CDs. There is usually existing language giving the studio the right to release a separate record in exchange for a set royalty. The numbers are always negotiable.

Another right the studio retains is the right to *dub* or double their performance. If the studio doesn't like your voice, even your speaking voice, it can automatically replace it with someone else's. If the studio doesn't like your body, or it doesn't want to put it at risk, it can replace your body with a double, which we discussed in chapter 17. It's an issue that can be negotiated. It can hit hard, especially when the entire vocal performance is dubbed, and it happens.

SCREEN AND ADVERTISING CREDIT

Even though you thought you had carefully negotiated your credit provision, if you look in the boilerplate section, you'll notice a huge chunk of additional verbiage regarding credits that can significantly reduce the studio's obligations. Most people ignore these provisions, even though they severely limit the studio's obligations to accord credit.

First, you don't get your credit unless you have performed "substantially all services called for," which, you may have noticed, is a fairly vague statement. Actors in particular don't get credit unless they appear recognizably in a role in the final production. So if they cut you out, you don't get credit. The obligation to give credit in advertisements applies only to paid advertisements (see chapter 17) issued by the studio. Such ads must be under the direct control of the studio and relate primarily to the production. Further, the obligation to give credit doesn't apply to the following: so-called *teaser* or *special advertising*, publicity, and/or exploitation relating to the production; any members of the cast, the authors, directors, or producers; trailers or other advertising (including *promotional films*) on the screen, radio, or television; *institutional, group, or list advertising;* credits on the screen at the end of the production; newspaper or other periodical advertisements of 1200 lines or less; or byproducts, record-album jackets, and similar packaging, merchandising productions, or commercial tie-ins. There is no obligation to give credit when the studio is paying for an *award ad*, which is an advertisement, usually in one of the trades, to help you get nominated or win an award, such as an Emmy or an Oscar. The creative talent isn't entitled to anything but regular credit, that is, credit in the billing block (see chapter 17). This is true even if someone else gets his name in the *artwork;* i.e., his name is included in special print or graphically woven into the pictures used to advertise the production. All references to size are defined by the height of the letters, unless your agent negotiated that size also refers to thickness and width. Usually the studio will bury a line in the boilerplate stating that everything else besides the issue of size is to be determined at the studio's discretion.

REPRESENTATION

The contract requires the creative talent to make certain statements (referred to as *representations*) about themselves. For example, one statement the creative talent promises is true is that he or she is under no obligations to others and therefore is free to work for the studio. As a result, if the creative talent happens to be under contract to someone else, the studio is in a better legal position to defend itself against another studio claiming it has exclusive rights on the talent. Another representation is that whatever work is done is wholly original.

Usually there are also some commitments about rendering services for the studio. For actors, these commitments will include *retakes* and *looping* (redoing part of their vocal performance, either because of inadequate sound quality of the recording made during production, or to record replacement language, e.g., PG words for television broadcast). They usually also include doing publicity for the production. Sometimes these commitments become the studio's wishful thinking when temperaments clash, but since they're in the contract, they give the studio the right to terminate the creative talent if they're too difficult to deal with, which stops the cash flow.

Another clause that usually is thrown into the boilerplate specifies that the studio is not obligated to use the creative talent's services. It can hurt a creative talent's reputation to get fired, not be used, or have his or her performance end up on the cutting-room floor. Consequently, this clause protects the studio from getting sued. Of course, if you have any clout, a smart attorney will negotiate a pay-or-play deal (see chapter 17).

TRANSPORTATION AND LIVING EXPENSES

Although these issues are usually handled in the initial negotiation, sometimes the boilerplate is used to define what a location is (typically more than fifty (50) miles away from the creative talent's place of residence). There's usually also some undefined but reassuring language saying that if the creative talent is rendering services at the studio's direction on location, then the studio will reimburse the creative talent for first-class transportation and reasonable first-class living expenses. Such reimbursement may be taxable and reported by the studio to the Internal Revenue Service if required by law.

SUSPENSIONS, STRIKES, AND OTHER FORCE MAJEURE EVENTS

These provisions are generally the most complicated and therefore the butt of the most jokes when people get together and complain about studio contracts. The idea behind these clauses is to provide the conditions under which the studio can suspend you—and stop paying you money or ultimately fire you—if something goes wrong. If you're a legalese nerd, these sections of the contract are fun to read, because the studios seem to have anticipated every possible disaster that could occur. There are many reasons a studio can blow the whistle, shut down production, and stop issuing paychecks. Almost anything that interferes with the development or shooting of projects can be described as a *force majeure* (major force) event. The reasons you can be suspended fall into three basic categories: things that you do, things that other people working on the production do, and things that happen because of events having nothing to do with the production.

THINGS THAT YOU DO

These include illness, incapacity, default, or similar matters.

The studio generally will not stop production if you're ill for more than a week or two, unless they've shot so much with you that the film can't be completed without you. Productions have been stalled for Elizabeth Taylor's illnesses as they were on *Cleopatra*, but most players won't get such privileges, especially if they can be dubbed, doubled, or cut out. If you have some clout, you might get some specific time periods added to the contract that indicate how long the production company must wait for you to recover before they can replace you. Other clauses can take into account further delays for medical opinions and require efforts by the studio to shoot around you.

Physical appearance is obviously a point that applies to actors and can be a touchy subject. While the contract won't necessarily state that you can't gain weight, the language is usually broad enough to address your fitness to do the role or to ask for a change in your physical appearance until a picture is completed. These demands make sense. Look at Judy Garland's performance in *Summer Stock*. She gained and lost somewhere in the neighborhood of thirty pounds during the picture, and it was obvious on screen. The studio went with the footage they had anyway, so she went from plump to thin by the time the production got to the final musical number.

The same principle applies with regard to plastic surgery and hair color: If you were a blond during principal photography you've got to remain—or be transformed back into—a blond for the retakes and reshoots.

This is something actors have to remember when they're about to grab that hot fudge sundae: The studio might be able to fire you for not looking the way it expects.

THINGS DONE BY OTHER PEOPLE ON YOUR PRODUCTION

These are occurrences in which production is prevented, interrupted, or delayed by reason of the death, illness, or incapacity of the director or a principal member of the cast. These occurrences can be tricky, because when someone else gets ill, it doesn't mean necessarily that production must stop. If a director becomes ill, another director can be brought in to complete production. With regard to a performer, the situation clearly depends on the role and how far along the production was. When Brandon Lee was accidentally shot just before completion of *The Crow*, the studio decided it had enough footage to complete the picture, so no suspensions were in order.

Sometimes suspension provisions can be used by the studio as an excuse to kill a production that's going sour. That's when pay-or-play clauses and other negotiated protections can be helpful. Even if the studio can legally stop paying for a short period, you should have enough protection to get them to resume payment and/or release you from your obligation to perform.

THINGS THAT HAPPEN HAVING NOTHING TO DO WITH THE PRODUCTION

These incidents are also known as the force majeure provisions. They cover virtually any event during which development and/or production is prevented or interrupted. Usually the contract will also include the word "interfere" to give the studio the widest latitude to define a disaster. Lots of things fall into this category: Almost any form of natural disaster is covered. In addition to fires, floods, and earthquakes, all of which occur regularly in California, a bad windstorm that blows down the sets can be deemed a force majeure and stop production (and therefore your salary). Other goodies usually include any labor dispute, strike, military uprising (not unusual in foreign locations), war or governmental action, or any disruptive event beyond the studio's control.

A word about *strikes*. Just about once a year, one of the unions threatens to strike. There's a lot of huffing and puffing, but generally no one on either side wants a strike. If any union goes out, eventually everyone is affected. An actor's strike can stop production cold. A writer's strike may not stop production immediately, but sooner or later the stories stop flowing in and production grinds to a halt. A long strike can cripple productions and put lots of people under, especially small production companies and creative talent wavering on the edges of the business. These people simply can't hold out until the money begins to flow again.

Here are some tips that might be helpful with respect to suspension provisions:

———

Tips on Suspensions

Tie yourself to others *You might try to add a provision stating that you can't be suspended due to* force majeure *unless the entire cast, director, and producer are also suspended. This gives you a great deal of protection, because a studio is not likely to suspend the director or the producer, since they hold the keys to the production.*

Recall Notice *Another handy provision to request is the right to work elsewhere on twenty-four hours recall notice. This will help you avoid starving to death or being in breach of your contract if you do some pick-up work while waiting for production to resume.*

Time Periods *Check out the clause that sets the duration of suspended production, after which you can back out of the contract entirely. You don't want the studio to be able to suspend production for a year and still have the right to force you back to work.*

These clauses are difficult to negotiate, but if you've got the resources and a tough attorney, you'll increase your freedom to work and prevent being locked into a project that gets back-burnered or completely shut down.

———

MORALS CLAUSES AND OTHER RESTRICTIONS

These clauses give the studio the right to fire you and deny you screen credit for a variety of so-called moral reasons. These reasons can, of course, include sexual behavior, but the language usually extends further to include criminal acts, political statements, or even statements ridiculing the studio or the production. In a town that has more fear of public perception than respect for actual morals, you can guess why these clauses came to be and why some studios are adamant about keeping them in the paperwork.

There's an interesting history to morals clauses. They started appearing during the silent-film era, when stars' wild parties and drug use resulted in some deaths and bad publicity for the studios. The sexual accusations against, and subsequent trial of, then-popular comedian Fatty Arbuckle; the public protest against Mae West's performances; and the drug-related death of director William Desmond Taylor all inspired the studio heads to have strict morals clauses written into the contracts. With these protections, the studios could control, or at least fire, the stars who were causing the most embarrassment. These clauses started to drop out of contracts in the 1940s until the McCarthy blacklisting era reared its ugly head. Suddenly, the studios were searching for reasons to fire their contract players, who began to be exposed as possible former or current communists. The morals clauses found their way back into the contracts, with new provisions that defined political beliefs as a morals issue. Unlike in days past, the studios used these provisions to fire people for their unpopular political views, rather than sexual or criminal acts.

These days, you can generally get the studio to modify these clauses, since hypocrisy is pervasive in a town that glorifies its own sexual hedonism and exploits its clout in almost every political arena. Some studios will delete these clauses entirely, or at least soften them. As an example, a studio may remove language about firing you if you have a criminal record. However, it's likely to retain the right to fire you if your criminal behavior makes it impossible to report to work: Because you're in jail, for instance, the foreign country you're filming in won't let you cross the border.

Not surprisingly, studios are very touchy about you slandering their film production in public. Your contract may restrict you from making any use of the name of the role you play, the character or characterization portrayed, or even the title of the production. Some go even further and state that the creative talent may not portray any role, character, or characterization that is the same or similar to, or which makes fun of the name of, any role, character, or characterization portrayed by the creative talent. This kind of language created some trouble for Clayton Moore, who portrayed the Lone Ranger, when he wanted to play the character in personal appearances having nothing to do with the actual productions. When these clauses have made their way into the morals section or elsewhere in the contract, they can be tough to remove.

OTHER GOBBLEDYGOOK

There can be really boring stuff in the contract, but it can be important to understand. For example, see if the studio has given itself the right to *equitable or injunctive relief.* If so, it means that it has the right to force you to work or stop you from working for others, or that the studio is exempt from court orders. The studio has to go to court like everybody else. They can seek the right to stop you from doing something, but they cannot get this right by contract.

INSURANCE

Insurance often comes up as an issue in the boilerplate. The studio has the right to purchase almost any kind of insurance it wants to cover you (and its investment in you). *Cast insurance* is a regular part of any budget, and the studio has the right to name itself and not you the beneficiary if anything should happen to you. This is not unusual. The thing that might cause you problems is the medical exam the studio requires so it can get its insurance. If you have a chronic illness, you may not be able to get insurance, and the studio can fire you. One thing you can do to make it easier on yourself is get a contractual right to have your own physician perform the examination.

AIRLINE TRAVEL AND OTHER HAZARDS

Boilerplate provisions often include language restricting your right to travel on anything but a commercial airline. Furthermore, it's a breach of your contract if you engage in any hazardous activity. Is the studio going to fire you for flying your own plane or skydiving? Probably not, unless it's looking for an excuse. Like the others, these clauses can be negotiated.

What can you do to protect yourself with regard to these boilerplate provisions? The studio is usually fairly intransigent in making any changes. There are probably two reasons they're so difficult to negotiate. One is that the force majeure provisions have been part of boilerplates since the beginning of the industry. Since disasters do happen, studios want to preserve their right to back out of production. After all, we're talking about tens, if not hundreds, of thousands of dollars a day in salaries if production is suspended. Truthfully though, we think the real reason these provisions don't get changed is that no one, including the studio lawyers, really understands them. Most of them are virtually incomprehensible, and it can give you a headache just to try to untangle some of the baroque language that's evolved.

Given the tremendous attorney costs that could be involved in moving a stubborn studio to change some of the boilerplate language, most people don't bother. The approach most people seem to use is to cross their fingers and hope that nothing bad happens. Usually only the bigger creative talents have the resources to take on boilerplate negotiations, but don't forget that in Hollywood almost everything is negotiable.

CHAPTER NINETEEN

Breaking the Contract

CHOOSING TO BREAK THE CONTRACT

What do you do if you find yourself in a contractual situation you don't like? The role is wrong, the budget is too low to achieve your artistic vision; the producer has put all his relatives on the payroll, and they don't know what they're doing; or you get a better offer. Once again, we have a short answer and a long answer to this dilemma. The short answer is, don't break your contract, at least not without the advice of a competent attorney, a lot of soul searching, and a discussion with your agent, though not necessarily in that order.

The long answer is, if you have a legally binding obligation and you break it, you can get sued. It doesn't matter why—for example, if you're worth more money now than when you got into the obligation and therefore deserve a higher salary, or the chemistry between you and someone else just isn't there. There's an even more compelling reason to avoid breaking a contract. If you get a reputation in town for being difficult, no matter how attractive or smart you are, you may find it hard to find work again. As we've discussed all through this book, Hollywood is really a small town with a small-town mentality. Everyone talks to one another, and there's too much of a flood of creative talent coming through the doors to put up with much bad behavior.

GETTING FIRED

No one likes to get fired. Still, we can give you a word of solace. In a town as volatile as Hollywood, people get fired all the time. Most of the studio executives lose their jobs every time there's a management shakeup, which occurs quite often. Inexperienced directors get fired because they're too nervous. Experienced directors get fired because they're too old. Tall actresses get fired when short actors don't want to have to look up. Unless your behavior is really bad, like you show up too stoned to work, it's not that unusual to get the old heave-ho. So get up, dust yourself off, and maybe call your agent or lawyer to see if the studio owes you any money or favors for letting you go.

The Rules of the Game

Now that we've reviewed how the players play and the workers work in Hollywood, plus some of the issues related to protection of properties and the kinds of contracts creative talent enter into, we're ready to see how the parts fit into the whole. Every project in film and television is set up with a business structure that determines who's paying for the production, what kind of people can work on it, how it's sold, how it's distributed and marketed, where it's exhibited, and the way profits get distributed. We'll explain here the rules of the game for structuring productions.

Unquestionably, some of what follows is fairly esoteric, and if all you need is to keep up with party chatter, a light skimming of this section may very well do. However, if you want to be an effective participant, especially if you hope to gain any business or creative control, this section describes the basic deal structures for motion picture and television production.

Chapter Twenty

Motion Picture Production

STUDIO PICTURES

What are the major studios we keep talking about? There are the long-time survivors, in no particular order, including MCA/ Universal, Paramount Pictures, Time Warner (formerly Warner Bros.), Disney, Twentieth Century–Fox, and Columbia. MGM was one of the great studios for over fifty years until it was stripped apart by various financiers, leaving only a film library, controlled mostly by Ted Turner, and a billboard of a lonely lion, though it's recently been revitalized with new executives and new production financing. Newer, but well-established, is Tri-Star. There are also some so-called mini-majors, which come and go. New Line Cinema, which was a mini-major with a relatively long history for an independent, was recently bought by Ted Turner. The Samuel Goldwyn Company both produces and distributes independently produced properties. Orion was a mini-major player for about fifteen years before it ran into financial trouble and had to shelve or sell the films it then had in production.

Disney has diversified by having a string of different kinds
of production companies: There's Walt Disney Pictures for the
purely G-rated (General Audiences) productions; and Touch-
stone Pictures and Hollywood Pictures for PG (Parental Guidance) and some R (Restricted) pictures. In addition, Disney
has distribution agreements with independent producers such as
Miramax, which produces more adult and offbeat fare. Sometimes these deals are referred to as *output deals*, because the
agreement is for a studio to exclusively distribute all of the
product of a production company without exercising direct control over the productions.

The big studios produce an average of ten to fifteen pictures a year, more when there's a particularly ambitious executive in charge. The majors are all involved in film and television
production. All of them still have the big physical plants with
soundstages (huge warehouse-sized buildings where filming is
done) and such elements as legal departments, music departments, prop departments, and *commissaries* or restaurants.

Of course, big studios are not the only entities producing
projects these days. There are a variety of ways that projects get
brought to and through the pipeline to theaters and TV sets.
One of the main distinctions between a studio picture and other
productions is that when the studio is producing under its own
name, virtually all above-the-line and below-the-line creative
talent will be union members. In an independent production, you
may find seasoned talent working at lower rates with or without
the approval of the union. You might also find the director
employing his or her film-school pals and neighborhood talent
to keep the budget down.

Since the 1930s, the studios have naturally been the biggest
targets of the unions, so the big studios are all union signatories,
which adds at least 30 percent (and usually more) to any budget.
Union people simply make more money, get more overtime, and

get terrific union *fringes* (sums added to the cost of personnel because medical and other benefits the employer must pay in connection with hiring union personnel). The studios negotiate as a block with the unions, and each of the unions has published basic agreements that detail the working conditions and rules that have been negotiated between the unions and teams from the major studios. Union rules are no secret: You can get copies of each of the basic agreements from the unions. See chapter 9 for more on the unions.

Add the inflated cost of using union people to the enormous charges already incurred by the studios for its own fees, costs, overhead, and interest, and you understand why "studio picture" has come to mean expensive. An average studio picture costs in the neighborhood of $26 million to produce, with an additional $10 to $15 million to promote and distribute. The classic studio picture has been structured, or set up, in much the same way since the beginning of the industry. Up until a project is approved, or *greenlighted,* the studio *absorbs* (pays for) all costs associated with the project, including the cost of buying the book, script, or life story and hiring the writers, along with possible fees for the producer who brought in the project. As soon as the project comes in the door (meaning the studio has either purchased or optioned the story), it's considered to be in *development.*

A studio will have a number of projects in different stages of development at one time. It's not unusual for a major studio to have more than one hundred projects in some stage of readiness at one time, and perhaps 10 percent of those will actually make it to production (and only 10 percent of *those* will ever see a profit). The studio also absorbs all overhead, i.e., costs of running the studio as well as the costs for the staff who work on the project, such as secretaries, lawyers, and creative executives.

Once an executive at the studio who has the power (usually

the president of production) decides to go forward on a project, a budget is set up. The budget will include all the known costs, such as the literary material and any creative talent already attached. The budget also includes negative costs, which are all costs the studio anticipates it will incur in preparing, filming, and editing the film until it has a completed negative.

Negative Costs

The negative of a production is like the negative of a photograph. When you take a picture with your camera, the film is exposed to light and the image is imprinted on the negative, which can then be processed and made into a photograph. Likewise, when a film or TV project is shot, you get a negative of the film. Negative costs include all costs of film production, including added sound, music, and special effects.

The studio adds a huge expense to every project, in the form of distribution fees, costs, interest, and overhead, which is another reason why studio pictures are so profoundly expensive. In the past, studios generally financed their own productions. However, the recent trend is for some of the studios to get outside financing, since the studios have been suffering cash-flow problems because of the mergers and acquisitions that have driven their debts so high. The important thing to understand about a studio production is that everyone who works on the project is hired directly by the studio, most of those hired for the project belong to a union, and the studio pays for the whole thing, or at least arranges for its own financing.

NEGATIVE PICKUPS

We'll discuss some of the many variations on the structure known as a *negative pickup*, but essentially it implies that a project is completely financed, filmed, and edited outside and independently of the studio. The term originated from the fact that a completed negative (picture, sound, music, special effects, titles, credits) ready for duplication and distribution is literally delivered to the studio by the producer. This structure was developed for a number of purposes. First, the studios have offices all over the world to get their own product into distribution, and the distribution systems are only efficient if they are used. In other words, it doesn't make sense to keep an office open in Peru if the studio doesn't have product for its staff in that country to promote and sell. Acquiring negative pickups keeps the studio pipeline fed. A studio can increase its production from ten to fifteen films a year to twenty-five or more, plus add a movie of the week or television series to its catalog, through negative-pickup deals.

There are some companies, like the late, great Orion, that have bigger distribution networks than they can feed, either by design or inheritance of another company's distribution system through the endless games of merger and acquisition that occur constantly in Hollywood. These companies function primarily by acquiring product through negative pickups, rather than making their own product.

Another great reason for a studio to deal in negative pickups is that, by their very definition, they are not made by the studio, and therefore such productions do not have to employ a union crew. As we've discussed previously, using non-union people can reduce the production costs enormously. Even if the lead actors and director are union people, a production company that is formed for the sole purpose of doing negative pickups can make a separate deal with the Screen Actors Guild. They don't have to employ union camera people, teamsters, and others. A studio film with a negative cost of $25 million could cost half that or less without union involvement. Of course, this issue has engendered tremendous acrimony from the unions, and from time to time, you'll read about one of the unions picketing some production company you've never heard of.

There are other reasons a production might be done as a negative pickup, not all of which are kosher. There was a period of time in the 1950s to 1970s when enormous tax shelters were available for investors in motion pictures, so a slew of companies located in Guam, the Philippines, and the Bahamas sprang up— most of them with American and European investors (who never stepped foot in these countries) behind them. These tax loopholes have been closed up over the years, though there's always room for financial creativity in the entertainment business.

Sometimes a studio has reason to be nervous about doing productions in foreign countries. The country may be hostile toward America for reasons that have nothing to do with Hollywood. In these cases, an American company won't get cooperation from the locals or be able to get its film and equipment out without paying exorbitant surcharges. Under these circumstances, a studio may arrange to have an independent company play the advance role in dealing with the country's government and businesses. The independent company has a different name from the studio, and the studio hopes that will make the production less vulnerable to attack.

NEGATIVE-PICKUP DEALS

The basic negative-pickup deal is relatively simple. The concept is that the studio reimburses the production company for the negative cost of the picture, then distributes the picture for a period of time in the territory that has been agreed upon. Generally the production company will share in some form of the profits the studio makes, after the studio pays itself back for the negative cost and the distribution costs. The profit participations are much like the schemes we describe in chapter 17. These deals can get complicated. It's not unusual for a studio to advance the production company some or all of the money to make the picture. However, it's still considered a negative pickup because theoretically the studio is not exercising control over the production; but as you might imagine, the rules often shift when the studio has actually put out some money up front. The studio lawyers put in a lot more approvals as well as liens on the negative (which gives the studio ownership in the exposed film), in case the production falls apart. Legions of studio executives start appearing on the set. The current favorite directors, production managers, and stars are signed on. Suddenly this little negative pickup starts to look suspiciously like a studio production, and then the unions start screaming. The negative pickup has simply become a cheaper way for the studio to make a picture without losing control.

———

Completion Bonds

One way to tell if a project is a true negative pickup—and not a facade to hide the studio involvement—is whether or not the production has acquired a completion bond. If a production is really independent, it must usually borrow the money from someone other than a studio to complete the picture. Very few individuals have that kind of money, and if they do, it's because they know better than to try to finance a production out of their own pocket.

The source of the backing can be banks, individuals, or companies set up specifically to supply credit to the film industry, such as Credit Lyonnais. In order to secure these loans, a producer must often purchase a form of insurance that guarantees that the picture will be completed even if something goes wrong. To obtain this protection, the producer will go to a company that specializes in this form of insurance.

The completion-bond company will enter into an agreement with the production company that states that for a fee (usually 6 percent of the overall budget), the company will guarantee to supply the funds to complete the picture. In exchange, the completion-bond company is given strict controls over the production and the right to take over production if it looks to them like the production is in trouble.

For example, if the company is going over budget, the director seems reckless, or a lead actor gets sick, the completion-bond company can literally take over the picture and complete it. When the film The Adventures of Baron Munchausen *got into financial difficulties and its budget started to go out of control, the completion-bond company had to step in and make decisions that got the film completed. The bond company would prefer to avoid taking over a film, since it's run by money people rather than movie people, but its job is to protect the investors.*

Acquiring a completion bond adds a rather large expense to the cost of a negative pickup, but it's what ultimately makes most of these productions possible, since a true arms-length investor wants a guarantee that someone is minding the store.

ARTICLE 20

Someday you might be dining—or waiting tables—at the current "in" restaurant in town and overhear someone using the phrase "Article 20" when referring to a project. This is another deal structure the studios have developed primarily to avoid having to use union people while still maintaining control of the project. It relates to both movie and TV production.

_____

Article 20

Article 20 refers to an exception in the union agreement the studios have with IATSE (International Alliance of Theatrical Stage Employees), the union that represents many of the crew people. The Article states that the studios' policy is not to evade unions or to offer union people less favorable terms than they'd get from the union.

Having stated the principle, this language allows the studio to do just the opposite, by letting the studio finance a production company that doesn't have to follow the union agreements. In other words, it's a rule that was made to be broken.

_____

How does Article 20 work? Essentially, the studio sets up a company for the sole purpose of completing one project. Since the company is not a union signatory, it can make its own deals with the unions, usually at more favorable rates; meanwhile, the studio finances the whole thing. The production company is the titular decision maker, while the studio maintains virtually total control over the project. This structure is especially useful for producing non-union pictures in the United States, because it allows a studio presence on the set as opposed to a negative-pickup situation, in which the studio is not supposed to provide direct oversight.

Usually the Article-20 structure calls for an outside law firm, i.e., not the regular studio legal staff, to prepare the paperwork. This way the studio can maintain the facade that the production company, which is more often than not set up solely for this one project, is really running things. A *financing agreement* is made, which states that certain funds will be loaned to the production company with the understanding that the studio financier owns the film upon delivery, along with a *production agreement,* which looks a lot like a negative-pickup deal. The latter sets up certain conditions, concerning such matters as the script and the creative talent, which must be delivered to the studio on certain dates.

Article-20 deals have been very popular for the last ten years or so in Hollywood, providing a constant source of irritation and embarrassment for the unions, which naturally look upon them as a breach of solidarity. The current trend seems to allow key players to enjoy all or most of their union benefits—regardless of whether they participate in an Article-20 production—including pension, health and welfare benefits, the same amount of time off for lunch as other union members, and overtime.

INDEPENDENT PRODUCTIONS

As we've discussed, most established producers either work for the studios or arrange to have their projects financed through studio deals of one kind or another. For true independents, or those who do work that is out of the mainstream, the negative pickup is a viable way to get financing. Whether or not the studio loans money up front, the independent producer can sometimes use the distribution deal it makes with a studio to obtain financing from banks or other sources.

It's almost impossible to distribute a film yourself, since it's incredibly costly and the studios also control exhibition—that is, the method of getting pictures into neighborhood theaters. We'll discuss some of the challenges of the exhibition market below.

People who are starting out sometimes make their first movies on credit cards and family loans. The trade papers occasionally report about someone who's made a pretty good film for a small fraction of what a studio film costs, and who then gets a studio or a mini major to *pick it up* (a term derived from the negative pickup) and get it into the theaters. It's a way to get started on a shoestring, and for those who do offbeat or sensitive material, it may be the only way to put something together. While maxing out your credit and pawning the family jewels may not be the wisest idea, as a strategy it reminds us that the studios are not the only game in town. Almost anyone can rent a camera and get some actors to help them tell a story. After all, that's what it's all about, isn't it?

Want Someone to Finance Your Film?
Here's What You'll Have to Bring to the Party

Whether you get financed by a negative pickup, an Article 20, or any variation of the above, if you want to produce a project yourself and have someone else pick up the tab, here is a list of things you'll probably have to bring to the financier for approval:

1. An approved screenplay.
2. A valid budget for the picture, based on the approved screenplay, presented in a budget format the financier approves.
3. A completed storyboard and/or script breakdown. These are fairly detailed. The financier wants to see drawings of how the picture will look from scene to scene, or at least a breakdown of how it will be shot, which we described in chapter 2.
4. A production schedule with a projection of the cash flow required for the picture's entire production. The schedule sets various dates from the start of production and photography until completion and delivery of the picture: tentative Start Date for principal photography, dates for director's cut completion, date for completion

of dubbing and scoring, and date for delivery of the completed picture.

5. Contracts which document the engagement of a production auditor and unit production manager, both of whom must be approved by the financier. This agreement can get very sticky, as the financier will probably want to put the financier's person on the job. After all, the auditor and unit production manager control the purse strings.

6. Evidence that you have acquired all right, title, and interest in and to the picture and all literary material upon which the picture shall be based. This evidence is absolutely critical. No one with any experience will touch a project unless there are clear rights to make the picture and fully exploit the rights to the material. Check out chapter 15 for more on rights.

7. A laboratory agreement with a laboratory the financier approves. This usually gives the financier access to the negative and controls the access others are given to the film.

8. Certificates of insurance which prove you've acquired the proper insurance in connection with the rights, liability, and cast.

9. Signed agreements with certain creative talents, such as the executive producer, director, and principal cast.

10. A signed financing agreement, if there's more than one source of funding—and sometimes a completion bond, if it's a true negative pickup.

MARKETING AND EXHIBITION

The studios not only control the bulk of motion-picture production and distribution in this country, they also exercise control over theaters and theater chains in most markets, not to mention sales to television, cable, and airlines. This is partly because they have the most product and the most money to promote it, which in turn gives them the most muscle to get theater operators to look at their product first.

MARKETING

The marketing divisions of studios are generally powerful and often fairly independent from the production arm. As a film is developed and produced, the marketing department will start building its strategy for marketing the product. Since the marketing can cost half again as much as the production itself, this is a serious business. Decisions are made as to what kind of release the picture should have. Will it be a blockbuster, opening simultaneously in 1500 theaters? Is it a small film that needs time to find its audience, with a limited open in a few-hundred theaters? Is it a terrible bomb? If it is a loser, should the studio make 1500 prints and get the most saturation for the two or three weeks it will be in the theater, or should the picture be *shelved?*

The marketing department will prepare a *campaign* for each picture, creating all material to promote the film. The films are usually audience tested, through advertised *sneak previews* or in Hollywood at the Preview House, where people view the nearly completed film and give their comments. It's from these early previews that the marketing department prepares and adjusts the campaign. Marketing plans include posters, advertising in newspapers and magazines, and trailers for television and movie theaters. The campaign will change as the movie gets closer to *release,* and will be adjusted again as the marketing department figures out what it has. Sometimes, particularly in the cases of *big*-budget blockbusters, the studio will have a "making of" film made for distribution on television. All of the marketing material prepared will be approved and reapproved by the studio and the creative talents who have contractual approval provisions. See chapter 17 for a discussion of some of the approval rights creative talent can obtain with regard to marketing.

EXHIBITION

Each studio negotiates the terms of distribution with theaters for each picture. The theaters take in money at the box office and return a percentage to the studios. The average amount the theater keeps of the box-office receipts is about 50 percent, but theaters may keep only 10 percent of the box office of big movies in their first weeks of distribution, with their take increasing as the weeks go by. The big money for most theaters comes from selling candy and popcorn: They generally get to keep all the money they take in from those $4.00 boxes of popcorn. We discussed the specifics of how distributors set up deals with theaters in chapter 17.

Blind Bidding

Sometimes the studios tacitly encourage theater operators to take their not-so-good product by promising to give (or withhold) their successful product. Is this legal? Not really, but it happens. There are government regulations prohibiting studios from exercising such tactics as blind bidding, *in which studios force the theaters to make bids on films they haven't seen, in order to get the films they know they want. Of course, the studios carefully train their marketing people to avoid the appearance—if not the fact—of unfair practices.*

The government has also attempted to prevent studio monopolies by forcing the studios to sell their movie theaters (known as the *Paramount Decree*, after the studio that got nailed first). Until recently, the Paramount Decree was a fairly effective way for the government to limit the domination of the studios by taking away their control of the means of distribution. For almost forty years, at least in this country, movie theaters were owned independently, which gave the independent producers some chance of getting their product into good theaters, although the studios still dominated due to their sheer size and their volume of output in the market. The Paramount Decree is now history, falling to the deregulation craze of the latter 1980s.

Now that studios are buying up movie theaters again with the government's blessing, many independents are forced to seek distribution through the studio system or turn to the venue of "art houses," which simply don't have the clout to compete. Great films often rise to the top, no matter how humble their beginnings, but they won't make money, at least good money, unless they get booked into a theater people want to patronize. It's one of the factors that makes distribution a tough game to play. After initial theatrical release, films are distributed internationally country by country. After that, they may be distributed in videocassette or put together in packages and sold in groups to television networks, cable companies, and airlines. There are antitrust rules in force with regard to these deals as well, but the studios have more freedom to sell their duds along with their hits by putting them together in one package. Of course, some films don't get packaged or put out on home video at all. Disney has made multiple fortunes by holding its classic full-length animated features back from the market, then re-releasing them in theaters every decade or so as each new generation gets introduced to jewels in the Disney crown.

CHAPTER TWENTY-ONE

Television Production

Just as there are a variety of ways motion-picture deals may be structured, there are a number of ways that television productions are put together and the product distributed. Note that when we talk about television deals here, we mean network TV and syndication as well as cable; in fact, we include anything that you can see on that living-room screen. Programs produced directly for the home-video market are produced in similar ways, though for now they are distributed through video stores, as opposed to some form of broadcast. As with movies, sometimes the means of production and distribution are still controlled by the same people, due to the relaxation of many government regulations that have shaped the business in the past. Television in particular is rapidly changing, because of new technology and the growth of new markets.

That Highway in the Sky

As a side note, it's not clear how the so-called information highway will affect the entertainment industry when we get those promised

500 channels feeding into our TVs or computers, which perhaps may someday serve as TVs. As of the writing of this book, this market hasn't matured.

However, agents, creative talent, and studio executives are starting to make regular pilgrimages to Seattle and the San Francisco Bay Area, the homes of the multimedia boom; and the entertainment industry is romancing computer-industry giants. The major studios are, meanwhile, all launching interactive divisions to exploit their own properties. It's our guess that to the extent the computer industry wants to reach mass audiences, it will seek out the successful players in entertainment, and the deals will evolve based on variations on the themes we've discussed here. Of course, entertainment players will move in to the computer world as soon as it can deliver audience. Many of the skills of the entertainment business seem to be transferable, so the net result should be more work for a lot of people.

A television program may be produced by a studio, a network, a cable company, or an independent production company, but the creator of the product is not necessarily the distributor or the exhibitor. To describe the means of distribution and exhibition, we'll give you a very non-technical explanation of how the signals get into your home, and then we'll discuss the ways deals are structured.

BROADCAST TELEVISION

An individual city station will have a broadcast signal that it delivers from its tower: The stronger the signal, the farther it reaches and the more people it will reach. Before the newer technology of cable delivery, most people used an antenna to catch the signal and bring it to their TV. If the station is an *affiliate*, it means it has some arrangement with the major networks, ABC, CBS, NBC, Fox or, most recently, WB (Warner Bros. Network) or UPN (United Paramount Network), to carry the programs that the network has produced or licensed. The first networks in the country were radio networks that sprang up when it became technically possible to send programs simultaneously to local stations through telephone-wire hookups.

One significant way a network makes money is by selling national advertising time. There are ratings services that keep tabs of how many people are watching particular programs: The bigger the audience, the higher the ratings, and the higher the ratings, the more money the network makes from selling advertising time. Because traditionally the networks had lots of affiliates (though this market is shifting with the growth of cable), a network could cover a huge amount of territory and reach enormous audiences. Since the networks could guarantee a big audience, they attracted the large accounts of the biggest advertisers. The network affiliates agree to carry the advertising in exchange for having the right to broadcast the network programming, in an arrangement that is referred to as *barter*.

A local station, even if it's an affiliate, makes its money by selling local advertising time. For every 30-minute network program, perhaps twenty-two minutes will be actual programming, and the rest will be advertising. Of the eight minutes of advertising, the network will have the right to use a certain amount of that time for the national advertising they've sold, and what's left over the local station can sell. There are variations on this arrangement, and the networks and affiliates all have different revenue-sharing arrangements (often depending on the size of the market); but this is basically how it works.

Another way networks make money is to own their own local affiliates. The FCC has traditionally regulated these areas. The network may own a half-dozen or so *O & Os* (owned and operated by the network). Typically the O & Os are in major markets, and the networks make money from the national and the local ads as well.

We'll talk about networks as producers (as opposed to distributors) of programming below.

CABLE TELEVISION

Cable stations deliver their programs through the cable hooked up to your home. Local cable operators make their money by providing the cable equipment that carries the signal to your home and charging you a monthly fee for service. Local cable operators are separate entities from the national cable services that supply programming. If the cable service is national, the programming will be delivered to a satellite which sends the signal to dishes owned by local cable operators. The local operators then pick them up and transmit them via cable to your home. Of course, some people have purchased their own satellite dishes, which are becoming more widely available to the consumer market.

When a supplier licenses the right to a cable service to show its programs, it typically does so for a limited number of runs. For example, a movie may be part of a package that is sold for distribution via cable. The deal might allow for eleven runs of the picture over a certain period of time (sometimes referred to as a *flight*). The national cable services may sell national advertising based on the size of the audience they can deliver, and they may charge the cable subscriber a fee to receive their programming. The FCC (Federal Communications Commission) currently requires cable services to allow the community a certain amount of public access to use the cable service, which is a public service. Public-access programming is basically amateur and uncensored. It's the only place on TV where your Aunt Emily can show off her tap-dancing skills, and even though it's unpolished, it can be a lot of fun to watch.

SYNDICATION

Another way television gets distributed and exhibited is through syndication. In syndication, owners of programming will license distribution rights to local stations. The programs are sold locally, one city at a time, so they're not broadcast simultaneously from one place. The trend is to sell programs to station groups so, for example, the syndicator Chris Craft will license the rights to a series for all of its stations in one deal. Programming typically includes series that have initially run on the networks and that are ready to be *stripped* on local stations. A deal might allow a syndicator to run reruns of *I Love Lucy* five days a week or ten times a week. This explains why *I Love Lucy* may run at 2 P.M. in Cleveland and 2 A.M. in Cincinnati, or twice a day (or more) in other markets.

Other programming is developed specifically for syndication, either for unaffiliated stations or for affiliates during their non-*prime-time* hours (before 8 P.M. and after 11 P.M., give or take an hour, depending on the market). *Entertainment Tonight* was developed by Paramount specifically for syndication; it runs at a different time in each city, so the local programmers can place it wherever they want in the schedule. Like networks, the show's producer keeps a certain amount of air time for national advertising sales, giving the rest to local stations to sell. Originally, this system created a way for producers to form their own loose networks. Aside from producing programming, syndicators may also own some stations.

Financial Syndication Rules

Studios and independent production companies are no longer the only sellers in the syndication game. The FCC has recently lifted its re-

strictions on the networks prohibiting them from owning the program-
ming they broadcast. Why should the networks pay a license fee,
usually substantial, to have a program produced, then not get the right
to own it? Historically, the reason was that the FCC created financial
interest in syndication *(sometimes abbreviated as* fin syn*) rules.*

The fin syn rules were designed to prevent the networks from
controlling and dominating the entire industry, which they did for
the first twenty years or so of television. Much like the Paramount
Decree we discussed previously, fin syn was a way to prevent monopo-
lies in the entertainment industry. However, with the advent of cable,
the networks' dominance decreased significantly, and the government
recently relaxed fin syn rules. By retaining ownership, the studios
have the right to sell reruns to syndication. Now the networks can be
in the same game. As this book is being written, ABC is developing
a production-distribution deal with the recently formed company of
DreamWorks SKG.

———

Now that we've discussed some ways the signals get into
your home, we'll discuss the companies that make the product.

WHO PRODUCES TELEVISION?

Who produces television? There are many players in the television business. Four major sources produce the majority of the
television programming: the studios, the networks, independent
producers, and local cable and broadcast stations. The productions may be directed toward creating an ongoing television
series or one-shot programs, usually referred to as *long-form*
programming, either made-for-TV movies or miniseries.

STUDIOS
Most of the major studios do some form of television production.
They have executives who come up with ideas—or hire inde-

pendent contractors who come up with ideas—and then pitch these ideas to buyers such as the networks. Studios like Fox, Warner, and Paramount, which have started networks of their own, are distributing their new and old product nationally through local affiliates. When a network buys a program from a studio, it pays the studio a license fee to produce the series in exchange for the exclusive rights to broadcast the *first run* of the series on their network and a limited number of reruns. In a series situation, the network will agree to pay a per-episode fee and order a number of episodes, anywhere from just the pilot to the whole season (approximately twenty-two episodes). These licenses come with the rights to a certain amount of reruns.

The license fee virtually never covers the entire cost of production, unless the program is a big hit. When the fee doesn't cover the cost, the studio will *deficit finance* the production in the hope that the program will have enough episodes for a post-network afterlife in syndication or on the cable services. If the program does hit big, the producer generally renegotiates its deal with the network, usually after the fourth season, so that the license fee exceeds production costs.

Traditionally, the studio has remained the owner of the property so, after the initial run, the rights revert to the studio so it can arrange other distribution. If the show is a hit and lasts long enough to accumulate a certain number of episodes (one hundred seems to be the magic number these days), the studio can sell the series *off network* into syndication or cable. If the series has accumulated fewer than one hundred episodes, it can sometimes be sold to cable, but it's generally a hard sell.

NETWORK AND CABLE PRODUCTION

Even before the relaxation of the government regulations of product ownership, the networks had been producing their own programming. Now that they can own the distribution rights, they have been more active in creating their own programming. A network such as NBC will have its own creative executives come up with program ideas that they pitch to their own business people. If they sell the idea, they will commence production pretty much as a studio does. Of course, the networks must pay for the entire cost of production. Because the network or cable service has the right to sell it into syndication or to other media, they have developed sales forces much like those of the studios.

INDEPENDENT PRODUCTION COMPANIES

Since Lucille Ball and Desi Arnaz started Desilu Productions, there has been a strong tradition of independent production companies in television. These companies are often organized around a star such as Lucy, a very successful writer such as Matt Williams of *Home Improvement* and *Roseanne*, or a team of producers such as Marcey Carsey and Tom Werner or Paul Junger Witt and Tony Thomas. These are separate entities who contract with the studios, networks, and cable networks to make product. They'll often initiate their own programming and sell it to the highest bidder, which gives some of these companies a large amount of creative control. Some of them even have the clout to retain the licensing rights to their properties, which makes them major players in the game.

LOCAL TELEVISION

Local stations produce their own programming as well, generally for their local market. It's not unusual to see some sort of afternoon or evening magazine-type of program, a local host presenting an afternoon movie and, of course, local newscasts. Typically, these programs are not of enough interest to be sold to any other markets, but they keep people employed and out of the Hollywood rat race.

CHAPTER TWENTY-TWO

The Marketplace

Business is done everywhere in Hollywood, from studio offices to restaurants to athletic clubs. There are also some public venues where the game is played, such as film festivals, film and television markets, and conventions.

FESTIVALS AND MARKETS

You've seen the girls in bikinis at the Cannes Film Festival on the French Riviera. For every bikini-clad starlet, there are dozens of people at the festival trying to buy or sell product. Festivals such as Cannes are major marketplaces, especially for people who aren't working in the mainstream studio system. Producers and distributors rent screening rooms, distribute flyers, buy advertising space, and make a point of being seen at the restaurants with the hope that they'll attract buyers for their product. The same thing happens at MIFED (Fiera Internationale de Milano) in Milan, Italy, though the focus on this festival is television product. U.S. companies take the opportunity at Milan to sell their product into the foreign markets, which are an ever-growing marketplace for American product. That's why stars of shows such as *Beverly Hills 90210* get mobbed when they make appearances in Europe.

There are some film festivals of note in the U.S., such as the ones held yearly at Robert Redford's Sundance Film Institute, Telluride, in Seattle, and other cities. Winning an award at a festival gives a project some visibility, and a great deal of industry interest can be generated by making the scene at one of these events.

NATPE/NAB

The National Association of Television and Program Executives deserves particular attention, as it's become the chief U.S. marketplace for television programming other than network sales. The venue for this convention changes every year. New shows are launched there with lots of fanfare, and buyers are wined, dined, and sweet-talked into buying product. Syndication product is sold at the NAB, National Association of Broadcasters.

AFFILIATE MEETINGS

The networks put on elaborate yearly affiliate meetings, where new programming is introduced, and affiliates are pumped up to carry the network product for another season. There are lots of free buffets and plenty of hype, plus maybe the chance for affiliate personnel to meet their favorite network talent.

EPILOGUE

Final Thoughts

This book came out of our discussions about what it took to make it in Hollywood and stay healthy and happy after finding your niche. We have many friends who have fallen out of the game, either because they were naïve coming in or didn't know the ropes when opportunities arose. We wanted to teach the basics and explain some of the more complicated aspects of the business.

If you've learned anything, it might be that the business is huge and diverse, offering lots of opportunity and more than its fair share of heartbreak. As someone once said (we think it was Tallulah Bankhead), Hollywood doesn't make talent—it breaks talent. This is a chilling thought. Of course, not everybody goes for the golden ring of stardom or a high rank in the Hollywood pecking order. Plenty of people manage to live in Los Angeles and go to work at a studio or production company every day, with life and health insurance, families who recognize them when they come home, and a more-or-less normal life. Other people buy movie theaters, and still others just go to the movies, which is probably the thing that sparked their desire to get to Hollywood in the first place.

Final Thoughts

What we've learned is that surviving and perhaps thriving depends a lot upon how seriously you take yourself, your patience, and how hard you're willing to work. Of course, it helps a great deal if you're in love with the movies and television and seduced by the lure of Hollywood.

APPENDIX

Suggested Reading List

The best way to find out what's currently happening in the industry is to read the trade papers and other industry resources we discussed in chapter 5. The reading material here includes biographies and personal accounts of life in the industry, along with some further references you might find helpful.

BOOKS ABOUT THE CRAFT OF ACTING

Sanford Meisner On Acting by Sanford Meisner.

Thousands have tried to imitate his approach to acting, but few have achieved his success in teaching actors their craft.

Stanislavsky on the Art of the Stage translated by David Magarshack.

Much of the current approach to acting in America is due to Stanislavsky and his search for theatrical truth. Hollywood actors would be wise to also heed his advice about *developing* the ethics to succeed.

Konstantin Stanislavsky: Selected Works compiled by Oksana Korneva.

More gems of wisdom from this great teacher. Also useful reading is a trilogy of books by Stanislavsky: *An Actor Prepares, Building a Character,* and *Creating a Role.*

The Divine Pastime, Lies Like Truth, and *The Naked Image* by Harold Clurman.

Three books of essays that reveal Clurman's remarkable insights into theatrical values and principles.

The Way of the Artist by Julie Cameron.

Good reading for any artist, this book provides a twelve-week program for developing your creative sensibilities.

Other books on acting include *Lessons for the Professional Actor* and *To the Actor on the Technique of Acting* by Michael Chekhov; *On Actors and the Art of Acting* by George Henry Lewes; *Method or Madness* and *Advice to the Players* by Robert Lewis; *The Actor's Eye* by Morris Carnovsky; *Acting: The First Six Lessons* by Richard Boleslavsky; *Actors on Acting* edited by Toby Cole and Helen Krich Chinoy; *The Technique of Acting* by Stella Adler; *A Dream of Passion, the Development of the Method* by Lee Strasberg; *Respect for Acting* by Uta Hagen; *American Film Acting, the Stanislavsky Heritage* by Richard A. Blum; *On Screen Acting* by Edward and Jean Porter Dmytryk; *Conversations with Brando* by Lawrence Grobel; and *Acting in Film* by Michael Caine.

SCREENWRITING
Adventures in the Screen Trade by William Goldman.
> This and any other book by Goldman offers a wealth of experience and anecdotes about writing in Hollywood.

The Screenwriter Looks at the Screenwriter and *The New Screenwriter Looks at the New Screenwriter* compiled by William Froug.
> Two books of interviews with many of Hollywood's best screenwriters.

Although there is a specific structure that screenwriters usually follow, the success of a screenplay still depends upon the strength of its story, the development of its characters, and the power of its dialogue. Any aspiring screenwriter would be wise to read a healthy dose of the great dramatic literature. This would include plays by such American writers as Eugene O'Neill, Tennessee Williams, Arthur Miller, Clifford Odets, Maxwell Anderson, Thornton Wilder, William Saroyan, Lillian Hellman, William Inge, David Mamet; and foreign writers such as Henrik Ibsen, August Strindberg, Anton Chekhov, Maxim Gorky, John M. Synge, Oscar Wilde, and George Bernard Shaw. John Gassner's *Masters of the Drama* provides a useful guide to these playwrights.

Also good on the techniques of writing are: *Dramatic Technique* by G.P. Baker, *Theory and Technique of Playwriting* by John Howard Lawson, *The Playwrights Speak* edited by Walter Wager, and *Playwrights on Playwriting* edited by Toby Cole.

EDITING
When the Shooting Stops by Ralph Rosenblum.
> Chock full of stories about Mr. Rosenblum's successful career as an editor.

DIRECTING
Great Directors at Work: Stanislavsky, Brecht, Kazan, Brook by David Richard Jones.
> Film and TV directors would be wise to go back to their theatrical roots

to learn how to work with actors. This book talks about four of the best directors and how they brought out the best in their actors.

Kazan on Kazan by Michel Ciment.
   If you're a director, any book on Kazan is worth reading.
Stanislavsky Directs by Nikolai M. Gorchakov.
   Stanislavsky was a great director as well as actor, and his passion for the craft is evident in anything you read about him.
On Directing by Harold Clurman.
   Clurman directed himself and worked with many great directors. Although most of his comments are about stage directing, many are applicable to the screen.
I Was Interrupted: Nicholas Ray on Making Movies by Nicholas Ray.
The Genius: A Memoir of Max Reinhardt by Gottfried Reinhardt.
John Ford: The Man and his Films by Tag Gallagher.
Scorsese On Scorsese edited by David Thompson and Ian Christie.

PRODUCING

The Industry: Life in the Hollywood Fast Lane by Saul David.
Behind the Scenes by Rudy Behlmer.
Reel Power: The Struggle for Influence and Success in the New Hollywood by Mark Litwak.
The Power and the Glitter: The Hollywood-Washington Connection by Ronald Brownstein.
You'll Never Eat Lunch in This Town Again by Julia Phillips.
Spiegel: The Man Behind the Pictures by Andrew Sinclair.
Adventures in the Screen Trade by William Goldman.
The Deal by Peter Lefcourt.
They Can Kill You, but They Can't Eat You by Dawn Steele.
Working in Hollywood by Alexandra Brouwer and Thomas Lee Wright.
   Good descriptions of the different careers in Hollywood and interviews with seasoned professionals in each field.

MUSIC BUSINESS

All You Need to Know about the Music Business by Donald Passman. There is a lot of crossover between the entertainment industry and the music business, and this book does a great job explaining the practical and legal ins and outs of the music field.

LAW

The Entertainment Law Reporter edited by Lon Sobel. Covers current case law in the entertainment and sports industries.

Both USC and UCLA host legal and business seminars about various aspects of the business. The handbooks which are regularly published as part of the seminars are great sources of contracts and discussions of current issues in the business.

The Practicing Law Institute publishes entertainment law contracts. Check out your local law library in L.A.

SELF HELP BOOKS AND BOOKS ON THE CHARACTER TRAITS OF SUCCESS

The 7 Habits of Highly Effective People by Stephen R. Covey.

If you read any book about character, this is the one to read. If you apply his principles to your own life, you will give yourself the best chance for success.

The Book of Virtues by William J. Bennett.

Mr. Bennett has assembled stories throughout the ages on character and virtue.

On Character and *The Moral Sense* by James Q. Wilson.

The former is collected essays on principles. The latter is about right and wrong. Having a good moral compass in Hollywood is an absolute necessity.

First Things First and *Principle-Centered Leadership* by Stephen R. Covey.

The former book expands on Covey's first book *The 7 Habits of Highly Effective People*. The latter applies Covey's principles to leadership roles, and is therefore good reading for producers, directors, and anyone else in a leadership position in the business.

Think and Grow Rich by Napoleon Hill.

One of the best self-help books for a long time. An excellent updated version of this book is entitled *Think and Grow Rich: A Black Choice* by Dennis Kimbro and Napoleon Hill.

The Content of Our Character by Shelby Steele.

A National Book Critics Circle award winner.

Life Work by Donald Hall.

A testimony to the value of hard work.

You Gotta Believe! by Drew T. Brown, III.

A book that inspires by stating the simple truths about life.

Dumbth by Steve Allen.

Comedian Steve Allen has written over forty books, and this one has a lot to say that you could make use of in fashioning your career.

BIOGRAPHIES AND AUTOBIOGRAPHIES TO INSPIRE AND TEACH YOU

We've included some of our favorites here, but just about any book about people who have achieved success in their particular field will be helpful for learning how to fashion your own life.

It Would Be So Nice if You Weren't Here by Charles Grodin.

Mr. Grodin tells you how his persistence and hard work paid off during his successful acting career. Also includes lots of helpful hints about breaking into the business.

A Life by Elia Kazan.

Great insights into life, acting, and directing by the director of such film classics as *On the Waterfront, East of Eden,* and the original stage productions of *Streetcar Named Desire* and *Death of a Salesman,* among many others.

My Life in Art by Konstantin Stanislavsky and *Stanislavsky, a Biography* by Jean Benedetti.

Books about the great Russian actor/director, which provide an inspiring account of how one man changed the course of theatrical history. His approach has had a profound effect on directing and acting in this country.

The Fervent Years by Harold Clurman and *Real Life Drama* by Wendy Smith.

The former book is the story of the Group Theater, by one of its founders. The latter is the best book written about this historic group. No other theater group in America has created as original and vibrant work as the Group Theater or left as large a legacy through the work of its members, such as Elia Kazan, Sanford Meisner, Lee Strasberg, Stella Adler, Clifford Odets, and others.

All People Are Famous by Harold Clurman.

In this autobiography Clurman writes not only about himself but also about many of the great artists he worked with.

Brando by Charles Higham.

Good material on how Brando's early work ethic contributed to his stunning success as an actor.

Laurence Olivier: A Biography by Donald Spoto.

Good material on what led Olivier to be the most celebrated English actor of his time.

The Mystic in the Theatre by Eva Le Gallienne.

Any biography about the legendary actress, Eleonora Duse, is worth reading.

Laurette by Marguerite Courtney.

You may not remember this great American actress, Laurette Taylor, but she went through more cycles in her career than a washing machine. Good reading also for documenting the destructiveness of drugs to one's career.

Other biographies about stage greats include: *Slings and Arrows* by Group Theater member Robert Lewis; *The Fabulous Lunts,* about husband and wife greats Alfred Lunt and Lynn Fontanne, by Jared Brown; *Chaliapin,* about Stanislavsky's idol, by Victor Borovsky; *Sarah Siddons: Portrait of an Actress,* about the great English tragic actress, by Roger Manvell; *My Life in the*

Russian Theatre by Stanislavsky's partner, Vladimir Nemirovitch-Dantchenko; *If You Don't Dance They Beat You* by director Jose Quintero; *The Divine Sarah: A Life of Sarah Bernhardt*, about Duse's rival, by Arthur Gold and Robert Fizdale; *One Naked Individual* by Group Theater co-founder Cheryl Crawford; *Tragic Muse: Rachel of the Comédie-Française*, about the great French nineteenth-century actress, by Rachel M. Brownstein; *Ellen Terry and Her Secret Self*, about the great English actress, by her son Edward Gordon Craig; *Gordon Craig: The Story of His Life*, about the theatrical visionary, by Edward Craig; *The Flash of Lightning: A Portrait of Edmund Kean*, about the remarkable Shakespearean actor, by Giles Playfair; *Prince of Players, Edwin Booth*, one of America's first great actors, by Eleanor Ruggles; *Garrick*, about one of the top dogs of eighteenth-century English stage, by Margaret Barton; *Mr. Macready, 19th Century Tragedian*, about another product of the fertile English stage, by J.C. Trewin; and *The House of Barrymore* about the American theatrical family that keeps on ticking, by Margot Peters.

A partial list of biographies and autobiographies of film stars includes: *Shelley: Also Known as Shirley* by Shelley Winters; *Montgomery Clift* by Patricia Bosworth; *Steve McQueen: Portrait of an American Rebel* by Marshall Terrill; *Life is Too Short* by Mickey Rooney; *Cary Grant: The Lonely Heart* by Charles Higham; *The Ragman's Son* by Kirk Douglas; *Life on the Wire: The Life and Art of Al Pacino* by Andrew Yule; *Robert Duvall: Hollywood Maverick* by Judith Slawson; and *What's It All About?* by Michael Caine.

GENERAL BIOGRAPHIES ON GREAT ARTISTS

Rodin, a Biography by Frederic V. Grumfeld.

Much can be learned by studying artists in other media and Auguste Rodin is one of history's best sculptors.

Martha: The Life and Work of Martha Graham by Agnes De Mille.

The choreographer who single-handedly revolutionized the dance world.

Education of a Wandering Man by Louis L'Amour.

Perhaps the most published American author, L'Amour recounts his development as a writer.

Arnold: The Education of a Bodybuilder by Arnold Schwarzenegger.

Ever wonder how Arnold propelled himself to the top of the Hollywood heap? Read about how he succeeded in his first career for some clues.

Vince by Michael O'Brien and *Lombardi: Winning Is the Only Thing*, edited by Jerry Kramer. Two books about one of football's greatest coaches provide great insights into what it takes to succeed and lead others to success.

The Greatest by Muhammed Ali.

It wasn't just talent that made Ali the greatest boxer of our time, but also his single-mindedness and lots of hard work.

Suggested Reading List

Benjamin Franklin's Autobiography by Benjamin Franklin.
One of our country's founders, Franklin has a lot to say about personal management. Carl Van Doren has also written a good biography about this self-made man.

Washington: A Biography by Noemie Emery.
There is a lot to learn about perseverance and leading others from the father of our country. Books about Jefferson, Adams, and other founding fathers are also excellent reads.

The Last Lion by William Manchester.
Manchester has written a fascinating two-volume account of Winston Churchill. Great reading for anyone who wants insights into how to survive the inevitable ups and downs of life.

Most of these reading suggestions come from *The Playhouse West Reading List* compiled by Robert Carnegie, artistic director of Playhouse West School and Repertory Theater. The authors gratefully acknowledge his permission to make use of this list.